D1236873

PROPHET IN POLITICS:
Henry A. Wallace and the War Years, 1940 - 1965

PROPHET IN POLITICS:

HENRY A. WALLACE AND THE WAR YEARS, 1940 - 1965

EDWARD L. and FREDERICK H. SCHAPSMEIER

The Iowa State University Press, Ames, Iowa

EDWARD L. and FREDERICK H. SCHAPSMEIER are Iowa-born twins with remarkably similar careers. They received their Ph.D. degrees from the University of Southern California and have coauthored many articles on all facets of American history. Books written by the Schapsmeiers include *Henry A. Wallace of Iowa: The Agrarian Years, 1910–1940* and *Walter Lippmann: Philosopher-Journalist*. Both are professors of history, Edward at Illinois State University and Frederick at Wisconsin State University at Oshkosh.

Composed and printed by
The Iowa State University Press

FIRST EDITION, 1970

International Standard Book Number: 0–8138–1295–3
Library of Congress Catalog Card Number: 70–114795

To Our Brother and Sister-in-law
HERMAN and GRACIA SCHAPSMEIER
in Gratitude for Their Encouragement

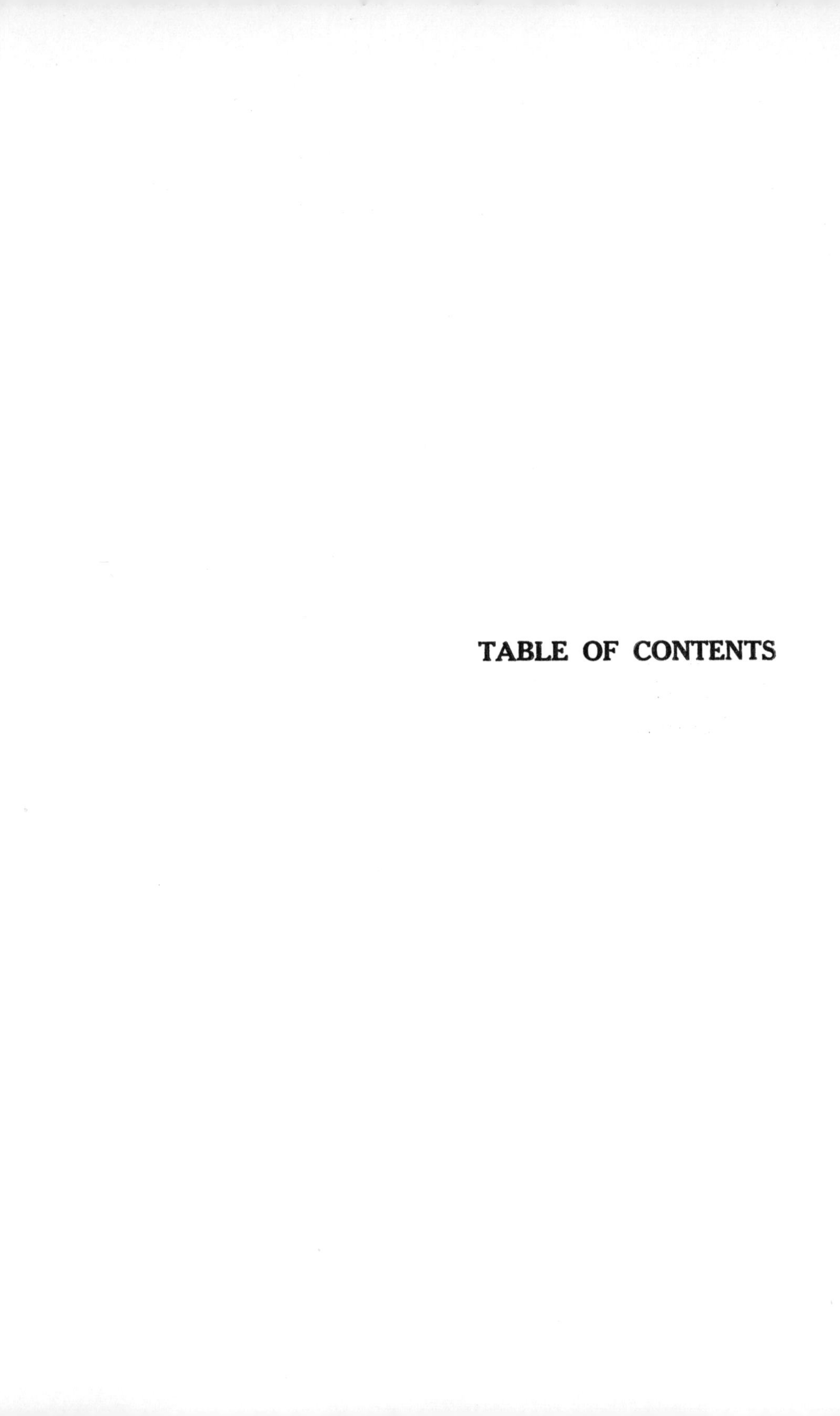

TABLE OF CONTENTS

FOREWORD ✠ BY LINUS PAULING

IN the first volume of their study of the origins and development of Henry Wallace's political philosophy, Edward L. and Frederick H. Schapsmeier discussed his family background, his early life, his service to the United States as Roosevelt's Secretary of Agriculture, and his election as Vice-President to serve during Roosevelt's third term. This second volume is an engrossing account of Wallace's place in world history during 1940–1965, a period which may well be considered by future historians as the most critical and decisive in the history of the world.

In these volumes the brothers Schapsmeier present an account of Wallace's actions and writings that permits a clear picture to be formed of his nature and character. He showed qualities of leadership, adeptness in adjusting policy to needs in the operation of government, and such realism as to suggest that he might well have been an effective President, might have succeeded in developing the Democratic party into a genuinely liberal one, and might have introduced his spirit of idealism into world affairs. He was an idealistic reformer, dedicated to morality and to his vision of a world of the future in which human beings would live in peace and from which, in the course of time, poverty, ignorance, and disease would be abolished—a world characterized by international cooperation.

At the Democratic Convention in 1944, in his address seconding the nomination of Roosevelt, Wallace described the sort of world he foresaw—a world from which segregation and discrimination based upon race, color, sex, or religion would be abolished. He might well have been selected as the Democratic candidate for the vice-presidency if he had had the strong support of Roosevelt and had not been strongly opposed by a group of ultraconservative Democrats led by Edwin W. Pauley, who were opponents of internationalism, economic reform, abolition of poverty, and civil rights. To these conservatives Henry Wallace—with his strongly held conviction that capitalism was in need of reform and greater morality—constituted a threat that could not be ignored; they were successful in averting the threat of his nomination and initiated the cold war, a period of militarism that has led to the tragic events of the past two decades.

Who can say what the world have been like if Wallace had

remained as Vice-President in 1944? There is the possibility that his accomplishments would have fallen far behind his ideals. But there is also the possibility that he could have been successful in averting the cold war. If Wallace had remained as Vice-President in 1944, there might have been no American involvement in a war in Korea, Vietnam, Cambodia, or Laos. The military dictatorships sponsored by the United States in many countries might not have come into existence. Tens of thousands of people who are now political prisoners might have remained free. International treaties might have been made that would have saved the United States and the Soviet Union hundreds of billions of dollars.

This book clearly raises the possibility that if the situation had been a little different and the Democratic Convention in 1944 had remained in session and carried out the first ballot with Wallace as the Vice-Presidential candidate, we might have a far better world today. I know of no other book indicating so clearly the possible importance of the action and influence of one man.

ACKNOWLEDGMENTS

FOR READING this book in manuscript form we wish to thank: James L. McCamy, Professor of Political Science at the University of Wisconsin; Boris Pregel, Vice-President of the Board of Governors and past President of The New York Academy of Sciences; Alfred Schindler, former Under Secretary of Commerce; Michael Straight, former editor of *The New Republic;* Bernard L. Gladieux of the New York firm of Knight and Gladieux—Management Consultants; and James W. Wallace, Chairman of the Board, Pioneer Hi-Bred Corn Company. Their comments and suggestions were greatly appreciated. We, of course, are responsible for all interpretations and conclusions.

A research grant from Illinois State University helped to make this project possible. We are grateful for this material assistance.

Our gratitude is extended to the many archivists and librarians who gave willingly of their time to aid us. Finally, we wish to thank Mrs. Alberta Carr for her superb typing and proofreading.

EDWARD L. AND FREDERICK H. SCHAPSMEIER

INTRODUCTION

BEING the legatee of a venerable family tradition, Henry Agard Wallace assumed the role of a crusader for rural rights as if predestined to do so.

All during the 1920s and early thirties he used *Wallaces' Farmer* as a forum for making known the grievances of midwestern farmers. The fighting editor also used the family farm journal to proffer solutions for the economic difficulties then plaguing the nation. In so doing he moved into the ranks of those rural leaders who would devise plans and programs to revive agriculture. This third of the Henry Wallaces of Iowa spoke up like an angry prairie prophet against the injustice of poverty amid plenty. He joined the administration of Franklin D. Roosevelt in 1933 in order to help create a new society where social justice would prevail.

While the complete story of his role as Secretary of Agriculture was related in the authors' first volume, *Henry A. Wallace of Iowa: The Agrarian Years, 1910–1940,* it should be noted here that he not only helped formulate New Deal farm programs but worked zealously to further other economic reforms. Accepting

The prophet that hath a dream, let him tell a dream.
JEREMIAH 23:28

the biblical injunction seriously about being "thy brother's keeper," he took it upon himself to champion the cause of the common man. As if possessed by a vision of a new and wonderful world, he tried to explain to the American people how they could reach the Promised Land of universal peace and abundance. His philosophy was not always understood, but the message he preached did appeal to the idealistic expectations of those who were innocent victims of the Great Depression.

As he interpreted the New Deal to Americans, Wallace also strove to engender in the public's mind the need for religio-economic reforms. This meant an alteration of attitudes, so that a revitalized society could be erected upon new institutional outlooks. A moral concern for the welfare of others, cooperation among all classes of people, and a willingness on the part of the United States to work with other nations were important aspects of his dream for universal affluence and international amity. His own horizons extended far beyond the cornfields of Iowa, and he was determined to induce others to think also in global terms. The essence of his rhetoric of reform was that mankind possessed the ability to create a new world. Faith in future change constituted the basic drive that propelled him along a course in which prophet and politician became indistinguishable.

In 1940 Franklin Delano Roosevelt personally selected Henry Wallace to be his vice-presidential running mate. The Secretary's administrative ability had been amply demonstrated as head of the Department of Agriculture. Furthermore he was a New Deal philosopher, which earned for him the reputation as an outstanding spokesman for liberalism. President Roosevelt appreciated his internationalist views and considered him to be one of his most loyal cabinet members. Despite strong opposition to the Iowan at the Democratic National Convention, by a coalition of big city bosses and southern political leaders, he was nominated as the vice-presidential candidate because Roosevelt insisted on it.

It was obvious from the outset that F.D.R. intended to make Wallace a working Vice-President. Even before the day arrived for him to take his oath of office, the Vice-President-elect was dispatched on a delicate mission to Mexico. After he assumed the official responsibilities of the vice-presidency, Henry Wallace was given administrative duties far beyond those of any of his predecessors. He would be called upon to assist in war mobilization and to aid the war effort itself. While doing this, he continued to preach the need for continued progress toward building a world where war and want were to be forever abolished. His soaring idealism inspired many and troubled others. Were his millennial expectations beyond mankind's ability to achieve? As a prophet in politics, he did not think so. But political realists regarded him as a dreamer of dreams, or as one who disregarded the profane for the prophetic in ways which invited inevitable disillusionment.

The great historian Arnold J. Toynbee once asserted, "Our greatest challenge today is the 'morality gap' between our cumulative accelerating advance in science and technology and our appalling failure in our relations with each other (relations of *all* kinds: industrial, political, family, racial)." No man in recent history tried harder to close this morality gap than did Henry Wallace. Regarding his political career as a divine calling, he earnestly strove to make science serve man, not Mammon. Preaching brotherhood, he spoke of racial equality when others remained silent. And finally he endeavored valiantly to obey the God of love and not the gods of war.

This book is about a magnificent man of faith who chose to serve God by serving humanity. The reader must, in the final analysis, judge for himself whether the political career of Henry Wallace was a triumph or a tragedy.

ABBREVIATIONS

For the convenience of the reader a list of commonly used abbreviations is presented here. These may appear in the text or in footnotes.

ACP American Communist Party
ADA Americans for Democratic Action
ALP American Labor Party
BEW Board of Economic Warfare
CIO-PAC Congress of Industrial Organization Political Action Committee
COHP Columbia University Oral History Project
EDB Economic Defense Board
FDRL Franklin D. Roosevelt Library
HAW-FDRL Papers of Henry A. Wallace located in the Franklin D. Roosevelt Library
HAW-UI Papers of Henry A. Wallace located at the University of Iowa
HAW-LC Papers of Henry A. Wallace located in the Library of Congress
HSTL Harry S. Truman Library
NAACP National Association for the Advancement of Colored People
NAS National Academy of Sciences
ICC-ASP Independent Citizens Committee of the Arts, Sciences, and Professions
NC-PAC National Citizens Political Action Committee
NDAC National Defense Advisory Commission
NDRC National Defense Research Committee
OEM Office for Emergency Management
OEW Office of Economic Warfare
OPM Office of Production Management
OSRD Office of Scientific Research and Development
PCA Progressive Citizens of America
RFC Reconstruction Finance Corporation
RG Record Group
SPAB Supply Priorities and Allocations Board
UDA Union for Democratic Action
UN United Nations Organization
UNRRA United Nations Relief and Rehabilitation Administration
USDA United States Department of Agriculture
WPB War Production Board

PROPHET IN POLITICS:

Henry A. Wallace and the War Years, 1940 - 1965

CHAPTER 1

PRELUDE TO WAR: MARSHALING THE NATION'S

BY JANUARY 20, 1941, the day Henry A. Wallace was sworn in as Vice-President, events in Europe were at a critical stage. Adolf Hitler had already dictated peace terms to France and was now directing the fury of his power at Great Britain. A mighty *Luftwaffe* was relentless in its air strikes, the *Wehrmacht* seemed invincible on the continent, and German submarines stealthily prowled the Atlantic Ocean at will.

Wallace viewed a Nazi victory with foreboding; but he, as did a considerable portion of the American public, harbored an ill-founded hope that his country would not become a direct participant in the conflict. He believed President Franklin D. Roosevelt was capable, somehow, of keeping the nation out of war, although it was not completely clear to him how this could be achieved.

F.D.R. was determined to aid Britain, but he did not believe the American people would support open participation in the European struggle. Preparedness maneuvers were disguised by calling them measures for national defense. Only partial mobilization was accomplished, but in so doing the nation's defense perim-

Be strong and of a good courage.
JOSHUA 1:6

RESOURCES

eter was extended to include the entire Western Hemisphere; and in this manner substantial assistance was given to England in its fight for survival. The United States, for all intent and purposes, engaged in an undeclared naval war while it mobilized its resources at home more fully. Administrative plans were deliberately formulated to convert the productive capacity of U.S. industry from peacetime output to materials of war. Roosevelt moved slowly, never proceeding too far in advance of public opinion, in laying the foundation for a gigantic war machine.

Obstacles existed everywhere. Industrial production in 1941 was relatively low or even nonexistent in many vital areas. Years of depression had made manufacturers cautious and reluctant to expand plant capacity. By the time a need for retooling and replacement of obsolete equipment became clearly evident, critical shortages of key materials already existed. The war had cut off sources of certain strategic goods, and stockpiling had not as yet been carried on with any sense of urgency. Obviously, some form of government supervision was needed quickly to ensure orderly procurement, then to guarantee proper allocation of these scarce items, and finally to establish production priorities for war needs.

To complicate matters, the gradual increase in defense activity stimulated the economy. Unemployment dropped, wage levels rose, and prices went up, as consumer demand exceeded output. Despite increases in the cost of living which hurt that segment of the population whose incomes were still comparatively low, F.D.R. refrained from taking steps to curb growing inflation. Political expedience forced him to forgo calling for sacrifices from a people hungry for material things and unwilling as yet to commit themselves fully to the immense task of preparing for war. Without any restrictions economic conditions varied widely, as the country enjoyed a surfeit of prosperity in some areas and shortages in others.

Even though mobilization was in disarray, Roosevelt refused to consider the appointment of a production czar. Bernard Baruch (who headed the War Industries Board in World War I) advised him to do this on numerous occasions. Many factors militated against such a move, at least as far as F.D.R. was concerned. A carefully orchestrated plan for war mobilization would have aroused the ire of militant isolationists, and this in turn would have caused greater disunity at home with resulting limitations on presidential freedom to act in other areas. Likewise, the President had been called a dictator during the depression, and he was not going to impose any system of controls which would give credence to that charge. Roosevelt's own concept of administration also prevented a well-planned program for mobilization from evolving, since he liked to play the role of arbiter between contestants. Any delegation of power was always diffused by limiting its purview or curtailing its impact by setting up a rival. Jurisdictional lines of authority between subordinates were deliberately blurred, so that F.D.R. remained the ultimate umpire in all disputes. This kept antagonists at bay and sustained a delicate balance between contending forces within the administration. This technique also gave Roosevelt the means whereby he could repudiate any policy by allowing a lesser official to accept responsibility for its failure.[1]

The disagreement and public quarreling which so enlivened the New Deal became an unfortunate part of the mobilization process. Wartime administrators found themselves ensnarled in needless conflict and confusion stemming from ambiguous and inefficient executive procedure. Many "dollar-a-year" men recruited from business never did comprehend the Roosevelt practice of duplicating jurisdictional realms or of allowing functions of several agencies to overlap.

A veteran of the intramural intrigues and political infighting of the New Deal period, Henry Wallace was suddenly plunged into another administrative maze when F.D.R. called upon him to assist in organizing the home front for war. The Vice-President was more businesslike though admittedly less artful in the practice of politics than his chief. He preferred clean lines of authority within well-defined spheres. As Secretary of Agriculture he had delegated power freely to trusted subordinates, while confining his administrative leadership to the policy-making level. Disliking details, which bored him, he devoted his primary effort to the task of determining future goals. His ability to plan ahead paid off time and time again for the Department of Agriculture. A substantial part of the credit for overall success of the entire New Deal can be attributed to his excellent long-range suggestions.[2]

A strange mixture of fact and fiction made up the public's image of Wallace. Seldom if ever was he considered an able administrator or an imaginative thinker. Instead, the press tended to create a caricature of a man who was presumed to be some sort of mystic or religious recluse. That he was a prophet in politics was true, but this was not fully understood within the context of his aims and objectives. His self-designated role was conceived in terms of how he personally could advance the twin causes of peace and social justice. Thus his affiliation with a party was secondary to the program to be achieved, and his basic devotion was to the cause involved, not the political organization. There is no doubt that Wallace felt an inner duty to speak for the voiceless masses. This compulsion came from a social conscience inculcated in him by his beloved grandfather and later sharpened by his own religious beliefs. His vocabulary, reminiscent of Social Gospel theology, and the idealized version of society he preached were obvious indicators of his Christian idealism. Why then was he so maligned and misrepresented by the press?

A congeries of reasons existed as to why Wallace became the target of vicious gossip, untrue anecdotes, and apocryphal stories. First of all he was different from the normal run of politicians. To professional newsmen he seemed to be a strange rustic saint out of place in the sophisticated and worldly atmosphere of Washington, D.C. He did not drink or smoke, never played poker, did not like ribald jokes, and disliked the trivial chatter so characteristic of cocktail parties in the capital city. Furthermore, his introvertive personality was misconstrued as deliberate aloofness, when in reality he preferred contacts with intimate friends to mingling in strange crowds. For relaxation he enjoyed spending a quiet evening at home in his modest apartment at the Wardman Park Hotel. The Vice-President was a voracious reader, and he spent many hours delving into history, economics, philosophy, and topics related to agriculture. Listening to the music of Beethoven or Latin American folk songs was his favorite cultural pastime, and invariably before bedtime he read portions of the Bible. For exercise he took long walks or played tennis. His left-handed style and lack of finesse on the tennis court were compensated by fierce determination to win and superb physical conditioning.

Indeed, Wallace's personal life did not conform to the usual behavior expected of a prominent political figure. Consequently when journalists wanted to liven up a feature story, they often distorted his religiosity and twisted the facts concerning his intellectual endeavors. Certainly the Vice-President was interested in things metaphysical and studied the sociological aspects of many religions, but it was not stressed that he regularly attended worship services at an Episcopal church. Only the more sensational aspects of his intense curiosity about spiritual phenomena were written up, such as interest in Oriental mysticism, theosophy, and the religious practices of American Indians.[3] His inquisitiveness also extended into the realm of science, and this too was often misrepresented to the public. His skill as a statistician (he pioneered in the development of biometrics) was made to appear as if he were a believer in numerology; astronomical observations made during the thirties to determine the influence of planetary movements on terrestrial climate were perverted into the charge he was a practitioner of astrology; and his attempts to figure out the aerodynamics of a boomerang were lampooned as the capricious behavior of a crank. Reporters did not always comprehend the fact that Wallace was a scientist of no mean talent. Had he pursued that profession uninterrupted from the time of his graduation from Iowa State College in 1910 until the time of his death in 1965, he would have achieved fame solely as a scientist. His fertile mind and insatiable curiosity would have prompted him to experiment in many more fields than genetics. Despite the demands of his political career, he continued to keep abreast of experimental work being done in the field of hybridization.

Preparatory to full assumption of vice-presidential responsibilities, Henry Wallace sought a better understanding of the history and nature of this position. After extensive briefings from both the Library of Congress and the Senate librarian, it must have been obvious to him that the vice-presidency per se was an auxiliary office with little inherent power. He may have been amused by the copy of Finley Peter Dunne's "The Vice-Presidency," sent to him by Professor David Lynch of Drake University, but Wallace did not intend to abide by Mr. Dooley's witty observation, "All that his grateful counthry demands fr'm th' man that she has illivated to this proud position on th' toe iv her boot is that he shall keep his 'pinyons to himself." The Vice-President regaled the members of the electoral college, at a dinner in their honor, with his rendition of Mr. Dooley; yet he regarded himself as more than one who would, according to the Irish humorist, rigorously enforce the nonexistent "rules iv th' Sinit."[4]

When Wallace took over his duties as presiding officer of the Senate, it became obvious to its members that he was not cut from the same cloth as his immediate predecessor. He never became a part of the Senate establishment. One of his first acts was to remove the facilities for serving liquor that John Garner had installed in the Vice-President's office. His relationship with individual senators was cordial, but strictly formal. Without possessing the gregarious quality of a backslapper or the effusive personality of a cloakroom manipulator, he had little influence on the Senate as a whole. Those liberals who shared his views on many issues respected him, but seldom did that admiration ever lead to relaxed or close friendships. The makeup of Wallace's personality was completely opposite to the hail-fellow-well-met type, and this worked to his disadvantage as a liaison between the White House and the upper chamber.

In addition, the Vice-President did not enamor the Senate with his undisguised boredom at their endless talk marathons. The proud and independent senators valued their right of unlimited debate; but Wallace, who was forced to listen, regarded it as an imposition on his time. He often slumped unceremoniously in his chair, closed his eyes, and pondered other questions than those being discussed *ad nauseum* on the floor. This was not meant as an insult, although some speakers thought so, but reflected his disinterest in seemingly unimportant aspects of the legislative process. Never having served in a representative body, he did not share the camaraderie or concern for parliamentary procedure that pervaded the tradition-bound upper chamber. He also found it impossible to genuinely like a senator when he disagreed with that individual on basic principles. This caused disdain for certain southern senators, and this in turn increased their resentment against him and his ideas.

On the whole Wallace did not enjoy his chore of presiding over the Senate, and thus he absented himself whenever possible. The constitutional right to cast a vote in case of a tie arose only rarely and, interestingly enough, the first time such an occasion presented itself he was absent. Perhaps the most satisfying vote he ever recorded, since it dealt with both human and natural resources, was the one which prevented the Senate from terminating the Civilian Conservation Corps.

If Wallace's duties as Vice-President had pertained only to his constitutional prerogatives, he would have slipped quickly into political oblivion. The real leader of the Senate was Alben Barkley of Kentucky. As Democratic majority leader he was a masterful debater, a storyteller par excellence, and a shrewd parliamentarian. Since Vice-President Wallace admired him greatly, he always took his cue from the Kentuckian regarding rulings from the chair.

In one humorous incident Wallace made good copy for newsmen hunting for human interest stories. The Senate gym attracted the Vice-President, since keeping physically fit was important to him. Even though everyone was sworn to secrecy, the story leaked out that in a friendly boxing match the Vice-President had landed a knockout punch on the jaw of Senator Allen J. Ellender of Louisiana. This unique turn of events elicited chuckles from surprised senators and, needless to say, few volunteered as future sparring partners for the vigorous Vice-President. Despite such isolated instances of joviality, the members of the Senate never really accepted Wallace into their exclusive club.[5]

The dormant administrative talents of the Vice-President were soon put to good use by the President when on July 9, 1941, F.D.R. indicated to him that whereas he was not yet ready to appoint an economic defense administrator, there was a need for ascertaining the "broad implications of our economic relationships in the light of what is going on in the world today." Roosevelt asked for the formation of a committee to implement this type of study with the personal comment, "I am sure that you know more about this field than anybody in town."[6] In this estimate F.D.R. was correct.

Even before receiving Roosevelt's request, Wallace had already taken steps on his own initiative to establish an unofficial committee for what was termed "interdepartmental discussions of the economic outlook." This group was assembled on July 16th for informal deliberations on the topic, "Prospects for Inflation." Invitations and agendas were sent to the following persons: Lauchlin Currie, administrative assistant to the President; Richard Gilbert, director, Defense Economic Section, Office of Price Administration and Civilian Supply; Isador Lubin, director of the Bureau of Labor Statistics; C. L. Wilson, director of the Bureau of Foreign and Domestic Commerce; Thomas C. Blaisdell of the National Resources Planning Board; Raymond W. Goldsmith, assistant director of the Securities and Exchange Commission; Michael Mehan of the Commerce Department; and Dr. E. A. Goldenweiser, director of research for the Federal Reserve Board. Meetings of a similar nature had been inaugurated by Wallace as Secretary of Agriculture. By taking the initiative, he often acquired information which he passed on to the President, and on the basis of such past assistance Roosevelt was prompted to rely on him for help in organizing the home front.

Exercising powers granted to him by the Reorganization Act of 1939 and by virtue of his 1940 Proclamation of Unlimited Emergency, Roosevelt decided to use Wallace's talents in an appointive office. The President, by issuing Executive Order No. 8839, officially established the Economic Defense Board (EDB) with the Vice-President as its chairman. Other members included Cordell Hull, Henry Morgenthau, Jr., Francis Biddle, Jesse H. Jones, and Claude R. Wickard. The EDB was to be a "policy and advisory agency" dealing with all "international economic activities." It was to concern itself with "exports, imports, . . . preclusive buying, transactions in foreign exchange and foreign owned or controlled property, international investments and extension of credit, shipping and transportation of goods among countries, the international aspects of patents, international communications pertaining to commerce and other foreign economic matters." Its general purview also included: (1) advising the President as to economic defense measures; (2) coordinating the policies and actions of the several departments carrying on activities relating to economic defense; (3) developing integrated economic defense plans and programs; and (4) making investigations and advising the President on the relationship of economic defense to postwar economic reconstruction and on the steps to protect the trade position of the United States and to expedite the establishment of sound, peacetime international relationships.[7]

Events abroad forced F.D.R. to speed up defense preparations. Britain's chances of survival were enhanced with passage of the Lend-Lease Act in March, 1941, and by Hitler's strange decision to launch Operation Barbarossa. On June 22 the massive assault on the Soviet Union began, canceling any plans for a German invasion of the British Islands. Now Roosevelt had to think of aiding Russia. An added duty given to the EDB was enforcement of President's Proclamation No. 2497, which as of July 17, 1941, blacklisted some 1,800 Latin American companies. This was done to prevent pro-Axis firms from transshipping goods to Germany after they had been purchased in the United States. To avoid conflicts in procedures regarding business dealings with South America, Coordinator of Inter-American Affairs Nelson A. Rockefeller, was also placed on the EDB as one of its permanent members. Roosevelt was, in effect, initiating a policy of economic warfare against Germany.

Because of the hydra-headed character of the Office of Production Management (OPM), this primary defense agency soon found itself in trouble. William Knudsen, a dollar-a-year executive from General Motors (who in 1940 was a member of the National Defense Advisory Commission), found it difficult to work with Sidney Hillman, former head of the Amalgamated Clothing Workers Union. These men were to handle civilian priorities, while Henry L. Stimson and Frank Knox, the secretaries of War and Navy respectively, controlled military needs. Demands for materiel began to cause major dislocations in supplies. F.D.R., in his typical fashion, sought to alleviate administrative logjams, not by replacing the OPM, but by superimposing another policy-making board over it. He therefore called upon Wallace again, this time to help straighten out the delays in production. The Vice-President was appointed chairman of the Supply Priorities and Allocations Board (SPAB). By issuing Executive Order No. 8875 on August 28, 1941, Roosevelt directed the SPAB to act as a "coordinating center for the execution of the powers and activities" of all aspects of defense mobilization. All the nation's resources were now to be systematically channeled into war production. Donald M. Nelson, a former vice-president of Sears Roebuck and Company and director of OPM's purchasing division, was made executive director of the SPAB. Other members included Knudsen, Hillman, Stimson, Frank Knox, Leon Henderson, Jesse Jones, and Harry Hopkins in his capacity as special assistant to the President.[8]

Vice-President Wallace labored diligently to make the unwieldy mobilization apparatus work. In both capacities, as head of the EDB and SPAB, he found the situation confused and disorderly. Shortages existed, he discovered, because of laxity in stockpiling strategic materials. Congress had not authorized such buying until 1939, and then it appropriated only a meager $10 million for that purpose. Jesse Jones, who was secretary of Commerce and head of the Reconstruction Finance Corporation, had also negelected to acquire supplies of natural rubber when they were available. Thus the SPAB had to establish select priorities for the use of this vital product just to conserve what was on hand. Furthermore, it was forced by necessity to curtail all nonessential construction while simultaneously seeing to it that steel output was increased, oil pipelines were built, and scarce metals were purchased abroad. During the first month of its existence, the production of war materials rose 15 percent and still another 26 percent the following month. The *Wall Street Journal,* which seldom praised Wallace, called the SPAB the "youngest, toughest, smartest, and—so far—most successful defense agency."[9] Alfred M. Landon, on the other hand, accused New Dealers of using the "national defense emergency as a smoke screen for their attempts to build a collective state."[10] Unfortunately this type of criticism, as leveled by the defeated Republican presidential candidate of 1936, only reinforced Roosevelt's proclivity to proceed with mobilization in slow stages rather than to impose rigid controls immediately over all facets of the domestic economy.

Wallace hoped that American productive power would supply such a torrent of materiel to Hitler's enemies as to make defeat of the Nazis possible without direct U.S. military intervention. He also believed Japan could be deterred from aggression if its leaders were truly aware of the enormous industrial might of the United States. Vice-President Wallace informed his friend, W. W. Waymack of the Des Moines *Register* and *Tribune,* that the press ought to publicize this fact, so that potential adversaries would be dissuaded from taking up arms. With conditions in the Far East growing constantly more menacing, and because of the Soviet Union's actions prior to the German invasion (when it partitioned Poland and attacked Finland), he wrote, "Russia and Japan both are in a position to be greatly influenced by the balance of power concepts and our speed of production is the dominant factor in forming their ideas as to where the balance of power will ultimately rest."[11] For this reason, confident the nation's power would become apparent to potential enemies, he advised Roosevelt in August, 1941, "I do hope, Mr. President, you will go to the absolute limit in your firmness in dealing with Japan."[12]

So that the American public would be aware of the complexities involved in the effort to build up the nation's industrial strength, Wallace notified Roosevelt that he and Milo Perkins were going to make at least "one important speech a month on the policies of the Economic Defense Board."[13] Perkins formerly had worked under Wallace in the Department of Agriculture and had headed the Federal Surplus Commodities Corporation before he was appointed executive director of the EDB. President Roosevelt had also designated Perkins to be chairman of the Joint American-Canadian Defense Production Committee. Henry Wallace and Milo Perkins shared the same general political philosophy and complemented one another well as an administrative team. The former thought in broad policy terms, while the latter handled the EDB's daily details. Both believed urgent steps were needed to consolidate national defense. When Wallace spoke to the American people about mobilization needs over a national radio network on November 12, 1941, he called for personal sacrifices on the consumer level and greater effort from defense plant workers. Speaking somberly and saying what F.D.R. had refrained from emphasizing, he stressed the theme of "production for victory." There was no doubt U.S. policy favored the defeat of the Axis. "None of us can expect to eat and wear and drink and buy on the basis of peacetime luxury living," the Vice-President announced, "Our country needs her copper, her aluminum and her steel to fight the battle of freedom on the seven seas and in all the continents of the world."[14]

Vice-President Wallace was not really cognizant of just how close to war the nation was at the time he sought to arouse the people to go all out for national defense. He abhorred Nazi and Japanese aggression as immoral and unjustified, and his innate dislike of war prevented him from openly advocating U.S. entry into world conflict as an active belligerent. American supplies and naval support for Britain, plus withholding of strategic goods from the Axis powers, would ultimately bring these totalitarian nations down to defeat. His negative opinion of the Soviet Union changed when it valiantly resisted the onslaught of Hitler's *Blitzkrieg*. The Vice-President, therefore, counseled Roosevelt to render aid to each and every victim of German aggression and to stand firm against Japan.

Unknown to him, the future course of American action would be determined by events beyond the nation's control. On

December 7, 1941, his role as a defense mobilizer would suddenly become transformed into that of a wartime administrator. This was a challenge not unlike the desperate days of the depression in that it brought forth a renewed burst of energy and idealism from Henry Wallace.

CHAPTER 2

WARTIME ADMINISTRATOR: THE BOARD OF ECONOMIC

THE Japanese government's fateful decision to launch a surprise attack on Hawaii stunned Vice-President Wallace.

Angered by this act of treachery, since he regarded the surprise air strike as a monstrous breach of morality, Henry Wallace believed his country was justified in taking up the sword against its foes. Heretofore he had earnestly hoped that such measures as military preparedness, hemispheric defense, and aid to Britain would forestall a state of open war between the United States and the Axis powers. Pearl Harbor and Germany's subsequent declaration of war accomplished what he was unable to do for himself. His aversion to war (bordering on pacifism) was replaced by feelings of moral indignation and righteous wrath. In clear conscience he could now support an all-out fight against such villainous acts which seemed to embody all that was evil and immoral. It prompted him to proclaim "Our God is a God of battles as well as a God of Peace"[1] and to assume divine retribution would be meted out to the malevolent Axis for their outrageous crimes against humanity. Their destruction, in his way of thinking, was a necessary prerequisite for a new world to follow; consequently, he advocated all means and any weapons to insure total victory.

A time to hate; a time of war. . . .
ECCLESIASTES 3:8

WARFARE

One such weapon was the atomic bomb, and Wallace was deeply involved in the initial stages of deliberations regarding its development. The original proposal for such a project was contained in a 1939 communication from Albert Einstein to the President. That letter, because of Einstein's great fame as a world-renowned physicist, prompted Roosevelt to seek further information about the feasibility of constructing some type of nuclear device. Both British and American scientists carefully examined the theoretical and engineering problems involved. Results of those investigations were collected by such organizations as the National Academy of Sciences (NAS), the Office of Scientific Research and Development (OSRD), and the National Defense Research Committee (NDRC). Each of the latter two were advisory agencies to the government and thus held quasi-official status.

Franklin D. Roosevelt appointed a so-called Top Policy Group in the fall of 1941 to assist him in the evaluation of much technical data that was being assembled. Its members were Henry Wallace; Henry L. Stimson, Secretary of War; George C. Marshall, Chief of Staff; Vannevar Bush, director of the OSRD;

and James B. Conant, chairman of the NDRC. The Vice-President was placed on this committee not only because of his involvement with mobilization but as one whose scientific background would qualify him to assess the practicability of such an endeavor. After appraising the findings of many physicists, the group was to make specific recommendations to President Roosevelt regarding a future course of action.

While a final report of the NAS was being prepared by a select committee of its own members, Dr. Vannevar Bush took care to keep the Vice-President briefed on important matters. He knew about Wallace's work in genetics and was fully aware that in the New Deal period the then Secretary of Agriculture was helpful in the establishment of a Science Advisory Board. Before the academy's final statement of conclusions was forwarded to Roosevelt, Arthur H. Compton (chairman of its investigatory commission) also made it a point to contact Wallace. After a friendly game of tennis, Dr. Compton brought up the subject of nuclear physics and government's future role in developing a fission-type weapon. The Vice-President was told that many physicists were confident a uranium–heavy water reactor could be constructed for purposes of making a U-235 bomb. The fears of certain scientists were also explained. Unless the United States invested heavily in such a project, Germany might forge ahead in this field. Compton's parting comment to Wallace was a somber reminder: "Please give this report your most careful attention. It is possible that how we act on this matter may make all the difference between winning and losing the war."[2] Bush and Compton were both using Wallace as a middleman because of his knowledge of science and easy access to the President.

Roosevelt received the NAS report on November 27, 1941. On the strength of optimism expressed by the scientists involved and encouragement given by Wallace, the President allocated additional funds for the NDRC to continue exhaustive studies on specific methods of producing an atomic weapon. The NDRC quickly formed a Uranium Committee, called S-1 Section, for purposes of exploring in detail the practicability of a uranium fission approach. A true sense of urgency permeated the work of S-1 after Pearl Harbor. Information from British scientists, the success of experiments at Columbia University, and current research results of American physicists convinced those on S-1 that a bomb could be made within a reasonable time. Because of the initial Allied defeats and the danger inherent in remaining too long on the defensive both in the Pacific and Europe, Henry

Wallace wanted work on this project to proceed as a high priority program. The United States needed a powerful offensive weapon. He called a meeting of the Top Policy Group on December 16, 1941. In addition to the Vice-President, only Stimson and Bush were present at the session that approved the recommendation of S-1 Section. General Marshall, who happened to be out of the capital on army business, was favorably disposed toward the development of any superweapon, but he was not present at this momentous meeting. Bush was so elated after the committee adjourned, he quickly notified Conant, who had been absent because of illness, that the green light had been given to move ahead on the fundamental physics problems involved in developing a pilot plant.

When the S-1 report reached Roosevelt after its approval by Wallace and the Top Policy Group, the President gave the go-ahead for full-scale action on this secret enterprise. Management of the program was assigned to the U.S. Army Corps of Engineers. On September 17, 1942, Brigadier General Leslie R. Groves was selected to supervise the massive endeavor to be known only as the Manhattan Project. At this point the Vice-President's active role in the undertaking ceased, although his knowledge of what was going on weighed heavily on his mind. He worried constantly about Germany's potential in winning the atomic race, and it also occurred to him that other nations, such as the Soviet Union, possessed capabilities for developing such a weapon. This was a major reason why he gave such serious thought to ways and means of fostering peaceful postwar relations with Russia while she was an ally.[3]

Whatever diplomatic or military mistakes caused the disaster at Pearl Harbor, they could not be undone. On the evening of December 7, 1941, as the news of naval losses continued to flow into the White House, F.D.R. met first with congressional leaders and then with his cabinet. Wallace was present at both meetings, when Roosevelt made it perfectly clear he meant to lead America to an ultimate triumph over all its adversaries. Congress passed a declaration of war against Japan on December 8th, and on the 18th it approved the War Powers Act. The President was given broad authority to array the nation's resources for total warfare. Soon after, the Vice-President sent Roosevelt a confidential note letting his "Commander-in-Chief," as he phrased it, know of his confidence despite the adverse turn of events in recent weeks. "For nearly nine years I have been a part of your official family," Wallace reminded him, and "these nine years have been unusually happy . . . the contact with you has been an altogether unique and heart warming experience." His concluding words revealed the depth of his faith in Roosevelt's leadership: "It has been truly providential for the nation that you have been our leader during these nine years. No one else had the insight to lead as effectively as you have done in meeting our problems both on the foreign and domestic fronts."[4]

Once the United States was actually engaged in warfare in both Europe and the Pacific, Wallace was extremely impatient with delays of any kind. He wanted mobilization speeded up and counteroffensives initiated in the various theaters of war. His zeal for action prompted him to write a lengthy letter to Roosevelt, urging him to assume the stance of an aggressive war leader. This missive, dated August 7, 1942, was typical of Wallace's many communications with F.D.R. They combined words of reassurance with advice and admonition. The Vice-President told his chief he had just read William B. Ziff's book, *The Coming Battle of Germany,* and its contents were worthy of consideration. Ziff, editor of an aviation magazine called *Flying,* claimed victory was possible only by centralized administration of war production, working closely with allies, and making effective use of air power. Wallace also took time to warn Roosevelt of the possibility that Japan might "launch a surprise attack on Siberia." The Vice-President concluded this bit of counsel, with a pep talk calling for quick countermeasures against Germany. "Hitler has not yet won the war, but it is of exceeding importance that our weight be thrown into the scales at the earliest possible moment. I trust you, yourself, with your unique combination of courage and judgment, will, after complete consultation but with the greatest possible speed, determine the time and place. 'Pour les vaincre, Messieurs, il faut de l'audace, encore de l'audace, toujours de l'audace.' "[5]

A steady flow of memoranda from Wallace reached the President's desk in those first crucial months of 1942. They covered a variety of subjects and sometimes proffered military advice. The Vice-President, for instance, recounted the substance of his conversations with Maxim Litvinov of the Soviet Union. Russia's ambassador had insisted the number of German troops stationed in Norway, Holland, and Belgium was much lower than recent estimates of U.S. military experts. Litvinov obviously meant to convey the impression that a second front could be established without undue difficulty. While not identifying his source, Wallace reported another item of intelligence that had reached his ears. He told F.D.R. of rumors that Hitler was planning some sort of peace offensive aimed at getting Britain out of the war. Reflecting some misgivings over the beleaguered island's ability to fight on, he commented, "It is, therefore, a question of fate, whether England, in the coming fall, will remember its relationship with Europe and change its foreign policy."[6] This observation, of course, ignored the pugnacious and determined stand taken by Winston Churchill against any capitulation or arrangement of any kind with the Nazis.

Another warning Wallace saw fit to make involved the possibility of a German invasion of Gibraltar. "My own feeling is that Hitler will move through Spain against Gibraltar and Africa," the Vice-President added, "unless he is certain we are too strong for him."[7] Although Wallace was wrong about an invasion of Spain, F.D.R. had anticipated German penetration of the Mediterranean and responded, "You and I think alike. I told Winston last January to read up on Wellington's Peninsular Campaign. We have both done it."[8]

The President greatly appreciated Wallace's general concern, even though advice tendered was not always followed. He had a way of rejecting such suggestions without hurting the Vice-President's feelings. Roosevelt knew that Henry, whom he always addressed on a first-name basis, had the best interests of the administration and country at heart. Frequently Wallace's comments were of genuine significance. On one occasion the Vice-President alerted his chief about an impending shortage of sugar unless import restrictions and acreage quotas were terminated quickly.[9] He furthermore pressed the President to adopt stringent anti-inflationary measures. One such device advocated was a program in which payroll deductions would automatically be made from the earnings of workers, rather than relying upon purely voluntary purchase of war bonds. Most important of all, he constantly urged Roosevelt to consolidate all aspects of war production into one agency and to centralize import-export activities under one supreme authority.[10] In his dual capacity as chairman of the Supply Priorities and Allocations Board and the Economic Defense Board, he—more than anyone else—realized the vast confusion that still existed in home front mobilization machinery.

On December 8th the members of the SPAB met in Wallace's Senate Building office to "consider the emergency created by the attack on the United States by the naval and air forces of the Empire of Japan." At the Vice-President's urging the following declaration was adopted: "From now on, every action of this Board and by related civilian agencies of the Government must be keyed to one goal—complete victory in this war which has been thrust upon us."[11]

Henry Wallace sought to infuse a similar sense of emergency into activities of the Economic Defense Board, which was renamed the Board of Economic Warfare (BEW) on December 17, 1941. Roosevelt, via executive order, bestowed additional powers upon this agency, so that it now possessed authority to negotiate directly with foreign governments in matters pertaining to the shipping and procurement of all strategic materials.[12]

In order to increase the BEW's efficiency, the Vice-President established three main departments: Office of Imports, Office of Exports, and an Office of Warfare Analysis. Most of its 3,000 technicians were assigned to duties dealing with acquisition of goods from all over the world (especially Latin America), a lesser number dealt with export licenses and permits (to prevent transshipment of useful material to Axis nations), and a select few were instructed to work on postwar planning. From his association with the SPAB Wallace knew that raw materials once obtained from the Far East now had to be secured elsewhere. He felt that nothing should be allowed to interfere with the BEW's attempt to procure what was needed for the war effort. Progress in streamlining operations induced him to write to his longtime friend Addison M. Parker of Des Moines, "I think we are getting a straight channel of power established now in a most excellent way and that we shall demonstrate productivity here in these United States in the most astounding fashion."[13]

No sooner had F.D.R. expanded the scope of the BEW's work than complaints from Cordell Hull started coming in. The Secretary of State maintained Wallace's agency was impinging upon traditional prerogatives assigned to his department. In his memoirs written in 1948, the Tennessean justified these protests because the President had "virtually creat[ed] a second State Department."[14] Cabinet jealousies could not be ignored, so Roosevelt pacified Hull by rescinding portions of his earlier order. A new directive was issued, "Defining Additional Functions and Duties of the Board of Economic Warfare," which curtailed Wallace's authority. The BEW's power to "determine the policies to be followed in the procurement and production of imported materials for the war effort and civilian economy" was reaffirmed, but "execution and administration" was to be retained by the several departments or agencies already involved in matters of foreign commerce.[15]

Not only did Wallace find it difficult to implement BEW policy through State Department channels but additional delays were incurred when he was forced to enter into prolonged negotiations with the Reconstruction Finance Corporation. In typical Rooseveltian fashion, the President allowed the BEW to make policy, but its funds were controlled by another agency. The Reconstruction Finance Corporation (RFC), headed by Jesse Jones (who was also Secretary of Commerce), had established numerous subsidiary corporations, which were major instruments in securing military supplies with funds appropriated by Congress. After the BEW secured purchase contracts for vital materials from abroad, it had to submit its request to RFC officials for payment. Jones insisted that all legal arrangements be scrutinized and thus forced renegotiation of numerous contracts to correspond with his concept of good business procedure. Additional trouble occurred when BEW projects conflicted with those of such RFC subsidiaries as: the Metals Reserve Company, the United States Commercial Company, the Rubber Development Corporation, and the Defense Supplies Corporation. The Vice-President wanted all procurement consolidated in the BEW so his agency could devise and carry out its own programs without duplication or interference from either RFC or State Department personnel. When it became clear F.D.R. meant to continue the practice of divided authority, Wallace pleaded for cooperation, "Make everyone realize the depth of your feeling about the greatness of the responsibility . . . of the hour. We must get the maximum of these foreign raw materials at once. No delays—no excuses—no holding back. . . . If you can by something you say, make State and Commerce not merely acquiescent but enthusiastic and eager in their cooperation, it would be grand."[16]

Needless to say this overlapping of jurisdiction did not make for efficiency or speed in carrying out transactions, since operations of the BEW were hindered by endless bureaucratic processing. To clear the channels of operation, Henry Wallace worked out a *modus operandi* with the State Department that proved to be satisfactory for both parties.[17] His efforts to arrive at some kind of practical arrangement with Jesse Jones were something else again. The Commerce Secretary was a zealous guardian of all authority vested in the RFC by Congress, and he resisted any attempt by others to encroach upon his personal domain. He liked to drive a hard bargain and prided himself on his ability to make profitable deals. This business-oriented penchant for economizing proved to be a liability when time itself was of the essence and under circumstances where Axis agents outbid

American buyers by paying higher than normal prices for scarce goods. Jones was also part of a conservative faction within the New Deal which shared none of Wallace's political objectives. Roosevelt planted seeds of trouble when he placed Wallace and Jones in the same administrative harness.[18]

The prima donna complex of Roosevelt's New Deal cabinet marred his war administration. Compounding the difficulty was F.D.R.'s refusal to discipline or discharge those who were not handling their duties properly. This helped create a bureaucratic maze which invited disputes and delays. When journalists began to refer to Henry Wallace as an "Assistant President,"[19] this only intensified envy among the Vice-President's former cohorts. Harold Ickes, for instance, was deeply resentful when F.D.R. asked Wallace to develop plans for adequate oil and gasoline supplies, since the quarrelsome curmudgeon had already been designated petroleum coordinator.[20] Unfortunately, the battle of the Potomac raged while prosecution of the real war suffered.

On January 15, 1942, the SPAB met to discuss an agenda consisting of such vital topics as synthetic rubber; the stockpile program; aluminum requirements of the Union of Soviet Socialist Republics; and increased copper, lead, and zinc production through price incentives. Midway through this particular meeting both Henry Wallace and Donald Nelson were summoned to the White House. President Roosevelt surprised them by announcing, "I have come to the conclusion that American war production should be placed under the direction of one man."[21] The Vice-President thought momentarily he had been chosen to head a new superagency, but F.D.R. tapped Nelson for the job. Roosevelt's decision was one which Wallace nevertheless applauded. Demands of war made greater efficiency imperative. Establishment of the War Production Board (WPB) seemed to fulfill that objective.

Now the Vice-President had but one administrative responsibility, as the SPAB was superseded by the WPB. Consequently his energies were directed toward making the BEW an effective organization. Focusing upon much broader issues than the day-to-day tasks of procurement, issuing licenses for exports, and preparing reports on economic conditions of enemy countries, Wallace meant to forge his agency into an instrument not only for guaranteeing ultimate victory in war but for winning the peace. To do this, he first sought to justify the war on moral grounds, then he strove to prepare public opinion for America's role in the postwar era. In these endeavors Henry Wallace became a leading ideologist of World War II.

CHAPTER 3

IDEALISM, IDEOLOGY, AND IDEAS FOR THE POSTWAR

MILITARILY the initial stages of World War II were fraught with peril. Japan's rising sun flew over vast portions of the Pacific, Red Army divisions could not stop nor even protect themselves from the savage blows of German panzer units, and weary British soldiers fought tenaciously to maintain precarious positions in North Africa.

Behaving like a giant dazed by sudden affliction, the United States did not yet possess the ability to strike back at its tormentors with offensive action. In Henry Wallace's judgment the worldwide conflict was definitely a life and death struggle between forces of freedom and the demonic might of those who would enslave all mankind in perpetual darkness. It appeared to him that some hellish fury had been unleashed upon humanity in an attempt to destroy the existence of all goodness and decency. The voice of God in man's conscience cried out in protest against evil militarists. Spiritual indignation surged within him and could not be quieted. He felt that if democracy were to survive, and with it the best hope of the human race, moral righteousness must triumph over evil. Terror of totalitarianism

For, behold, I create new heavens and a new earth.
ISAIAH 65:17

WORLD

had to be extinguished permanently from the earth. His justification for using force stemmed from the Old Testament example of Israel being called upon by God to destroy wicked nations. The United States was the Lord's instrument for liberating the world and leading it along a new course.

Total victory as envisioned by Henry Wallace included more than just military success against the aggressors. In his mind it encompassed a complete conquest over war itself. He was obsessed with the vision of a world to come where human beings would live in perpetual peace. Not only war but also want, ignorance, and disease were to be vanquished forever. A new world beckoned, and Wallace was enraptured by the promise of its fullfillment. Deeply inspired by his religious conviction, the Vice-President elected to speak for suffering mankind as a prophet of peace. Only this idealistic prospect of a better world, where all people could live in universal peace and prosperity, made the death and destruction caused by war endurable. His beloved grandfather had spoken often of the "New Jerusalem" that would come to pass when men of goodwill banded together to gain ascendancy over the satanic forces of wickedness. The noble venture to which the Vice-President committed himself was to lead all citizens of the world to that type of Promised Land. Needless to say, many of Wallace's ideals were projections of hope far exceeding the scope of historical reality.

For Wallace it seemed the height of folly not to think beyond the time when the war would be won. He feared a repetition of what had happened after World War I. No plans or permanent foundation for international cooperation had been laid while the fighting took place. Everything was left until hostilities ceased, and by then it was too late. To prevent a recurrence of the tragic events of the post-Armistice period, Wallace asked Roosevelt for more authority, so the BEW might start laying the groundwork for future economic cooperation on a global basis. He told the President, "Our feeling is that we are writing the postwar world as we go along and that we need some of the RFC powers now to do a good job of it. Those powers can be used to get in raw materials from abroad more aggressively than they have been used in the past. The administrative machinery thus set up to help win the war will be the most effective economic means through which we can win the peace later on. Without labeling it as such, we can thereby get an international ever-normal granary functioning before we ever come to an armistice."[1]

In his correspondence with Roosevelt, the Vice-President insisted on the need for specific planning relative to international reconstruction and postwar reconversion. As a starter he thought future food production should be handled to eliminate both competition and surpluses at home and abroad, while permitting prosperity and equitable distribution all over the globe. The domestic program, as it operated through the Agricultural Adjustment Act of 1938, was to be extended on a worldwide basis via an international ever-normal granary. For this reason Wallace recommended to Roosevelt that the United States, Argentina, and Canada enter into an immediate International Wheat Agreement as the first phase of such a project. A mechanism of this type would provide a method for "getting a definite hold on some of the problems which will be with us after the war."[2]

On another occasion he complained to the President about lack of congressional appropriations for the purpose of carrying out "necessary planning and blueprinting" for postwar needs. Indicating his concern over this unfortunate situation, Wallace reminded Roosevelt, "Woodrow Wilson had no carefully worked out plan for demobilizing the army, relocating the war workers, reconverting the war industries, . . . [or] protecting the farmers."[3] His own feeling was that a well-defined public works program should be prepared in advance to prevent a postwar depression from occurring. The Vice-President advised F.D.R. to seek immediate authorization from Congress for the establishment of an official "planning agency."[4] Specific proposals for national, state, and local projects could be drawn up with provisions made for funding them from the federal treasury. He labeled this a program of "Lend-Lease on the domestic front." His goal was to head off the expected unemployment after the war by using intelligent governmental planning and federal expenditures to stimulate the economy.

In the broadest context Wallace's economic thought reflected his acceptance of Keynesian compensatory spending, the Progressive principle of positive government, and the economic theories of Thorstein Veblen. He was influenced profoundly by the ideas of Veblen, who was a founder of the institutionalist school of economics and whose ideas provided the conceptual framework for his own political philosophy. Wallace accepted Veblen's assertion, that economic abundance was possible for the United States and the world at large if only the productive capacity of industrial nations were harnessed for the good of humanity. Veblen contended that capitalists deliberately curtailed domestic production to sustain high profits at home while simultaneously inducing governments to engage in imperialistic ventures to secure additional markets abroad. According to his interpretation this international competition for new outlets promoted tensions and precipitated wars. To prevent that type of conflict, Veblen proposed such remedial steps as free trade, economic interdependence, mutual cooperation between nations, and a world organization which he called a "pacific league of neutral nations." In a real sense he was advocating a common market on an international scale. He believed that by integrating the national economies of all countries, two beneficial results would occur. First, by pooling technological know-how and unleashing productivity, the possibility of attaining universal affluence was made a plausible goal. Second, an interlocked economic structure made self-sufficiency impossible; hence nations would be less prone to resort to armed force to resolve differences.[5]

As a young man Henry Wallace had read and absorbed many of Veblen's ideas. He initially adapted Veblenian concepts to agriculture, but soon their application in wider terms became evident to him. Institutional economics complemented his concern for social justice and supplied a rationale for reform both on a national and international scale. Many of the Vice-President's pronouncements, considered impractical schemes and idealistic visions by political opponents, were merely elaborations on themes originally posited by Veblen. Need for social inventions, abolition of poverty, anti-imperialism, economic cooperation in global terms, and the need for an effective international organization to foster peace were all extensions of Veblenian precepts.[6] Wallace's program for the postwar era, therefore, was based on his experiences of the twenties and on his expectations that institutional economics would work on a dimension never before attempted. His grand scheme, which indeed did have an abstract quality about it, was to secure for the world a future state of peace and prosperity. That would be the real millennium or, in the lexicon of the Social Gospel, the Kingdom of God on earth.

When asked to deliver an address to the Woodrow Wilson Foundation meeting concurrently with the American Society for Public Administration and the American Political Science Association, Vice-President Wallace used the occasion to spell out his program for the postwar world. His speech was broadcast nationally on December 28, 1942, the eighty-sixth anniversary of Woodrow Wilson's birth. Wallace definitely identified his own ideals with the Progressivism of Wilson. Of the last war President, he said, "The 'New Freedom' for which Wilson fought was the forerunner of the Roosevelt 'New Deal' of 1933 and of the world-wide democracy which is the goal of the United Nations in this present struggle."[7]

By identifying Wilson's war aims with those of World War II, the Vice-President again cast America's role as crusading to make the world safe for democracy. The cornerstone for this new universal society was to be a "federated world organization" fashioned specifically to keep the peace. Wallace explained:

> Obviously the United Nations must first have machinery which can disarm and keep disarmed those parties of the world which would break the peace. Also there must be machinery for preventing economic warfare and enhancing economic peace among nations.
>
> Probably there will have to be an international court to make decisions in cases of dispute. And an international court presupposes some kind of world council, so that whatever world system evolves will have enough flexibility to meet changing circumstances as they arise.[8]

Speaking as though he were the Woodrow Wilson of World War II, Henry Wallace set about systematically to announce a set of objectives equal in scope to those contained in the Fourteen Points. Fusing Progressive principles with his own version of institutional economics, he called for the establishment of a world organization that would achieve the following: "Preserve the liberty of the United Nations—liberty in a political sense, equality of opportunity in international trade, security against war and business depression due to international causes, and unity of purpose in promoting the general welfare of the world." On the domestic scene he called for "careful planning," so that mistakes of the twenties would not be repeated. Listeners were reminded their country would emerge from the war a creditor nation, that a high tariff policy would again be disastrous, and that "maintenance of full employment . . . should be the joint responsibility of private business and of government."

The Vice-President was persuaded in his own heart and mind that history truly had provided mankind with one more opportunity to bring to fruition the type of world envisioned by Wilson. "Now at last the nations of the world have a second chance," he vowed, "to erect a lasting structure of peace . . . such as that which Woodrow Wilson sought to build but which crumbled away because the world was not yet ready." He implored all Americans to help transform a tragic but necessary war into a bold venture aimed at creating a universal society based on justice and peace. Wallace was convinced his nation's destiny, was to take the lead in forging a better world—an abode for humanity for which countless generations yet unborn would give praise.[9]

Just as Henry Wallace had assumed a self-designated role of philosopher for the New Deal in the thirties, he soon gained stature as a leading liberal ideologist for the war. His many speeches reiterating Wilsonian ideals helped influence public opinion to support American participation in a future international organization. As his popularity increased, he received many more invitations to speak than he could possibly accept. Requests from publishers were also extended to him. H. S. Latham, the vice-president of Macmillan Company, asked him to consider writing a book for them which would "deal vividly, dramatically, concisely, with . . . war aims and what the United Nations are intending to do, and what will be the future of the world when the war is won."[10] Another request came from Donald M. Stuart, representing Scott, Foresman, and Company, inquiring whether the Vice-President would be interested in writing a "World History of the Common Man."[11]

Interestingly enough Franklin D. Roosevelt joined the parade of those urging him to apply his writing talent along these lines. The President wanted four books written, each to deal with one of his Four Freedoms, and he expressed a wish that Wallace would accept an assignment to do one of them. The only advice F.D.R. offered as to content related to the manner in which conservative critics should be treated. "Personally, I would use a gentle panning of the opponents of the Four Freedoms—but in a light vein," he suggested. "For instance, one could make comparisons between them and the nobility of France at the beginning of the French Revolution; with the small, but noisy minority who opposed the Magna Charta; with the rioters of Athens who drove out many wise men; and with the rambunctious children of Israel who made Moses so angry he smashed the Tables of Stone."[12]

Another significant Wallace speech, rivaling Roosevelt's Four Freedoms in public popularity, was his "Price of Free World Victory," which was originally given to the Free World Association at New York City on May 8, 1942. The text was so widely circulated in booklet form that it made the phrase "free world" a household term. In seeking clearance from Roosevelt, which he did for all his major speeches, the Vice-President indicated the purpose of his talk was twofold: to arouse in the American people a fierce determination to fight for "complete victory" and to "encourage downtrodden people of the world" by instilling in them hope for the future. Prior to its delivery Wallace had pondered how best to inspire the masses and infuse in them the will to fight on until totalitarianism was crushed. He wanted to propagate for the free peoples of the world a philosophy that would undermine fascism and all other militaristic modes of thought. Going far beyond Winston Churchill's famed "blood, sweat, and tears" speech, he hoped to rally subjugated populations to resist their oppressors, at the same time holding out to them the promise of a brighter future based on a new era of worldwide democracy.

Incorporating ideas about Germany and the Soviet Union gained from Joseph Davies (former U.S. ambassador to Russia who wrote *Mission to Moscow*), Serge Chakotin (Russian psychologist and author of *The Rape of the Masses*), and Herman Rauschning (an anti-Hitler exile who once belonged to the Nazi party), Henry Wallace delivered a powerful speech. It caught the attention of millions at home and abroad as an eloquent justification for fighting to total victory. At the outset the war was defined as a struggle to the finish. But mere conquest was not the final goal;

preservation of freedom was the basic objective. He exhorted, "As we begin the final stages of this fight to the death between the free world and the slave world, it is worth while to refresh our minds about the march of freedom for the common man. The idea of freedom—the freedom that we in the United States know and love so well—is derived from the Bible with its extraordinary emphasis on the dignity of the individual. Democracy is the only true political expression of Christianity."[13]

Although many political scientists would challenge the validity of equating democracy with Christianity (even in broad terms), it seemed obvious to Wallace. Furthermore, he maintained that the historical development of democracy paralleled expansion of education and the rise of an enlightened populace. This explained why the Soviet Union lagged behind other Western nations in the evolvement of democratic institutions. "Russia, for example," asserted the Vice-President, "was changed from an illiterate to a literate nation within one generation and, in the process, Russia's appreciation of freedom was enormously enhanced." He insisted that common people everywhere, including those in the Soviet Union, were steadily moving toward the attainment of democratic freedoms and economic security. World War II, as he interpreted it, was to be the beginning of a true "people's revolution." Using the logic of historical determinism, Wallace claimed such a mass movement would inevitably lead to the "century of the common man." That was the precursor of a millennium to come, a virtual kingdom of God on earth in the eschatology of Social Gospel theology, and not the thousand-year Reich of Hitler. Mankind was on the move, progressing from tyranny to freedom and from the debilitating chains of poverty toward permanent prosperity. The ultimate aims of the war, in Wallace's words, were:

> The people in their millennial and revolutionary march toward manifesting here on earth the dignity that is in every human soul, holds as its credo the Four Freedoms enunciated by President Roosevelt in his message to Congress on January 6, 1941.
>
> These four freedoms are the very core of the revolution for which the United Nations have taken their stand. We who live in the United States may think there is nothing very revolutionary about freedom of religion, freedom of expression, and freedom from the fear of secret police.
>
> But when we begin to think about the significance of freedom from want for the average man, then we know that the revolution of the past hundred and fifty years has not been completed, either

> here in the United States or in any other nation in the world. We know that this revolution cannot stop until freedom from want has actually been attained.[14]

Within the context of Wallace's ideological system, the German Führer was the incarnation of a satanic force preying upon the weaknesses of mankind. "In a twisted sense," the Vice-President attested, "there is something almost great in the figure of the Supreme Devil operating through a human form, in a Hitler who has the daring to spit straight into the eye of God and man." The Nazi leader was doomed, he predicted, since the people's revolution could not be stopped. Through victory in war men everywhere would break the bonds of totalitarian slavery and achieve both political and economic freedom. He vowed, "When the Nazi psychologists tell their master Hitler that we in the United States may be able to produce hundreds of thousands of planes, but that we have no will to fight, they are only fooling themselves and him. The truth is that when the rights of the American people are transgressed, as those rights have been transgressed, the American people will fight with a relentless fury which will drive the ancient Teutonic gods back cowering into their caves. The Götterdämmerung has come for Odin and his crew."[15]

With intense passion he proclaimed, "No compromise with Satan is possible. . . . We shall fight for a complete peace as well as a complete victory." His final rubric in this litany of triumph was the invocation: "The people's revolution is on the march, and the Devil and all his angels cannot prevail against it. They cannot prevail, for on the side of the people is the Lord. . . . Strong is the strength of the Lord, we who fight in the people's cause will not stop until that cause is won."[16]

This specific address was well received, especially by fellow liberals, since it justified the war in moral terms and set forth noble objectives. Eleanor Roosevelt wrote Wallace, "I wanted to tell [you] . . . how much I am impressed by the effect that your speech on the People's Century has had on young people."[17] Although most critics thought the Vice-President had good intentions, some believed the sentiments expressed were far to idealistic. Defeat of Hitler was in the self-interest of the United States, but they did not think it realistic to presume Germany's demise was the prelude to a world utopia. Morale was raised at home and expectations abroad were lifted when Wallace's forceful words were given wide dissemination. Excerpts from his talk soon found their way into editorials, sermons, movies, and even comic books. Overseas broadcasts, including those from underground radio installations, elevated the Vice-President to a position of spokesman for world liberalism. Joseph Goebbels, the Reich's chief propagandist, sneered at Wallace's "effusions," but he nonetheless ordered Dr. Otto Dietrick to refute them.[18] Like Wilson, Wallace also aroused the hopes of conquered people that Americans were doing battle solely for lofty principles and altruistic aims.

In the Merrick Lectures delivered at Ohio Wesleyan University in 1943 (and subsequently published in book form as the *Christian Bases of World Order*), the Vice-President dwelt again on the theme of how the great conflict then in progress could truly be the war to end all wars. He began the series by pointing out that three political philosophies were contending for global superiority. They were defined in this manner: "The first, based on the supremacy of might over right, says that war between nations is inevitable until such time as a single master race dominates the entire world. . . . The second—the Marxist philosophy—says that class warfare is inevitable until such time as the proletariat comes out on top, everywhere in the world, and can start building a society without classes. The third—which we in this country know as the democratic Christian philosophy—denies that man was made for war, whether it be war between nations or war between classes, and asserts boldly that ultimate peace is inevitable, that all men are brothers, and that God is their Father."[19]

Christianity to Wallace meant religion "based on the social message of the prophets [and the] . . . insight of Christ." Here again he equated the principles of democracy with doctrinal teachings of the Social Gospel, claiming both emphasized the brotherhood of man and fatherhood of God. All religions (e.g., Judaism, Mohammedanism, and Hinduism) and all denominations (Roman Catholic and various Protestant groups) were considered to be proponents of democratic Christianity insofar as they "in one way or another preach the doctrine of the dignity of each individual soul, the doctrine that God intended man to be a good neighbor to his fellow man, and the doctrine of the essential unity of the entire world." His interpretation of the "gospel of Christ" was essentially limited to the words of the Sermon on the Mount.[20] In the Vice-President's thinking such precepts as love, charity, and humanitarianism were the essential tenets of all higher religions and were not related to specific dogmas or ceremonial worship. Many orthodox clergymen obviously did not agree with his definition of Christianity. Wallace's spiritual approach, therefore, did not have as widespread support from organized Christianity as one might suppose.

Continuing his lectures, the Vice-President caused great consternation among political conservatives and cautious observers of the Soviet system by his oversimplification of Russian history. Infused in his interpretation of Marxism were assumptions that were debatable. Whereas Wallace had read Karl Marx, he ignored important doctrinal additions of Nikolai Lenin to Communism and felt sure that the expulsion of Leon Trotsky in 1929 ended the desire of the Soviet Union to export its revolutionary teachings. The 1943 dissolution of the Comintern by Joseph Stalin gave Wallace an additional reason to believe Communism was no longer a revolutionary ideology to be used for subversive purposes. He took it for granted that the wartime alliance could be extended into a permanent friendship. However, he overlooked the fact that Soviet national self-interest dictated a policy of expediency in collaborating with the United States as a temporary ally only. The Vice-President presumed immediate coexistence was possible because Marxism had undergone changes which made it compatible with democracy as practiced in the United States. He thus argued, "The future well-being of the world depends upon the extent to which Marxism, as it is being progressively modified in Russia, and democracy, as we are adapting it to twentieth-century conditions, can live together in peace."[21]

In his eagerness to establish the fact that Soviet-American friendship was based on firm foundations, Henry Wallace placed far too much trust on what he hoped would come to pass. He never doubted Stalin's motives and took at face value Soviet statements about future cooperation. Those stationed in Russia found the Soviets hard to get along with; and Roosevelt knew, though he never revealed this to his Vice-President, that Stalin harbored expansionist ambitions in Europe and Asia. Wallace's overwhelming desire to counter the isolationists, many of whom were now taking an anti-Communist stance, drove him to the extreme of making postwar cooperation dependent almost entirely upon American actions. Note his logic as he explained why the postwar period might end in disaster:

> We shall decide sometime in 1943 or 1944 whether to plant the seeds for World War No. 3. The war will be certain if we allow Prussia to rearm either materially or psychologically.
>
> That war will be probable in case we doublecross Russia.
>
> That war will be probable if we fail to demonstrate that we can furnish full employment after the war comes to an end and

> Fascist interests motivated largely by anti-Russian bias get control of our government.
>
> Unless the Western democracies and Russia come to a satisfactory understanding before the war ends, I very much fear that World War No. 3 will be inevitable.[22]

The burden for maintaining amicable Soviet-American relations was placed to a large extent upon the United States. Nothing was said about the possibility of Russian duplicity. His fear was not that the Soviet Union might act irresponsibly, but that a nascent fascism in the United States would become an obstacle to peace. Wallace seemed to think the huge military-industrial complex built up to win the war might tempt possible reactionary elements of the business community to think about imperialistic adventures abroad. One form of this drive for world hegemony manifested itself, in his view, as an anti-Communist crusade. He was sure that eventuality would pose a threat to peace far more dangerous than a policy of working amicably with the Russians.

While Franklin D. Roosevelt and Cordell Hull were the actual architects of the United Nations Organization (UN), Henry Wallace worked both privately and publicly to ensure its final establishment. He helped prepare public opinion for U.S. membership, while at the same time seeking to implement measures designed to make international cooperation a success. At times his pronouncements about the proposed UN were extremely idealistic, imputing to it such peace-keeping powers as it would never possess, while on other occasions he proposed practical steps to ensure economic stability after the war. To Roosevelt he privately urged such proposals as subsidizing foreign travel for American citizens (to foster goodwill and also render financial assistance to other countries via tourism), an ever-normal granary on a world scale, international control and regulation of cartels, and the internationalization of major airports all over the globe.[23] The Vice-President also had Milo Perkins and other Bureau of Economic Warfare officials work out details of reconstruction plans for war-torn countries that were later implemented by the United Nations Relief and Rehabilitation Administration (UNRRA).

Wallace's thinking was definitely cast in terms of international solutions for all economic problems. He publicly advocated other measures that were far in advance of what F.D.R. thought feasible. In *The Century of the Common Man* (1943), a compendium of articles and speeches, Wallace declared openly, "People of our country and of the world will have an opportunity to act boldly and imaginatively to organize the greatest utilization of the world's resources that history has even seen." If the alternative for the growing population of the planet was to be plenty or penury, his option was to strive for universal abundance. He reiterated his favorite argument: Modern technology had provided the means for abolishing poverty, if only men motivated by moral principles would create institutional agencies to harness the world's resources for the benefit of the masses. He saw the UN (as a world organization) as the key, to a new epoch of affluence. Note Wallace's total commitment to internationalism:

> It is vital, therefore, that the United Nations' covenant must provide the machinery to assure "freedom from fear"—an international peace law, an international peace court, and an international peace force. . . .
>
> We must prevent international cartels of the German type and perhaps substitute for them a United Nations agency to restore stable conditions in raw material markets, on price terms that assure producers fair incomes and promote expanded consumption.
>
> To prevent worldwide unemployment, there will probably have to be a United Nations investment corporation, under whose direction public and private capital can be put to work for worldwide reconstruction.[24]

Did Roosevelt underwrite these ideas? The President indicated to Wallace he was "delighted" with *The Century of the Common Man,* but no explicit endorsement was ever made concerning these proposals.[25] F.D.R.'s concept of a world organization was much more modest in scope at this time and considerably more practical in the way he hoped it would keep the peace. There was no doubt in the Vice-President's mind, despite these real differences, that his chief agreed with him. By not informing Wallace of his disagreement, and certainly no American President could commit himself to a policy of permitting an international body such sovereign powers over the United States, Roosevelt allowed his Vice-President to believe their respective plans for after the war were identical. They were not. Roosevelt envisaged the Big Four (the United States, Britain, Russia, and China) as the world's policemen; they would give the UN its power. Wallace, on the other hand, presumed the UN would have supremacy; and nations, including the United States, would subordinate themselves to a world government.

Because Henry Wallace was such an eloquent spokesman for the internationalist viewpoint, many liberal Democrats began to look upon him as the "peace President." He seemed the natural successor to Roosevelt. The height of Wallace's public popularity came in 1943 when he made a triumphant goodwill tour of Latin America. This came about after he received an invitation from the Chilean ambassador, and Roosevelt suggested the trip be expanded to include visits to other nations in both Central America and South America. This allowed Wallace to do what he felt should be done; namely, to prove to all Latins that the good-neighbor policy was a genuine attempt to solidify inter-American friendship.[26]

CHAPTER 4

GOODWILL AMBASSADOR TO LATIN AMERICA: THE

HENRY WALLACE developed a many-faceted interest in Latin America long before becoming the Vice-President.

In the course of his investigations concerning economic factors affecting agricultural prices, made during the twenties and thirties, he became very much aware of how the world market was influenced by South American products. When he took over as Secretary of Agriculture in 1933, Wallace pushed hard to regain lost markets for U.S. farm commodities. He wholeheartedly supported the concept of reciprocal trade and the idea of complementary agricultural production among nations of the Western Hemisphere.

Wallace approved the reciprocal trade agreement which was negotiated with Cuba in 1934, because that Caribbean republic could not finance imports from the United States unless it first could export its sugar crop. Trade was a two-way street, and while that meant some curtailment of the amount of sugar beets raised domestically, the overall gain for agriculture was beneficial. His long-range goal was to encourage Latin countries to cultivate what could not be grown in the United States and to head off native

Woe unto him . . . that useth his neighbour's service without wages. . . .
JEREMIAH 22:13

TRIUMPH OF POPULAR DIPLOMACY

production of what could best be raised in Central America or South America.

Roosevelt's attempt to implement the good-neighbor policy, Hull's reciprocal trade program, and Wallace's efforts to eliminate competition in the realm of agriculture did not immediately erase the ill will and mistrust Latin Americans harbored against *norteamericanos*. Both Japan and Germany took advantage of this long-standing suspicion to increase their trade with Latin America. The Reich's design exceeded that of merely securing commercial advantages. It intended to bring Latin America under its sway by undermining U.S. economic influence.[1]

Loss of markets in Central America so alarmed Wallace in 1936 he felt the necessity of bringing it to the personal attention of the President.[2] Efforts were redoubled in the Department of Agriculture to halt this encroachment on traditional U.S. markets. The division of foreign agricultural relations was instructed to devise ways and means of bettering trade relations. Special seminars were conducted for bureau chiefs, and an educational program was planned whereby Central American countries would be induced to raise more tropical plants. It was hoped this would result in increasing the number of products which could be sold in U.S. markets, thus providing dollar credits for them to buy more extensively from the United States.

At this time Wallace initiated an intense program of self-education on Latin America. He studied Spanish, read many books on the history and culture of Western Hemisphere nations, and started a collection of recorded Latin American music. His facility with the Spanish language increased to where he could read and speak it without undue difficulty. He even acquired a Spanish edition of the Bible and used it for his evening devotional reading. Accompanying the Christmas gift he sent to F.D.R. in December of 1936 (a book on Mexico and Central America), Wallace enclosed the following message: "Con mís mejores desos cordiales para la Novidad y un feliz Año Nuevo, le envio á Ud. un libro sobre Mexico y America Central que le interesá á Ud. como la espero."[3]

This in-depth study of Latin America convinced Wallace that to give meaning to the good-neighbor policy and to solidify an inter-American consciousness, some concrete steps would have to be taken to foster real unity. Writing for the *New York Times Magazine* in 1939, he outlined a program for promoting genuine Pan-Americanism. In his judgment twin pillars of such a movement were "culture unity" and "economic reciprocity."[4] The former could be advanced by a cultural exchange program (e.g., students, books, radio programs, and art exhibits) and the establishment of an inter-American university. Physical ties with the Americas were to be strengthened by completing the Pan-American highway as quickly as possible and by increasing other means of transportation to South America via air and sea. War in Europe and tensions in Asia made it imperative that the United States seek new sources for such raw materials as rubber, abaca, and cinchona (for quinine). Now was the opportune time for U.S. financial and technological assistance to be put to use in aiding Latin countries to develop a capacity for production of these desired items. An opportunity existed for Central and South American nations to become permanent producers of articles needed by the United States. Such sales would ensure the necessary dollar balances for U.S. products, thus creating a sound basis for reciprocal trade.

Speaking before the Commonwealth Club of San Francisco in 1939 and presuming that the United States would not become involved in the war, Wallace elaborated on his concept of Pan-Americanism. Inter-American harmony was an ideal means for the New World to demonstrate to the Old World (with its constant wars) how international cooperation could work. Cultural and economic unity of the Western Hemisphere would set an example—albeit on a regional basis—of how harmonious relationships could be established between groups of nations. He explained:

> As an ultimate ideal, the bulk of the American people will always respond to Woodrow Wilson's dream of a League of Nations, and to the vision of the prophets of Isaiah and Micah of a universal, charitable peace.
>
> Our strength today is not equal to the task of composing the differences which exist in Europe and Asia. Our task, in cooperation with the twenty Latin American republics, is to do a first-class job of laying a foundation for democracy on this hemisphere—for the kind of democracy that will conserve our soil and people for thousands of years to come.
>
> We shall hope for the day when the Old World is no longer preparing for its wars. We shall hope for the day when the New World can help put an end to war. For the New World is determined to live and act for peace.[5]

After the election of 1940 and before Henry Wallace was sworn in as the Vice-President, President Roosevelt made use of his running mate for a unique diplomatic mission. Josephus Daniels, U.S. ambassador to Mexico, had notified F.D.R. that trouble was brewing south of the border.[6] A presidential election there had been held in July, and losing candidate General Juan Andreu Almazán had refused to concede the contest to his victorious rival, General Manuel Ávila Camacho. The inauguration was scheduled for December 1, 1940; but as that day approached, it appeared certain the ceremony would be marred by civil disturbances. By placing Vice-President-elect Wallace at the head of a special delegation, Roosevelt hoped to enhance the prestige of Ávila Camacho and cement good relations between the two countries. Other members of the American entourage included such dignitaries as Senator Dennis Chavez of New Mexico; Representative Sol Bloom, chairman of the House Committee on Foreign Affairs; and Mayor Maury Maverick of San Antonio, Texas. James LeCron of the Department of Agriculture also accompanied Wallace as his special assistant.[7]

From the day Henry Wallace arrived in Mexico his presence was a salutary one. His decorum was perfect for the occasion, he insisted on mingling with the common people, and his ability to speak to Mexicans in their native tongue evoked an enthusiastic response from the masses everywhere he went. Wallace was hailed as a popular hero in Mexico City, and upon him was bestowed the special honor of addressing the Mexican Congress. His speech was delivered in Spanish and drew thunderous applause. The trip was a resounding success in popular diplomacy—a tribute to his personal ability. A few minor incidents occurred, some heckling by pro-Nazi elements, but the inauguration proceeded without serious interruption. A crisis was averted, and Mexican-American relations were greatly strengthened by the visit of the Vice-President-elect.[8]

After high-level discussions with President Ávila Camacho and other Mexican officials, Wallace notified F.D.R. that prospects for amicable settlement of outstanding differences were very bright. The Mexican government wanted a commission established to resolve problems stemming from oil expropriations, conflicts about water rights, and controls over U.S. investments. A request was also made for lower tariffs on beef and vegetables. In return the new Mexican President promised wholehearted cooperation in defense of the continental coastline.[9] Having seen an abundance of inexpensive books bearing German and Spanish identification as to place of origin, Wallace proposed to Under Secretary of State Sumner Welles that the United States open an information library in Mexico and also provide scholarships for Latin students to study at American universities.[10] Furthermore a lengthy report to Cordell Hull included the warning that conditions warranted constant surveillance of activities carried on by the Falangist, Nazi, and Communist parties in Mexico. Suggestions for cementing hemispheric solidarity included proposed aid to Mexico from the Export-Import Bank, a fair solution to the petroleum problem, an equitable division of water resources, careful handling of the Chamizal dispute (a touchy boundary question), and the possible construction of dams on the Rio Grande River.

Although President Roosevelt rejected the idea of a joint U.S.-Mexican commission, he did react favorably to all the proposals relayed by Wallace.[11] Nelson A. Rockefeller, Coordinator of Inter-American affairs, responded to Wallace's recommendations to Sumner Welles, and notified the Vice-President that libraries would be established in Mexico and throughout Latin America. Scholarships were also to be made available for Mexican scholars to attend U.S. institutions of higher learning.[12]

The direct contact Wallace had with Mexican officials prompted him to redouble his efforts in furthering the goals of the good-neighbor policy. Following his return to Washington, D.C., he continued to correspond with President Ávila Camacho and other members of his administration in Mexico. Wallace also conferred regularly with Welles and Rockefeller on ways to maintain amicable relations between the United States and Latin America, and he personally appealed to the Rockefeller Foundation with regard to agricultural projects it might finance for the Republic of Mexico. Wallace was overjoyed when Rockefeller secured $500,000 in federal funds for an Inter-American Institute for Education and Research, especially so when he was asked to serve as one of its trustees. The Vice-President was convinced that foreign exchange programs would foster U.S.-Mexican goodwill. His own daughter Jean was induced to attend Mexico University during the summer of 1943 and while doing so took part in projects sponsored by the Friends Service Committee.[13]

Another wise step was taken when Rockefeller established an Agricultural Division within his agency of Inter-American Affairs. Dr. Earl N. Bressman, Wallace's close friend and former assistant director of the Office of Foreign Agricultural Relations (USDA), was named by Rockefeller to direct the new bureau. Its primary task was to encourage Latin countries to increase production of such desirable products as rubber, sugar, quinine, vegetable oils, tropical fruits, cocoa, tea, flavoring extracts, herbs and various drugs.[14] Wallace, then chairman of both the Supply Priorities and Allocations Board and the Economic Defense Board (of which Rockefeller was also a member) indicated his hearty concurrence by notifying Rockefeller, "I have examined your project authorization for agricultural and mineral technical advisory service, and wish to express my full approval of it. . . . It is needed urgently both in connection with our new program for increased armaments and the fact that any interference with shipping in the Far East will throw an extra burden on the resources of critical and strategic materials in Latin America."[15]

As part of a vast mobilization team, the Vice-President had to concern himself with Latin America as a potential source of needed goods, but his feelings went beyond that. During his brief stay in Mexico he saw poverty that made him sick at heart. Wallace's sympathetic attitude made the *campesinos* regard him as a genuine friend. A poverty-stricken peon from the Yucatan region, for instance, wrote Wallace that his visit to Mexico "won the sympathy and affection of the whole country." He complimented the Vice-President for being an American of high station that truly "loves the Latin American countries."[16] This was not an isolated sentiment; many Latins, particularly the poor, regarded him as their only spokesman. Knowledge of this trust spurred Wallace to promote the kind of foreign policy that would fulfill the hopes and aspirations of the common man everywhere. He may, however, have overestimated the value of popular diplomacy, since he was relatively speaking an amateur in the field of international relations.

While in Los Angeles to deliver a talk commemorating the 132nd anniversary of Mexico's independence, Henry Wallace met Miguel Alemán (the equivalent of the Secretary of Interior in Ávila Camacho's administration). He encouraged the Mexican official to promote a program of hybrid seed corn distribution so that food production might be increased. With technical and financial assistance from the Rockefeller Foundation, such plans were implemented When Alemán succeeded Ávila Camacho as President of Mexico, he established a Mexican Corn Commission to further enhance the quality and quantity of his nation's staple food.

In his commemorative address, the Vice-President spoke of the Mexican Revolution of 1910 as a first step of a twentieth-century movement of all common peoples toward a better way of life. Candidly he stated that the American government was glad to see the end of "dollar diplomacy" and "other forms of imperialism." Both the United States and Mexico were now fighting to rid the Western Hemisphere and the world of another insidious form of imperialism—that imposed by Germany and Japan. "This terrible world war, in which we are both now engaged, on the same side," he asserted, "is not without its compensations in the form of new appreciation for each other."[17]

The Vice-President assured his Los Angeles audience, many of whom were Mexican-Americans, that Roosevelt's administration was keenly interested in helping Mexico raise its income level. As proof of this attitude, he explained: "Take the matter of living standards of war workers. The governments of both countries are interested in protecting these standards, and so it is of great significance that the contracts under which the United States is getting materials in Mexico comply with the progressive labor laws of Mexico."[18] Here he had reference to the so-called "Labor Clauses" the Board of Economic Warfare inserted into its contracts with Latin American producers. The official BEW policy regarding these agreements read as follows:

1. A general obligation to maintain such conditions of labor as will maximize production;

2. An obligation to comply with all laws of the country of origin, so far as they affect labor relations . . . ;
3. A series of specific obligations regardless of the actual provisions of the law, to furnish adequate shelter, water, safety appliances, etc.;
4. An obligation to consult with the buyer as to whether the wage scale is such as to maximize production; and
5. A provision that the seller will cooperate in a plan to improve conditions of health and sanitation and will pay half the costs of the improvements, if the U.S. Government will pay the other half, it being understood that the total cost shall not exceed an amount stated in the contract.[19]

The State Department approved use of labor clauses insofar as it would "maximize production and minimize those conditions of health, safety, housing, sanitation and labor which may tend to limit . . . productivity."[20] Jesse Jones, in contrast, opposed them as wasteful and unnecessary. As spokesman for conservative Republicans, Senator Robert A. Taft of Ohio, publicly challenged the wisdom of, in his words, "setting up an international W.P.A."[21] Henry Wallace thought otherwise. He considered this attempt at improving living conditions necessary both in terms of bolstering the war effort and as a justifiable means of actually implementing the good-neighbor policy. In honor of the fifty-second anniversary of the Pan American Union, the Vice-President explained, "Pan-Americanism is an ideal which transcends this hemisphere and which can serve as a pattern for an international society where people can live and work in freedom, in friendship, and in peace."[22] The United States must amply demonstrate its desire to assist, not exploit, Latin America. And by so doing, it would set an example to the world of how big and little nations could live together in peace and harmony.

Because his speeches were widely acclaimed for their idealism and evidence of friendship toward Latins, Henry Wallace was a popular figure in Latin America even before his 1943 goodwill tour of Central America and South America. Fairness and generosity while conducting business with Latin countries as head of the BEW also gained for him a reputation unique among South Americans.

Capitalizing upon this popularity, the State Department laid out a travel itinerary in 1943 for the Vice-President, including stops in Costa Rica, Panama, Chile, Bolivia, Peru, Ecuador, and Colombia. He was to leave Washington, D.C., on March 16 and not return until April 25. Wallace insisted that protocol arrangements be kept simple by subordinating formal functions and official ceremonies to grass roots tours of farms and factories. He did not wish to be the recipient of lavish ceremonial gifts, and word was passed ahead that the Vice-President would consider recordings of Latin American folk music as worthy presents. Wallace's primary objective was to meet and mingle with the common people. In order to encourage informality, his official retinue consisted of only two persons—Laurence Duggan, adviser on political relations to the Department of State, and Hector Lazo, assistant director of the Bureau of Economic Warfare Office of Exports. Señor Lazo was a Harvard-educated Guatemalan who proved to be a valuable escort because of his general background and knowledge of Latin customs.

In addition to his grand objective, that of furthering the good-neighbor policy, Wallace was very much interested in examining BEW projects in Latin America. His agency had spent millions of dollars in Latin American countries during the fiscal years of 1942 and 1943. These expenditures, broken down into two categories, were distributed in the following manner:

Region	*Procurement Contracts*	*Development Programs*
Mexico	$ 91,525,000	$ 4,729,000
Central America	37,874,000	7,258,000
South America	582,896,000	22,874,000

Since the United States relied heavily upon its sister republics for goods inaccessible anywhere else, successful implementation of BEW procurement and developmental programs were absolutely vital for America's war effort and obviously were of enormous benefit in developing their economies. Many BEW projects related to the promotion of production of scarce items such as rubber. Latin American nations were also recipients of lend-lease ($135,858,000 as of 1944), but this too fostered increased output in needed products in addition to compensating various countries for lost European markets.

By the time Henry Wallace completed his goodwill tour, twelve Latin American countries had declared war on Germany and a total of twenty had broken diplomatic relations with Axis nations. On a few occasions this was done as an immediate result of his visit. But in severing ties with Axis nations, Latin countries had deprived themselves of from 25 to 50 percent of their imports and from 10 to 40 percent of their exports. Thus it was not only equitable but quite necessary that the United States compensate for this lost trade as a price for their cooperation.

Although of short duration the Vice-President's trip was an

unqualified success in every way. The massive receptions accorded Wallace were truly awe inspiring. The Baltimore *Sun,* always very critical of Wallace, admitted in an editorial, "Whatever his shortcomings in other respects, he was an admirable ambassador of the good-neighbor policy, for he spoke the right language in more ways than one. . . . By personal example he sought to prove that Americans are simple people, every day, homely, neighborly folk."[23]

Basically, Wallace's down-to-earth demeanor captivated his guests. He did not act like the typical VIP. Without artificial affectations to impress local dignitaries, Wallace won the hearts of his hosts. He spoke their language, displayed genuine interest in their culture, and mingled freely with the masses. The Latin press, both right and left on the political spectrum, joined in the chorus of praise for the Vice-President. Although the Chilean government had been considering the action for years, it declared war on Germany immediately after his departure. Ecuador had special stamps printed to commemorate Wallace's visit; and even some of the newspapers in Argentina, a nation that was not visited because of its pro-German leanings, printed complimentary statements about his presence on the South American continent.

United States diplomats were astounded at the enthusiastic response to Henry Wallace. Claude G. Bowers, the American ambassador to Chile, informed Sumner Welles that "never in Chilean history has any foreigner been received with such extravagance and evidently sincere enthusiasm." In his report to Cordell Hull he commented further, "My judgment after the first three days of his stay is that it is one of the best things in Chilean-American relations that has happened since the 'good neighbor' policy was enunciated. . . . The enthusiastic reaction of the common people cannot be explained away by press preparations, party orders or anything else than the idea that here was a man representing the United States fresh from Washington who was their friend and deeply interested in their welfare."[24]

Assessments of other U.S. ambassadors were the same. Edwin C. Wilson in Panama cabled the Secretary of State: "I feel that Mr. Wallace's visit was an outstanding success. His informal manner, his knowledge of and interest in Panamanian problems and the fact that he speaks Spanish made an excellent impression, and, as President de la Guardia remarked to me, 'A visit like this really brings us closer together.' "[25] The newspaper *El Panama America* echoed Ambassador Wilson's evaluation when it editorialized, "We would say to Mr. Wallace from your visit springs hope for Latin America. . . . It has erased many scars and old wounds . . . of the 'Big Stick.' "[26]

Such an outpouring of love and admiration from the crowds was a source of deep personal satisfaction for the Vice-President. Throughout his trip huge throngs continually chanted praises wherever he went, and this in turn confirmed for him the value of personal diplomacy. The event was an emotional one, a spiritual experience, reinforcing within him a feeling that he must continue to champion the cause of common people. The voiceless masses not only in Latin America but everywhere in the world needed a spokesman. His conscience compelled him to assume the burden of representing their aspirations and yearnings. Wallace wanted these people whose lives were a daily struggle for existence to share in the abundance of a better world to come.

After participating in a dedicatory ceremony of the Tropical Institute of Agriculture in Costa Rica, a project he helped bring to fruition, Wallace was invited to address that country's Congress. In his speech, delivered in Spanish, the Vice-President declared it was possible to attain universal social justice on an international scale. This meant harnessing the "immense worldwide productive capacity" for the "greatest blessing of mankind." The good-neighbor policy was infusing meaning into Pan-Americanism so that living standards might be raised throughout the Americas. Wallace excited the expectations of his Latin listeners when he told the Costa Rican legislators, "We in this blessed hemisphere who have a common past of love of liberty can and must help the rest of the world to attain the realization of the Christian principles of justice and well-being for all. We must remain united in this great world crusade and we must hold our heads high. We of this hemisphere must make freedom from want a reality on earth."[27] This was the heartening message Vice-President Wallace preached throughout Central America and South America.

Very often, visiting U.S. officials forgot promises upon their return home, but Wallace took his pronouncements seriously. He not only worked for bold plans to aid the entire economy of Latin America but also took practical steps to render immediate assistance. He used his influence to see that minor differences were settled, to promote tourism, and to encourage the sale of Latin American products in the United States.[28] Time was spent working with officials of the National Broadcasting Corporation, for instance, to see that radio programs presented an authentic version of Latin music and manners. As a member of the General

Advisory Committee of the Division of Cultural Relations he recommended exchange programs to foster better understanding between the peoples of Latin countries and those of the United States.[29] Wallace's interest in Latin America never wavered. Until the time of his death he was actively engaged in genetic research devising new types of hybrids to increase the corn yield for the Indians of Central America.[30]

Wallace's intent was to use the BEW as a major vehicle for implementing social and economic reforms as a part of the good-neighbor policy. He realized there were some who regarded Latin America as an area to exploit and then to ignore once the war was over. Confrontation with these political foes posed a great threat to his political leadership for instigating world reforms. No sooner had the Vice-President returned from his triumphant trip abroad than he was engaged in the most crucial administrative fight of his career.

CHAPTER 5

IDEOLOGICAL CONFLICT AND ADMINISTRATIVE

THE Democratic party in 1943 was fashioned around a broad coalition of northern liberals and southern conservatives, much as it had been in the 1930s.

Franklin D. Roosevelt had attempted by various means, including his celebrated purge in 1937, to insure the primacy of New Deal liberalism within the party. Yet when the war came, F.D.R. announced an end of domestic reforms, so that victory over Germany and Japan might be given top priority. He sought unity within his party as well as throughout the nation by putting the New Deal under wraps for the duration.

Politics was not adjourned, however, just because the President proclaimed it to be so. Most southerners had opposed the vice-presidential nomination of Henry Wallace. They disliked his idealism and distrusted his liberalism. Every move made by Wallace as a wartime administrator was scrutinized carefully by congressional conservatives. The Vice-President in turn never relented in seeking to keep alive the New Deal philosophy. Roosevelt had made his peace with the Democrats from Dixie, but Wallace had not. When the conservatives opposed him, he made no

Fight against them that fight against me.
PSALMS 35:1

CONFUSION: THE WALLACE-JONES CLASH

effort to placate them but struck out furiously.

In 1942 the first assault was made upon Wallace in a manner calculated to ruin him politically. This initial attack was launched by Martin Dies, a Democratic congressman from Texas. In his capacity as chairman of a special House Committee on Un-American Activities, Dies issued a statement to the press containing serious allegations regarding certain employees in the Board of Economic Warfare. Only after he released his list of charges to newsmen did Dies inform Henry Wallace about them. In a letter to the Vice-President, dated March 28, 1942, the conservative Texan claimed "at least thirty-five high government officials employed by the Board of Economic Warfare have public records which show affiliation with front organizations of the Communist Party." Specifically, however, he named but ten people who were purported to be members of Communist-front groups. While remaining silent about the other twenty-five, the Un-American Activities Committee chairman became most upset over one Maurice Parmelee. This gentleman had once written a book with the title *Nudism in Modern Life* (1931), and Congressman Dies was positive Parmelee still advocated the "widespread practice of nudism in this country."[1] All too many newspapers headlined these sensational accusations without first seeking corroborative evidence.

When Henry Wallace read the daily papers, he was outraged by the apparent recklessness of these allegations. He felt these wild charges were a smear tactic aimed at ruining the reputation of his war agency. Suspicions were reinforced when he finally received the Dies letter. The BEW had never been informed about any pending public revelations, nor had any of the accused been asked to testify before the committee. No private communication from the chairman had ever been received relative to the loyalty of any BEW employee, and no effort was made to verify the substance of the charges made in the public letter. It was signed only by Martin Dies—not by any other members of the Un-American Activities Committee. Obviously the gauntlet had been flung at Wallace. He did not waste time in replying to this challenge.

The Vice-President issued a public statement that bristled with contempt for the Texas congressman. He countered, "If Mr. Dies were genuinely interested in helping our war effort, he would have discussed this matter with me as it came to his attention. He did not. Rather, he is seeking to inflame the public mind by a malicious distortion of facts which he did not want to check with me. If we were at peace, these tactics could be overlooked as the product of a witchcraft mind. . . . We are at war, and the doubts and anger which this and similar statements of Mr. Dies tend to arouse in the public mind might as well come from Goebbels himself as far as their practical effect is concerned. As a matter of fact, the effect on our morale would be less damaging if Mr. Dies were on the Hitler payroll."[2]

Admitting immediately that one individual working for the BEW had once written on the subject of nude sunbathing, this attack was labeled by Wallace as but a "malicious use of isolated facts."[3] He defended the patriotism of his personnel and announced the BEW would seek an FBI investigation at once to clear the names of those whose loyalty was questioned.

The Federal Bureau of Investigation found nothing substantive in the accusations made by Dies to warrant a conclusion that anyone in the BEW was either subversive or a menace to national security. Maurice Parmelee was discharged from the BEW by Milo Perkins; and after protesting the loss of his job, he was given a position with the Railroad Retirement Board. C. Hartley Grattan was also pressured to resign. His removal was due, not to Dies, but to Jerry Voorhis, a liberal Democrat from California who was a member of the House Committee on Un-American Activities. He claimed that Grattan, as a member of the American League for Peace and Democracy, had voiced strong disapproval of U.S. involvement in the war against Germany prior to Pearl Harbor. It was never made clear whether he was merely a pacifist, a prewar isolationist, or pro-German in his sentiments. In any case Voorhis was successful in getting this particular person out of the BEW.

David B. Vaughan, accused by Dies of having Communist affiliations, filed a libel suit for $750,000. Because the chairman of the House Committee on Un-American Activities had handed out a press release without its being an official statement of the committee, he had forfeited his congressional immunity. Much to the embarrassment of Dies, his staff had confused this BEW employee with another man with the same last name who also lived in the Tauxemont Road area of Alexandria, Virginia. This case of mistaken identity exemplified the careless nature of the investigation conducted by Dies. The Texas congressman came through relatively unscathed when the falsely maligned David B. Vaughan took no further legal action after Dies made a public apology and paid his lawyer's fee.

Without a doubt the Dies-Wallace confrontation served no useful purpose in either furthering the war effort or strengthening internal security. Liberals interpreted the Texan's attack on the BEW as but a thinly disguised assault upon the entire New Deal. This was confirmed in their minds when, after the encounter between Dies and Wallace, the House Committee on Un-American Activities began to harass such organizations as the Union for Democratic Action (UDA). Although containing some socialists and left wingers, it was originally founded by the eminent theologian Reinhold Niebuhr as a non-Communist, liberal activist group to further the aims and objectives of the New Deal. When Frank Kingdon, president of the UDA in 1942, asked for a hearing before the Dies committee, he was refused. By not allowing the refutation of these public allegations, the Texas congressman infuriated New Dealers. Unfortunately the liberal community reacted by defending anyone investigated by the Dies committee. The political atmosphere surrounding the investigations of subversive activities negated any usefulness they might have had. Substitution of an ideological inquisition for judicious inquiry prevented the committee from detecting the small amount of Communist infiltration that did occur within the government.[4]

Conservative charges seldom discriminated clearly between

pragmatic reformers and fellow travelers; idealistic one-worlders and card-carrying Communists; or New Dealers (however practical or impractical they may have been) and radicals committed to some economic doctrine other than capitalism. True, the Popular Front of the 1930s and a desire to cooperate fully with the Soviet Union during the 1940s did make liberals extremely tolerant of known Communists. A crusade to destroy the Nazis provided a convenient anti-fascist catchall that often made comrades in arms of anti-Communist as well as pro-Communist elements within the spectrum of American liberal thought. By refusing to discern carefully between these constituent groups, men like Martin Dies confused the issue and helped perpetuate an unholy alliance. Because Communists could invariably claim violations of their civil rights due to heavy-handed tactics of the Committee on Un-American Activities, liberals of all persuasions banded together to resist these intrusions on basic American rights. This made liberals susceptible to the charge that they were defending Communism instead of the U.S. Constitution. Many New Dealers, especially Henry Wallace, were going to be victimized by this turn of events.[5]

Whereas such an individual as Earl Browder, the leader of the Communist Party of America, commended Henry Wallace for his wartime statements, so did certain prominent Republicans.[6] Wendell L. Willkie, for instance, concurred with many of Wallace's ideas for postwar planning. His best seller, *One World,* was a similar application of Wilsonian principles to international relations. John Foster Dulles, then chairman of a commission on postwar goals for the Federal Council of Churches, also agreed with many tenets of Wallace's thinking on foreign policy. He publicly agreed with the Vice-President by asserting, "Victory is too much looked upon merely as something that will bring relief from peril. We do not look to it as something that will bring the opportunity to achieve a great mission in the world. . . . The addresses by Mr. Wallace and the final chartering of our courses by Mr. Hull are beginning to create the content for the dynamic faith we need."[7]

The mixture of Christian idealism and Wilsonian internationalism in Wallace's thought represented a philosophic outlook deeply rooted in the historic tradition of the United States. Richard L. Strout of the *Christian Science Monitor* categorized the Vice-President as a thinker belonging to the utopian school,[8] because the millennial epoch of which the Vice-President spoke when he referred to the establishment of the "kingdom of God on earth" was definitely American in character. Wallace and other liberals of similar persuasion envisioned a new era where universal peace and abundance would make the world an earthly paradise. Their views were an indigenous American idealism with a sense of progress and mission, reaching from Thomas Jefferson to Woodrow Wilson and finally to Franklin D. Roosevelt.

One consistent critic of both utopian and Wilsonian schools of foreign policy was Walter Lippmann. By no means was this optimism of things to come shared by the renowned analyst (then writing for the New York *Herald Tribune*), who viewed international affairs in more realistic terms. Having once served in the administration of Woodrow Wilson, he found the experience a disillusioning one because the World War I President had aroused idealistic expectations relative to the postwar era which were unattainable. Wilson's undoing was laid to the following cause: "He failed because in leading the nation to war he had failed to give the durable and compelling reasons for the momentous decision. The reasons he did give were legalistic and moralistic and idealistic reasons, rather than the substantial and vital reason that the security of the United States demanded that no aggressively expanding imperial power, like Germany, should be allowed to gain the mastery of the Atlantic Ocean."[9]

In Lippmann's opinion idealists such as Henry Wallace in the Roosevelt administration were making the same mistake as Woodrow Wilson. The Vice-President identified war aims with total peace in the future rather than with specific objectives related to national self-interest. "National ideals," Lippmann contended, "should express the serious purposes of the nation, and the vice of the pacifist ideal is that it conceals the true end of foreign policy. The true end is to provide for the security of the nation in peace *and* in war."[10]

The onslaught of Martin Dies had failed either to dislodge Wallace from his position as head of the BEW or to lessen his stature within the Democratic party. Another Texan, however, was to be more successful. That man was Jesse Holman Jones. This Houston millionaire was a conservative Democrat who had served his party and country for many years. During World War I he honored Woodrow Wilson's request to direct military relief for the American Red Cross. Because of his personal wealth and contact with businessmen, he was called upon repeatedly to help raise funds for various political campaigns. In 1928 Jones brought the Democratic National Convention to Houston by pledging $200,000 to cover the costs involved. He also contributed another $25,000 to Al Smith's ill-fated presidential campaign.[11]

When the Reconstruction Finance Corporation (RFC) was

chartered by Congress on January 16, 1932, President Hoover appointed Jesse Jones to its board of directors. In 1933 F.D.R. elevated Jones to be its chairman. This unique federal corporation had been given $500 million in capital with authority to borrow an additional $1.5 billion. It was a mighty tool for recovery and served the New Deal well. As the RFC's power increased, so did that of Jones.[12] In time he headed other agencies dependent upon RFC funding, such as the Federal Housing Administration, Home Owners Loan Corporation, and the Export-Import Bank. After Harry Hopkins left the cabinet in 1940, Jones became Secretary of Commerce; and shortly thereafter the President also designated him federal loan administrator.

Although Roosevelt got along well with Jesse Jones most of the time, on certain occasions the President became exasperated with "Jesus" Jones, his secret appellation for the stubborn Texan. Generally some compromise was devised to settle any disagreement between the two men. Jones was not above circumventing a presidential directive if he personally disapproved of it. Essentially his base of strength lay with Congress, for it was they who provided the RFC with its funds and lending authority. War powers bestowed by Congress in 1941 greatly enlarged the purview of the RFC and permitted it to create subsidiary corporations, first for advancing national defense and then for furthering the war effort. Consequently Jones controlled literally billions of dollars for purposes of stockpiling and plant enlargement. Ruling his bureaucratic empire with a firm hand, he acknowledged only one master—Congress.

Henry Wallace and Jesse Jones were about as dissimilar as two people could be but had avoided conflict from 1933 to 1941 simply because their paths seldom crossed. However, in Roosevelt's wartime administration they were forced to work together closely for an extended period. Their cooperation was crucial, since both were involved in procurement activities and this required coordination of their efforts. The RFC was the BEW's banker, which made it imperative they collaborate as a team. Furthermore, their subordinates must necessarily pull together as one unit rather than standing guard zealously over bureaucratic prerogatives. Harmony under ideal conditions would have been difficult to sustain, but with the RFC and BEW it was an impossibility. Jones was a conservative who disliked Wallace's political philosophy, while Wallace was a liberal who disagreed with both Jones's political stance and style of administration. To compound the difficulties, Jones's and Wallace's chief assistants each harbored a mutual distaste for one another. Milo Perkins, the BEW's executive director, and William L. Clayton, assistant secretary of commerce and deputy Loan Administrator, were both from Texas; but Perkins had been a small-scale operator in contrast to the wealthy Clayton. Neither Jones nor his assistant were about to take orders from either Wallace or Perkins, whom they regarded as radical left-wingers knowing nothing about the business of buying strategic goods.

Despite Henry Wallace's victory over Martin Dies and the favorable publicity he received because of his triumphant tour of Latin America, the Vice-President's position vis-à-vis Jones was not as strong as outward appearances indicated. Midterm congressional elections in 1942 had emboldened conservatives. Republicans picked up ten Senate seats and over forty in the House of Representatives. Southern Democrats seldom lost, so when they saw fit to join with the G.O.P., a strong conservative coalition came into existence. This nullified any numerical majority the Democrats enjoyed insofar as administration proposals were concerned. Since the RFC was a creature of Congress and Jesse Jones had many friends among its conservative members, this allowed him to act quite independently with regard to agencies established by executive order only.

F.D.R. often humored and cajoled his Commerce Secretary, rather than issuing him firm instructions. Henry Wallace possessed neither the disposition nor the desire to emulate Roosevelt. He attempted to influence the President to discipline Jones, and when that failed Wallace took his case to Congress. Perpetual skirmishes between the BEW and RFC before congressional committees laid the groundwork for an explosion that came in 1943. In part it was a collision of overlapping agencies due to bad administrative policy on the part of Roosevelt, and undeniably it was a confrontation of two ideological positions within the Democratic party.

Wallace and Perkins designed BEW policies both to promote military victory and to further the cause of social justice. Jones and Clayton opposed this dual objective; they were interested only in winning the war in the most economical manner. This was the crux of their administrative and ideological differences. A good example of Wallace's philosophy causing dissension between the BEW and RFC was his attitude toward the so-called labor clauses. Inserted into BEW procurement contracts were provisions whereby the U.S. government underwrote compliance with certain minimum standards of welfare for the workers. Whatever extra cost was involved, Wallace believed, was well worthwhile if it proved to the Latins that the United States was not exploiting them.

Obviously this type of concern for the laboring class in Latin America made Wallace popular among the masses of Central America and South America. It proved to them the Vice-President meant what he said when talking about the United States being a good neighbor. Jesse Jones, on the other hand, simply regarded extra expenditures for implementing labor clauses to be poor business and an inexcusable waste of money. The Houston millionaire wrote in his memoirs, many years after leaving government service, that Wallace and his "social-reformer colleagues" had promoted a program which was "practically eleemosynary" in character. It constituted an international extension of New Deal reformism which to him was untenable. Thus Jones boasted that under his control the RFC had never been "concerned with reforming the habits and customs of foreign people."[13]

The cost-conscious business-oriented approach to wartime procurement practiced by the RFC outraged both Wallace and Perkins. They considered speed, sure acquisition of scarce materials, and international goodwill more important than mere price tags. The BEW and RFC also clashed for years over the means for guaranteeing adequate rubber supplies for war and civilian use. Jones's record of securing stockpiles of rubber, when the RFC was authorized to do so prior to Pearl Harbor, was one of lost opportunities and poor results. A Rubber Reserve Company was set up as a subsidiary to the RFC, with an advisory committee to work with rubber manufacturers; but this agency failed to prevent shortages of crude rubber from developing. Caution and parsimony on the part of Jesse Jones caused a complete muddle in rubber, ultimately making gasoline rationing necessary to reduce rubber consumption on the part of civilian automobile owners.

Without Wallace's foresight in 1938 when the Department of Agriculture engineered a trade of 600,000 bales of surplus cotton for 90,000 tons of raw rubber, actual military shortages would have occurred. Crude rubber was stored in Commodity Credit Corporation warehouses and this, along with a three-year supply of corn and wheat in the ever-normal granary (part of the Agricultural Adjustment Act of 1938), did much to enhance the war effort. Also, because of the four regional research laboratories established that year, USDA scientists began to investigate the possibility of making synthetic rubber from corn.[14]

When far-eastern production was cut off permanently, various BEW projects were authorized, such as securing wild rubber from Brazil, Haiti, and West Africa and having the guayule plant grown in Mexico and Central America. These programs were very expensive, as was the suggestion for developing synthetic rubber. The latter proposal called for government-owned plants to extract butyl alcohol from grain, and this in turn was to be converted into butadine from which synthetic rubber could be manufactured. Wallace also recommended that synthetic rubber could be produced from oil, since under his joint procurement program (with Harold Ickes) sufficient amounts of petroleum were available for this purpose.

When Jesse Jones was finally forced to agree that synthetic rubber was the only solution to the problem, he argued for private control of this new industry. Wallace pushed for government ownership because he believed it would be better for the postwar period. He had uncovered information suggesting that under a cartel arrangement between I. G. Farben of Germany and Standard Oil Company of New Jersey the American firm was prohibited from development of synthetic rubber. A similar arrangement had also prevented U.S. companies from developing atabrine, a synthetic substitute for quinine. Another consideration was the entire Latin American economy.[15] By keeping synthetics a government monopoly, adjustments could be made to continue purchases of raw rubber from hemispheric neighbors. Private industry would be less inclined to consider the political and economic aspects of the good-neighbor policy.

The extent of the RFC's bungling of the rubber program was made evident in 1942. On September 10th the "Report of the Rubber Survey Committee" was presented to Roosevelt. F.D.R. had appointed a special group consisting of Bernard Baruch (chairman), Dr. James B. Conant, and Dr. Karl T. Compton to investigate the mix-up in rubber production. This Rubber Survey Committee was highly critical of Jesse Jones's role and of the administrative confusion. Without detailing all the mistakes, the report found much fault with the President's administrative techniques: "These errors, growing out of procrastination, indecision, conflict of authority, clashes of personality, lack of understanding, delays and early non-use of known alcohol processes, are not to be recounted by us, nor shall we go into the failure to build a greater stockpile of crude rubber."[16]

Jesse Jones blamed this adverse report on Baruch, claiming it was a personal vendetta and not an objective assessment of his handling of rubber production. But the RFC head had trouble explaining away the criticisms leveled by a special Senate Committee Investigating the National Defense. Its chairman, Harry S. Truman of Missouri, had done a thorough job of ferreting out the reasons for a rubber shortage. Much blame was placed at the doorstep of the RFC. Jones had allowed the Japanese to outbid the RFC prior to Pearl Harbor, sometimes by less than one cent. Because Jones had set maximum prices to be paid, RFC officials sat by and let scarce supplies from the Far East fall into the hands of a future enemy. Not only was the Truman committee critical of the Rubber Reserve Company but it later condemned practices of two other RFC subsidiaries—Defense Plant Corporation and the United States Commercial Company; neither had performed its job properly. The former agency had failed to enforce priority regulations, thus letting scarce materials fall into the hands of black marketeers; and the latter company had permitted speculators to profit from their acquisition of essential goods.[17]

Stung by the Baruch report on rubber, President Roosevelt belatedly appointed a rubber director for the War Production Board on September 15, 1942. His choice was William Jeffers, president of the Union Pacific Railroad. Immediately, Henry Wallace contacted the new director and asked him to use only the BEW for procurement of rubber supplies. On the basis of an oral understanding with Jeffers, Milo Perkins was instructed to prepare a detailed plan for such an eventuality. The proposal, sent to Jeffers on January 2, 1943, would have placed the BEW in complete command.[18] Expecting confirmation of the arrangement, Perkins was surprised when informed by Jeffers on January 9 that thereafter the BEW would limit its function to making "recommendations for such projects as you believe warrant exploitation," while allowing the RFC's Rubber Reserve Company, under William Clayton's direction, to "take over their execution."[19]

When Wallace heard the news, he immediately protested to Jeffers, reminding the rubber director of the RFC's "record of incompetence" which constituted one of the "sorriest chapters in our whole economic history and now presents us with one of the gravest threats to our current war effort."[20] Anxiously seeking a change, the Vice-President also complained to James F. Byrnes, then head of the Office of Economic Stabilization.[21] When this too failed, Wallace took his case directly to President Roosevelt. His January 25th letter to F.D.R. claimed Jeffers' directive would deprive the BEW of part of its legitimate import powers, and by so doing would interfere with the war effort. He again explained the need for consolidating all procurement in the BEW and reminded the President of steps taken to avoid confusion in this field.[22] As head of the BEW Wallace had issued Order No. 5 to clarify the situation. All agencies involved in import activities were directed by him to coordinate their activities with the BEW and to allow the latter to assume leadership in this field. President Roosevelt did not ask Wallace to rescind his directive, but neither did he force Jeffers to retract his order.

Termination of the rubber fracas did not end the battle between Wallace and Jones. It was but a prelude to an even greater hostility. Order No. 5 rankled Jesse Jones. On January 19 the Vice-President wrote Jones in an attempt to explain the reason for his action. This order, he claimed, "separates sharply the responsibility of the Board's staff and the responsibilities of the staffs of Defense Supplies Corporation, Metals Reserve Corporation, Defense Plant Corporation, and the U.S. Commercial Company," and in so doing, "[serves] to increase substantially the efficiency of the work of our Government as it relates to the imports program, and will enable all of us more effectively to discharge our respective responsibilities under Executive Order 9128." Wallace was asserting that his organization, according to President Roosevelt's executive order, should have preeminence over RFC subsidiaries in policy decisions regarding all procurement from abroad. Delineating the functions of the BEW and RFC clearly, he concluded, "This Order follows the simplest principle that, with respect to all import work, the negotiation, contract preparation, supervision and administration of contracts will be discharged by employees of the Board, while corporate execution of contracts, disbursement of funds, the necessary accounting with respect to disbursements, and the acceptance of delivery of commodities and materials, will be handled by the financing agencies."[23]

Jesse Jones did not relish the idea of taking orders from Wallace, but several factors motivated him to seek a way out of an administrative situation that was causing such confusion. He had been subject to much criticism for his handling of rubber imports and was enough of a realist to know a purchasing agency ought to handle its own funds. After a talk with Roosevelt and consultation with RFC officials, Jones answered Wallace, "Your Order No. 5, issued while the President was in Casablanca, went beyond any reasonable interpretation of Executive Order 9128 and has proved unworkable. . . . We are prepared to proceed in all matters, but our respective staffs should get together and reduce the agreements we received Saturday, May 29th, to writing, and not have someone else attempt to do so. When this is done and we get the approval of the President I will ask Congress to instruct us to make funds available to U.S. Commercial Company under BEW management."[24]

In reply to this invitation Wallace suggested a speedier solution—the transfer of agency powers through the Bureau of the Budget. "I do not understand your objection to clearance with the Bureau of whatever order you and I might jointly agree upon," the Vice-President answered. Wallace could not refrain from chiding his colleague with the assertion: "Order No. 5 has worked astonishingly well in spite of the obstacles thrown in its way by some members of your staff. It would work excellently if you were to put an end to such obstructionist tactics."[25] In a communication to Roosevelt the Vice-President indicated, "Mr. Jones and I have agreed that, if you approve, the U.S. Commercial Company be turned over to the Board of Economic Warfare for the purpose of handling, with certain exceptions, the development and procurement of all strategic and critical materials as well as for the preclusive buying in which we are now engaged." He predicted with undue optimism, "Jesse and I are both hopeful this will result in greater peace in the family."[26] After F.D.R. concurred, Wallace informed the President the entire business could be concluded quickly if the RFC would expedite the matter without the usual delays. He added the warning, "McKellar and Byrd are lined up to get the BEW."[27]

These preliminary negotiations proved to be only a fragile truce and not a permanent settlement of administrative differences. Jesse Jones, who seemingly had agreed to the transfer of his RFC subsidiary (U.S. Commercial Company), made critical remarks before the Joint Committee on Reduction of Nonessential Federal Expenditures. Because of the strong anti-New Deal sentiments of its chairman, Senator Harry Byrd of Virginia, this committee's very existence was based on the premise that government spending should be cut drastically. Whether Jones did so by design or not, he spoke disparagingly of the BEW and implied strongly that much of its work was a wasteful duplication of that of the RFC. Immediately following Jones's appearance before the Byrd committee, Senator Kenneth McKellar of Tennessee could not resist attacking the BEW. He claimed it had grown into a large and wasteful agency despite the fact that a "congressional appropriation has never been made for the payment of a single person employed in the BEW." McKellar's allegations were meant to be political and subsequently drew a favorable response from southern colleagues and economy-minded members of the G.O.P.[28]

To set the record straight, Milo Perkins appeared voluntarily before the Byrd committee. Had Henry Wallace known how angry Perkins really was, he never would have allowed him to speak publicly. The BEW's executive secretary had suffered a personal tragedy when his eighteen-year-old son had been killed while training to be a Marine pilot, and he was in no emotional condition to undergo a grueling session before a hostile committee. With outward calm, Perkins forcefully refuted what Jones and McKellar had said. It was brought out that whereas the BEW was established by executive order, Congress did provide statutory authorization for administering exports and had appropriated money for salaries. Perkins placed particular emphasis upon the BEW's practice of pursuing an "extremely aggressive policy with regard to the import[ation] of strategic materials." When queried about the BEW's involvement in internal affairs of other countries, Perkins asserted that at no time had his organization "attempted to influence the politics or ideological side of friendly nations with whom we deal."[29]

More fuel was added to the smoldering fire when William Clayton also appeared before the Byrd committee. As Jones's right-hand man he naturally defended the RFC, while sharply attacking the BEW. He justified the RFC's practice of modifying some of the contracts negotiated by the BEW in terms of cutting down waste. Labor clauses, some one hundred of which had been inserted into contracts by BEW representatives, were pinpointed as evidence of unnecessary expenditures. When Senator Byrd asked Clayton whether Henry Wallace's Order No. 5 had actually helped the procurement program, the assistant commerce secretary replied, "No, I do not think it has."[30] From the tone of Clayton's testimony he obviously regarded the BEW as an interloper in a field where the RFC was decidedly the more competent agency.

By now the halls of Congress were buzzing, and the pages of newspapers were filled with commentary over the BEW-RFC conflict. Friends of the New Deal hurled critical barbs at Jesse Jones, and conservative allies countered with denunciatory charges against Henry Wallace. Both camps were treading in dangerous waters since the rancorous debate was reaching a point of no return. The BEW and RFC personnel were leaking news to the press (or more accurately planting stories with favorite reporters), and each side was violating President Roosevelt's specific injunction against public disputes during wartime. What started out as an administrative clash was now escalating into a personal feud on the one hand and an ideological struggle on the other. The Roosevelt administration was heading for a bitter internal fight of massive proportions, as congressional Democrats became involved in a contest of liberals versus conservatives.

Right at this explosive juncture, Milo Perkins had to face a Senate subcommittee holding hearings on appropriations for the BEW. To make matters worse, Wallace's archenemy Senator Kenneth McKellar presided as chairman. Taunting Perkins with question after question relating to the BEW's alleged wasteful procedures, the Tennessean made a specific point to prove its acquisition program was extravagant and ineffectual. Why did the BEW authorize huge expenditures for a dubious program of planting cinchona plants in Central America? Did it not take seven years for this plant to produce quinine? Perkins tried to explain the emergency nature of this project. Normally a seven-year period would be needed, but quinine could be extracted in three years by killing the plant. This was an expedient measure and expensive only if critical wartime conditions were overlooked. The executive director of the BEW could not refrain from casting aspersion on the RFC for allowing shortages of quinine to develop in the first place and specifically blamed the RFC for the countless delays in the acquisition of this vital medicine and other strategic materials. Of the BEW orders for $240 million worth of goods (during the period from April 13, 1942, to February 1, 1943), the U.S. Commercial Company had processed and paid for only $67 million. This was why Order No. 5 and transfer of this RFC subsidiary to the BEW were necessary. Speaking still more angrily, he pointed out other notorious examples of unjustified delays. For instance the Defense Supplies Corporation had purchased only $122 million of material when the BEW had ordered $237 million. The RFC's habit of procrastination, Perkins alleged, simply held up the war effort.[31]

Upon receiving the transcript of his testimony, the executive director of the BEW realized immediately he had added explosive fuel to an already inflammatory situation. Phoning Wallace, Perkins confessed, "it doesn't read as gently as . . . [I] thought it would." Regretting his harsh words and having already disregarded the advice he was about to give, Perkins suggested a "restrained approach" be taken henceforth in order to "do everything possible to stand off a fight."[32] This counsel was reinforced by a memorandum relating what James F. Byrnes, now war mobilizer, had said recently about the BEW-RFC controversy. "He told me he had just finished telling the President that the situation between you and Mr. Jones was so hot that he, Justice Byrnes, wouldn't touch it and that the President would have to get into it himself."[33] Obviously things were getting beyond the control of the two disputants and soon the Chief Executive would be forced to intervene. No one knew yet what that would entail.

William Clayton again entered the lists against the BEW by presenting a rebuttal. The assistant secretary of commerce denied outright that the RFC was responsible for prolonged delays in funding BEW orders. Any time lag between receiving BEW requests and payment for delivery was caused by the necessity of having to go over poorly negotiated contracts. He implied strongly that by doing so the RFC saved U.S. taxpayers millions of dollars. Clayton argued furthermore that when RFC handled procurement by itself as some of its subsidiaries did, all went well. Trouble might arise only because the BEW had entered a field where it was not qualified. Senator McKellar agreed wholeheartedly with Clayton and demanded that no BEW official be allowed henceforth to issue an order to the RFC.

Heretofore Henry Wallace had stayed out of the debate by allowing Perkins to answer Clayton. But Senator McKellar's comments so upset him, the Vice-President sent a prepared statement to the subcommittee for placement in the record. Wallace justified his action to Roosevelt by notifying the President he "felt obliged to release the attached statement in order to protect the war-time powers over imports of strategic materials. . . ." Wallace was fearful lest Senator McKellar carry out his opposition to the BEW with a reduction in appropriations. The House had approved $36 million for his agency, and any cut would automatically hamper its ability to function properly.

Whether Wallace's action was politically prudent can be debated, but the strong language used in his public statement was by all odds a horrendous error. The RFC was castigated severely for its "obstructionist tactics," its pernicious habit of trying to "harass" the BEW, and its general ineptitude in implementing import orders. Wallace blazed away at the RFC by accusing it of proceeding in a "timid, business-as-usual" manner despite extraordinary circumstances caused by wartime emergencies. He made the categorical charge it had "failed miserably" in discharging its duties to the nation. Throwing caution to the wind, Wallace asked Congress to make funds available directly to the BEW so that it might circumvent the "hamstringing bureaucracy and backdoor complaining of Mr. Jones and his employees."[34] Such a stinging rebuke was tantamount to asking Jesse Jones for a showdown—and in full view of the American public.

President Roosevelt was aghast at the severity of Wallace's attack on Jones. Acting hastily to repair what should have been resolved months or even years before, he now asked James F. Byrnes to act as peacemaker. On June 30 the war mobilization director had the two combatants meet in his office. For two hours he mediated what appeared to be a satisfactory settlement. Wallace would not have to retract his statement but was to issue an apology, prompt steps were to be taken to have the U.S. Commercial Company transferred to the BEW, and henceforth neither participant in the agreement was to criticize the other in public. Wallace issued what was purported to be a statement of regret for the incident, but when Jesse Jones read it in the newspaper his temper rose to a fever pitch. The Vice-President's press release read as follows:

> I have talked with Mr. Jones. He and I have agreed for the time being to continue the present arrangement.
>
> The Board of Economic Warfare will initiate steps which will result in a proposal to Congress . . . so that the BEW may be completely independent of RFC.
>
> I advised that in my [previous] statement . . . I had no intention to reflect upon his patriotism. I intended to assert that the delays in the RFC in acting upon projects had delayed the war effort.
>
> It did not state or intend to create the impression that his personal motive was deliberately or intentionally to delay the war effort.[35]

Disregarding prudence, Commerce Secretary Jones retaliated immediately by telling newsmen, "Mr. Wallace . . . repeats that delays of the Reconstruction Finance Corporation have retarded the war effort. This dastardly attack is as untrue as when he first made it. As for the rest of his statement, Mr. Wallace was not authorized to speak for me. I will continue to speak for myself and, as previously stated, I shall insist upon a Congressional investigation."[36]

Urged on by Senator McKellar and encouraged by his staff, Jones ordered a detailed, point by point rebuttal prepared of the accusations contained in Wallace's June 29th statement. This caustically worded document was released to the press on July 5. In it Jones insisted that Wallace's initial "tirade is so filled with malice, innuendos, half-truths, and no truths at all, that considerations of self-respect and of common justice to my associates force me to expose his unscrupulous tactics." The RFC's record was again defended by claiming it had "complied efficiently and speedily" to all procurement orders, and if delays occurred they were due to BEW "error and poor practices in some of the contracts." He further charged that the BEW was "inexperienced" and had repeatedly demonstrated "incompetence" in its work. "Squandering the people's money even in wartime is no proof of patriotism," he vowed. Continuing his bitter assault, Jones maintained Wallace and the BEW were more concerned with promoting postwar ideologies than in prosecuting the war. "It is my belief," attested Jones in his final blast at the BEW, "that Government should seek to preserve private business . . . whenever possible in the war effort . . . without resorting to methods bordering upon the hysterical."[37]

Throwing all caution to the wind, Perkins and Wallace prepared for battle even if that meant going before a congressional investigating committee. Wallace went to the White House, and after seeing Roosevelt he reported to Byrnes, "I talked with the President and he said he hoped there would be no Congressional investigation but if there were one in the Senate, that he hoped it would be by the Truman Committee. He suggested I talk with Harry [Truman], which I did. Of course Truman hopes there will be no investigation and would like to stay out of it. But he would go to bat, if necessary, to prevent the Byrd Committee from acting."[38] It appeared to the Vice-President that F.D.R. was going to back him up all the way. This in fact was not going to happen, but Wallace was fatefully unaware of it.

Newspapers all over the country headlined Jones's blatant allegations, and Republicans quite naturally took advantage of this rancorous intra-administration fight to make political capital. Representative Wigglesworth of Massachusetts introduced a resolution in the House for a complete investigation of the entire affair. He noted that the flurry of accusations indeed constituted "further evidence of dissension and lack of coordination on the home front."[39] Republican Senator Styles Bridges wanted both Wallace and Jones to appear before the Senate Military Committee because of the "very serious charges regarding the conduct of the war."[40] Senator McKellar again joined the fray by adding an amendment to the Senate appropriations bill that would have required majority approval of the BEW's board before any expenditure could be made.[41]

Continued public and congressional uproar caused by the increased tempo of the Wallace-Jones controversy appalled President Roosevelt. Congress was in a rebellious mood, and F.D.R. feared prolonged hearings would serve only to further embarrass his administration. His veto of the War Labor Disputes Act (Smith-Connally Bill) had been overridden on June 25, and an administration measure to roll back prices was killed shortly thereafter. Food Administrator Chester Davis had fought for higher prices for farmers and subsequently announced his intention of resigning. Still other domestic problems existed, including a race riot in Detroit and a threatened coal strike by John L. Lewis's United Mine Workers union. Conduct of the war also imposed heavy responsibilities on Roosevelt. Joseph Stalin was demanding a major second front, Chiang Kai-shek clamored for the recall of General Joseph Stilwell, and preparations for the impending invasion of Sicily demanded much attention. Amidst these distractions, F.D.R. once again asked James F. Byrnes to arbitrate the BEW-RFC squabble. Unfortunately Roosevelt sought no firm solution, only pacification of the contestants.

Armed with the President's orders, Byrnes once more played the role of peacemaker. He sent messages to Wallace and Jones instructing them to cease once and for all their public attacks upon one another.[42] Jesse Jones remained intransigent and replied as if he were the injured party. Stoutly maintaining his innocence in the whole affair, Jones claimed he had actually "tried to avoid any public exposure of any differences between the BEW and the RFC." Not only that, Byrnes was surprised to discover, he had "consistently refrained from any public criticism of BEW." Jones placed the entire responsibility on Henry Wallace. The Vice-President, he claimed, had made unfair charges publicly and had caused a $5 million appropriation for the RFC to be defeated. Furthermore, charged Jones, BEW officials fed "misinformation to certain members of the press, who have been unfriendly to the Administration, and [leaked news] to their pet columnist and radio scandalmonger" (a reference to Drew Pearson). Conceding nothing, the Commerce Secretary even added a request that his answer be shown to Roosevelt. The only concession was a statement that he would do his "best to comply with your suggestion of July 6th," which was a reference to Byrnes's first attempt to mediate the Wallace-Jones dispute.[43]

Henry Wallace undertook no such diatribe but presented a straightforward case directly to the President. On July 12 he addressed a lengthy letter to Roosevelt, proposing a final resolution to the entire problem. Wallace presumed F.D.R. would support him, since the facts justified it. Insisting to F.D.R. that proof did exist of "serious RFC delays to the war effort," the Vice-President asked for a clear-cut decision. "I should like to respectfully suggest that the situation is serious enough to warrant a thorough investigation by an outstanding committee which you might appoint for this purpose [e.g., the Baruch committee]. . . . I feel that you should differentiate between the man who is Vice-President of the United States and the man who is Chairman of the Board of Economic Warfare. If it should be proved that the very serious charges which I felt compelled to level at Mr. Jones are in error, then it seems to me that the public interest would be served by removing me as Chairman of the Board of Economic Warfare. If this approach does not appeal to you, we ought to go ahead promptly with the transfer to U.S. Commercial Company to BEW."[44]

Included with the correspondence was a letter from Irving Brant, who Wallace claimed was reliably informed that Jesse Jones "has been very careful to get your initials on all questionable programs so that he can escape personal responsibility if any serious investigation of RFC activities is ever undertaken by the Congress." This constituted another reason, the Vice-President asserted, for "continuing your policy of gradually stripping the RFC of its vast power."[45]

Wallace's letter indicated his political differences with Jones quite obviously were too great for him to be expected to work harmoniously with the RFC. But the Vice-President erred in thinking Roosevelt wanted to resolve this dispute in his favor. F.D.R. only desired an end to public feuding and had no intention of arousing the ire of conservative congressmen either by elevating Wallace over Jones or by singling out the RFC head for public chastisement. The bitter irony of this situation involved F.D.R.'s longtime laxity in disciplining subordinates. Such sins of omission now came home to haunt him. Presidential strictures to cease the political infighting were ignored as if circumstances were similar to the 1930s. Because crazy-quilt administrative structure and tolerance of interdepartmental wrangling had become so much a part of the Roosevelt style, neither Wallace nor Jones seemed to consider seriously what the President would do if he truly became incensed over their prolonged quarrel.

One thing Wallace had in his favor was his loyalty to the President. F.D.R. could count on him, whatever decision was made. But before Roosevelt had time to apply pressure, events went beyond the point of reconciliation. Unknown to Wallace the executive director of the BEW prepared another bristling statement in reply to Jesse Jones's latest set of allegations. Milo Perkins had been given great latitude in administering the functions of the BEW, and perhaps that freedom prompted him to act without consulting Wallace. Another factor that continually added to the emotional tension under which Perkins worked was the deep sorrow he endured over the death of his eighteen-year-old son. This tragic loss weighed on him unduly, since his only other son had been killed in a railroad accident at age fifteen. He could not reconcile the fact his son had been killed as a Marine pilot, while men like Jesse Jones seemingly bungled their responsibilities. Young boys were sacrificing their lives; yet, as he conceived it, incompetency was not punished on the home front. Perkins forced Wallace to cross the Rubicon figuratively speaking, when he sent a recriminatory letter to Senator Carter Glass. As chairman of the Senate Appropriations Committee he placed it in the record. Newsmen were astounded at its vindictive tone. Perkins lashed out bitterly against Jones and the RFC. "Mr. Jones has thrown up a smoke screen but he has not proved and cannot prove that he bought what the Vice-President charged him with not buying." Relative to the RFC's failures, Perkins charged, "If Mr. Jones would publish a simple statement indicating the imported raw materials actually warehoused in government stockpiles as of either December 7, 1941, or April 13, 1942, it would become apparent to everyone that he failed dismally to build the government stockpiles authorized and directed by the Congress some 18 months before Pearl Harbor."[46]

Headlines again featured the Wallace-Jones struggle, and radio commentators devoted entire broadcasts to discussions of its implications. President Roosevelt could hardly believe that Wallace had allowed this to happen. Under no circumstances did F.D.R. want the dispute to continue, nor did he desire public confidence to be shaken by further charges of any kind. His 1942 ban on "public criticism of other agencies of the Government" had been flaunted once too often. Without seeking an explanation from Wallace or taking time to consult with Jones, Roosevelt dictated identical letters to each man. The only differences were one line informing Wallace he had been relieved of his position as chairman of the BEW and a notification to Jones that he would no longer control RFC activities related to wartime procurement. In a most unusual step the President washed his hands of the entire affair by telling the pair, "I have come to the conclusion that the unfortunate controversy and acrimonious public debate which has been carried on between you in public concerning the administration of foreign economic matters make it necessary, in the public interest, to transfer these matters to other hands. There is not sufficient time to investigate and determine where the truth lies. . . . My action today is not intended to decide that question."[47]

That same day, July 15, 1943, a press release came from the White House announcing abolition of the BEW and transfer of its duties and personnel to a new agency. The newly created Office of Economic Warfare (OEW) was to be headed by Leo T. Crowley.[48] Henry Wallace remained silent, but Jesse Jones issued a statement commending the President for his "determination to have harmony and cooperation between Government officials and agencies in the war effort." He then praised Roosevelt for his selection of Crowley.[49] If Jones presumed the new OEW chief would pay deference to him, he was mistaken. Leo Crowley wrote to Jones in a formal and businesslike manner, informing the Commerce Secretary that his "first efforts [would] be along lines to take over such activities [as foreign purchasing] and consolidate them in the OEW organization." Pending transfer of the U.S. Commercial Company to his agency, Crowley let it be known he would "assume full responsibility for . . . directives" to the Metals Reserve Company and Defense Supplies Corporation. The OEW director commented tersely that to speed up fulfillment of purchasing orders, he would "appreciate your acting upon them."[50] This was just the beginning of the bad news. Jesse Jones was all but dethroned as emperor of the RFC when the OEW ultimately gained control over other subsidiaries such as the Rubber Development Corporation, the Petroleum Reserve Corporation, and the Export-Import Bank.

The OEW's total independence from the RFC was assured when President Roosevelt issued a positive executive order stipulating that Jones was to "supply necessary funds" for any requests approved by the War Production Board.[51] A resolution was then passed by the WPB's board approving all programs started by the old BEW. No basic policy changes were made. Leo Crowley now possessed the powers that Henry Wallace had sought for so long and had never received.[52] Crowley's assessment of the situation was that the entire BEW-RFC dispute was avoidable, had personalities not entered the picture.[53] After having precipitated the last crisis, Milo Perkins confessed that "90 per cent of the scum inside me has boiled to the surface," but feeling better psychologically could not repair the political damage to Wallace.[54] In the final analysis Henry Wallace probably lost the best chance he had to retain the vice-presidency and with it an opportunity to become President of the United States.

CHAPTER 6

PHILOSOPHER WITHOUT PORTFOLIO: PLANNING FOR

THE abrupt dismissal of Henry Wallace from his position as an important war administrator brought a crescendo of criticism from fellow liberals.

Those who desired to see the New Deal philosophy prevail within the Democratic party felt betrayed and bewildered.[1] Wallace's friends definitely felt that Jesse Jones was the one who deserved censure, not the Vice-President. In an effort to encourage him, Addison Parker remonstrated, "Don't be disturbed if you are a voice crying in the wilderness because you may recall the first voice that cried in the wilderness is still echoing through the ages and until it is heeded, there will be no peace, I fear, in this troubled world."[2] Wallace's Uncle Dan added the comforting reminder, "You may remember that I once told you that God has his hand on your shoulder, young man."[3] Although retaining the prerogatives of his elective vice-presidential office, Wallace had lost the source of real power. This did not discourage him, however, since he felt confident many Americans agreed with his political philosophy. He was determined to be heard and hoped thereby to influence the formulation of postwar foreign policy.

Cast thy bread upon the waters.
ECCLESIASTES 11:1

WORLDWIDE REFORMS

Although pursuing an independent course, his loyalty to Franklin D. Roosevelt never wavered. Even though he had been rebuked harshly, Wallace steadfastly regarded F.D.R. as the leader of world liberalism. Devotion to the cause of reform prompted him always to subordinate his own role to that of his chief's.

If anti-New Dealers thought Wallace's plummet from a position of administrative power would silence him, they were mistaken. On the very day he was removed as head of the Board of Economic Warfare, Henry Wallace was in Connecticut delivering a commencement address. This was a special event for him, since his own daughter Jean was graduating from Connecticut College for Women at New London. The Vice-President used this occasion to memorialize Milo Perkins's son George, who had been killed only a short time before while on a training flight at Pensacola, Florida. Wallace empathized with his BEW colleague, since he also had two sons in the armed forces. Henry (the fourth first-born son in the Wallace lineage to be so named) was in the navy, and Robert served in the army. Men were dying in war. Was their sacrifice justified? In a solemn manner Vice-President Wallace spoke these words of hope: "Somewhere there must be a perpetual song of resurrection, ringing forth continuously the message of peace and good will. And now I conclude this vivid personal experience by saying: May it be so that my George, your George, and all those who have sacrificed their lives will so inspire us to effective action that they will not have died in vain."[4]

Public attention was focused on Wallace as he journeyed to Detroit, Michigan, for a major speaking engagement. Organized labor regarded the Vice-President as their major spokesman, and speculation ran rife as to what Wallace would say to them. Would he denounce the Roosevelt administration? The liberal newspaper *PM* editorialized on July 25, 1943, the day his speech was to be given, "We cannot take it for granted that the Democrats will remain a New Deal party."[5] This Detroit address was significant in that Wallace publicly reaffirmed his faith in F.D.R. and the Democratic party. More important was the strong reaffirmation of his political philosophy. His voice ringing with emotion, Wallace clearly enunciated a domestic program and foreign policy for which he would fight. To ensure the creation of a "warproof world," he asserted, "World leadership must be more concerned with welfare politics and less with power politics, more attentive to equalizing the use of raw materials of nations than condoning the policies of grab and barter that freeze international markets, more interested in opening channels of commerce than closing them by prohibitive tariffs, more mindful of the need for a stable currency among all countries than in high interest rates on loans."[6]

Living up to the principles of brotherhood would impose upon America the obligation of eradicating deprivation at home and abroad, Wallace declared. Such humanitarianism would be, quoting the biblical phrase, "bread cast upon the waters." The United States "will have to fill many breadbaskets, help restore homes and provide medical care here and in other lands before our own peace will be secure." American productivity must be harnessed for the welfare of the world because mobilization for peace was the only way to avoid future world wars. Only isolationists and reactionaries would desire imperialistic nationalism or selfish, economic isolation. He branded this type of thinking a form of "American Fascism."[7]

Because a serious racial disturbance had erupted in Detroit shortly before the Vice-President's appearance, he deliberately took this occasion to speak on the imperative need for black and white Americans to live together harmoniously. This was not the first time he had spoken out on this politically touchy subject. He was in actuality one of the earliest of contemporary civil rights crusaders and certainly the first to identify racism as a basic evil which sustained segregation. More will be said later about his concern for minority rights, but at Detroit in 1943 Henry Wallace made an important point. He asked citizens of Detroit to think how absurd it was to wage war overseas to preserve democratic freedoms, while at the same time denying them to American Negroes. The Vice-President did not pull any punches: "We cannot fight to crush Nazi brutality abroad and condone race riots at home [fifty blacks had been killed]. Those who fan the fires of racial clashes for the purpose of political capital here at home are taking the first step toward Nazism."[8]

Public reaction to the Vice-President's speech was strong, whether pro or con in sentiment. His words quickened the spirit of many Americans who hoped the war would result in a rebirth of brotherhood and international cooperation. Expectations were raised that out of the bitterness of global strife a better world would emerge. Even his entreaty for assurances of civil rights for Negroes struck a responsive chord. Liberals hailed Wallace as a world leader who voiced the noblest ideals of all mankind. On the basis of this address Senator Joseph P. Guffey, chairman of the senatorial Democratic Campaign Committee, issued a statement that he personally desired the renomination of Henry Wallace in 1944 as Roosevelt's running mate.[9] Prior to Detroit certain columnists had already written Wallace's political obituary, but now all agreed the Vice-President was still a powerful figure in American politics.

Adverse response came primarily from southerners and G.O.P. conservatives. A considerable number of Democrats from Dixie did not like Wallace's utterances on the subject of civil rights and they, more than ever, were determined to block his renomination. Harrison E. Spangler, chairman of the Republican National Committee, lambasted Wallace for "labeling the 25,000,000 voters in America who are opposed to the New Deal as Fascists. . . ."[10] The Vice-President had used this term ill-advisedly to describe those specific capitalists he thought were motivated purely by desire for wartime profits. Wallace obviously was not referring to millions of Republicans but only to a small group of industrialists and financiers who, in his opinion, placed personal gain above the welfare of people. This was no doubt an overly ardent or even misleading description of a small portion of the business community based on fears that the great industrial-military complex built up during the war would be used exclusively for private welfare rather than public. While involved in war mobilization, Henry Wallace had discovered to his utter amazement that some firms with government contracts were sometimes greedy in their quest for monetary gain. It bothered him that patriotic soldiers were dying on foreign battlefields and at the same time some businessmen were getting rich without sacrificing anything at all. These were the pernicious few he condemned as "fascist," hence substituting a new symbolic epithet for "Wall Street" which had heretofore served as the *bête noire* of liberals.

There was no doubt that Henry Wallace was preoccupied with developing an American foreign policy based on humanitarian principles. Only then, he believed, could lasting peace be achieved. This was the meaning of his statement to Madame Litvinov (wife of the Soviet ambassador) that "the object of this war is to make sure everybody in the world has the privilege of drinking a quart of milk a day."[11] He did not think industrial nations could live in abundance, while allowing underdeveloped nations to exist in abject poverty. Such regions were not to remain colonies with their peoples subject to continued exploitation by big powers. Within this frame of reference, Wallace went far beyond the mere advocacy of foreign aid. The first step in preventing international conflict was to harness productivity of developed nations for the welfare of all the world's peoples. When cooperation replaced competition and free trade supplanted tariffs, the stage would be set for universal economic abundance. At Detroit the Vice-President had indicated he was not altering his views or retracting anything previously spoken. He, in fact, boasted, "I hope I shall always be an idealist."[12]

One interesting reaction to Wallace's altruistic views came from Guy Irving Burch, of the Population Reference Bureau. Burch told the Vice-President there were too many inhabitants on the planet to guarantee adequate diets for all. The "simple arithmetic" of sheer numbers, he claimed, made this goal unrealistic.[13] This coincided with criticism from political conservatives, who labeled Wallace's proposal global New Dealism and handouts to Hottentots and believed it would bankrupt America. Wallace's reply to Burch revealed the scientific basis of his thinking. During the 1920s he had worked out the statistical correlations between personal wealth, size of families, and social status of various segments of the U.S. population. His research demonstrated that the "birthrate goes down when education and standards of living increase." Relating this fact to Asia, he concluded, "When democracy, increased agricultural efficiency, increased industrialization and a higher standard of living permeate the East, you will find that their birthrate also will undergo the changes which we observed take place in the United States during the past one hundred years. To maintain these people in a backward status will bring about a more rapid increase in population than would otherwise be the case."[14]

Wallace's demographic study had convinced him the population explosion could be contained only when rich nations helped raise living standards all over the world. Fusing humanitarianism with practicality, he pointed out, "If the United States shoulders this responsibility she will profit thereby and there will be much less danger of either war or worldwide overpopulation (relative to resources) than if she does not take the responsibility."[15]

Franklin D. Roosevelt continued to allow the Vice-President to expound an ideology for World War II. Because of this Wallace always presumed F.D.R. held an outlook similar to his own. In seeking White House approval for an address to be given before the Chicago United Nations Committee to Win the Peace, he told Roosevelt, "If I know your heart, Mr. President, this speech, even though awkwardly stated, expresses in its broad principles either that which you have already said or that in which you have long had faith."[16] The theme of this speech focused on the concept that "economic democracy must be combined with political democracy." Wallace pointed out that democratic ideals in Western Europe had succumbed to fascism because of the dual evils of economic hardships and lack of social justice. Thinking in terms of the future extension of economic democracy, he declared, "In the world of modern technology, the possibilities of abundant production are so great that it is only a question of time until we can bring the blessings of freedom from want to every one."[17] Once this had been done, political democracy would have a chance to take root and flourish.

Henry Wallace tended to view the existence of international tensions solely within the dynamics of macroeconomic factors. Without detailed empirical data he thus argued almost in tautological terms that concerted and coordinated efforts be undertaken to initiate such international reforms as abolition of cartels, worldwide regulation of air space, promotion of international trade, removal of customs and passport barriers, planning for balanced production (e.g., international ever-normal granary), and channeling surpluses to backward countries. Once again, however, the practical side of Wallace emerged, as he hastened to explain the value of such an economic policy to the U.S. economy.

"Power projects on the Danube, irrigation works in India, [and] flood control in China," he declared, not only benefited the common man in those areas but in so doing "jobs will be created in Chicago and Detroit, and there will be a better market for the Iowa farmer right here at home." The key to a projected *pax orbis terrarum* was not in narrow nationalism as Wallace saw it, but rather in wise application of economic policy to stimulate economic growth everywhere. Americans would be the beneficiaries as a result of both increased trade and international stability. Closing his Chicago address with a prayerful plea, the Vice-President said, "May wisdom and understanding guide our President and the 96 Senators as they try to make the dream of universal peace a reality."[18]

At a press conference in Chicago, Wallace told reporters of the Windy City, "It is unthinkable that Mr. Roosevelt not be at the peace table." Just as he had been one of the first to call for a third term for F.D.R., he now took the lead in advocating a fourth. "There is no question but that the sentiment of the people is for Roosevelt as permanent chairman [of the Big Three]," he stated positively. "The Roosevelt name ranks highest with the people of other nations."[19] Without doubt Wallace very much identified his own plans for world peace with those of the President. Only with Franklin D. Roosevelt guiding the formulation of postwar policies could the Vice-President rest at ease.

Although detractors called Wallace a dreamer, certain aspects of his *weltanschauung* had a pragmatic quality insofar as his desire for world reform was based on the potentialities of scientific technology. While speaking to a group of visiting Latin American conservation technicians, the Vice-President elaborated on how productivity all over the world could be increased greatly by planning. "This is my thesis," he asserted. "The problem of peace, the problem of political democracy must of necessity express themselves against the background of philosophic reconciliation between the principles of liberty and unity." Nationalism had to be limited to allow worldwide regional planning in order to devise projects aimed at elevating living standards for large areas of population. He reminded his visitors that no prosperity via industrialization could be achieved without first guaranteeing ample food supplies. "The science of sustained yield, whether with soil, trees, or wild life that lives on the grass and wanders through the forests, or fishes that swim the water, is paramount to human welfare."

Always cognizant of nature's ability to nourish the spirit of man, Wallace cautioned, "It is possible for the exploiters to produce such a cataclysm as would make the fall of the Roman Empire seem a mere twinkle." He remarked candidly, "The problem is of a deeply religious nature. The appreciation of 'sustained yield' was woven into the Indian religion. For my part, I can't understand why the white man's religion can't be as good as the Indian's. I see nothing in the Bible to stand against our looking on Mother Nature in a deeply religious way. . . ."[20]

Not wishing to become totally a technocrat, Wallace tempered material reform with environmental considerations. His agrarian background, skill as a geneticist, and interest in conservation made him aware that the natural habitat of man should not be destroyed in the name of progress. As a member of Friends of the Land, an organization devoted to the promotion of better rural life, he continued to meet with former colleagues of the Agriculture Department. Frequently he wrote for its magazine, *The Land,* or addressed gatherings of its members. In one such article, "Soil Defense," he displayed considerable disquietude over the consequences of worn-out soil, depleted countrysides, and rampant urbanization. Wallace wrote, "Everything is made of our Mother, the Earth. Man is part of the living landscape, made of the same natural processes and laws. His body, his thoughts, and his spirit are the product of that landscape; that sun, soil, wind, and air. We are slowly learning to think in terms of a new science called ecology, in terms of inevitable relationships—to recognize that all living things under the sun—the clouds, the rocks, the soil, the streams; and the people and the spirit of the people—are all of the same going concern."[21]

At a meeting of Friends of the Land at Louisville, Kentucky, Wallace called attention to the fact that over a billion people dwelled in Asia: "Eighty per cent of them live on the land. Not more than twenty per cent of them can read or write. Their average family income is considerably less than one hundred dollars a year. They are scourged by disease and bitter hardships. It is our privilege and responsibility to help them to a better way of living, for the sake of ourselves as well as for them." Asiatic countries needed industry, but Wallace realized the basis of sustained prosperity was abundance in agricultural production. "It takes four families of these people to support one family living in town," he pointed out, while "here in the United States one family living on the farm can supply four families living in town."[22] Under conditions such as these both food and labor would be scarce, and any attempt at industrialization would be doomed to failure.

Thus the duality of Wallace's religioeconomic philosophy embraced both the spiritual and the material by supporting the application of scientific knowledge in both agriculture and industry to better living standards in so-called underdeveloped areas. For instance, he encouraged Mexican officials to take advantage of hybrid corn; aided nations in Central America to use scientific techniques in developing tropical horticulture; and used his influence to secure training for Chinese students in such skills as road building, terracing, and building bridges. When John Carter Vincent, counselor of the American Embassy in Chungking, forwarded to Wallace a request for assistance from the Nationalist government, the Vice-President took immediate action. The letter was from Dr. Tseng Yang-fu, minister of communications, and it asked for an arrangement to train students in practical skills. "One of the problems demanding immediate attention is the bringing up of enough engineers and technicians to undertake the immense responsibilities of a machine age . . .," wrote Dr. Yang-fu. "We have therefore worked out a Training Plan . . . with anticipation of most favorable response from your various industries."[23] Wallace contacted General Philip B. Fleming to see if his Federal Works Administration could help these students. General Fleming not only organized a training program but secured a subsidy for the first-year cost and gained the cooperation of other government agencies. All this was accomplished between June 14 and June 23, 1943.[24] This was an excellent example of how Wallace worked for practical projects to implement his overall ideas for international reform.

The BEW, as part of its wartime functions, had made detailed analyses of economic conditions in both allied and enemy nations. For this reason Wallace had a good grasp of China's current needs. This spacious land had held special interest for Wallace since a study of its Confucian period had given him suggestions about the feasibility of an ever-normal granary. From his reading of F. H. King's *Farmers of Forty Centuries* he realized how greatly the Chinese were rooted to the soil. He also knew the rural population was victimized by a land system that exploited them unmercifully. Wallace had sought to influence Kuomintang officials, especially T. V. Soong (acting president of the Executive Yuan and foreign minister), to initiate agrarian reforms. Chiang Kai-shek continually sought financial and economic assistance; but in the Vice-President's judgment there would be no economic stability in that vast country until China's agriculture operated on a sound basis.

President Franklin D. Roosevelt and Vice-President-elect Henry A. Wallace display victory smiles as they ride to the White House on election day, November 7, 1940. *(Courtesy Franklin D. Roosevelt Library)*

The Vice-President made many friends for the United States during his goodwill tour of Latin America in 1943. In addition to meeting with government officials, he made a concerted effort to meet the people as well. Here he is greeted by President Lopez of Colombia *(right)* with whom he visits a grocery store in Bogota *(center)*. His scientific interests took him to a laboratory engaged in research on the extraction of quinine from cinchona bark *(bottom)*. *(Courtesy University of Iowa)*

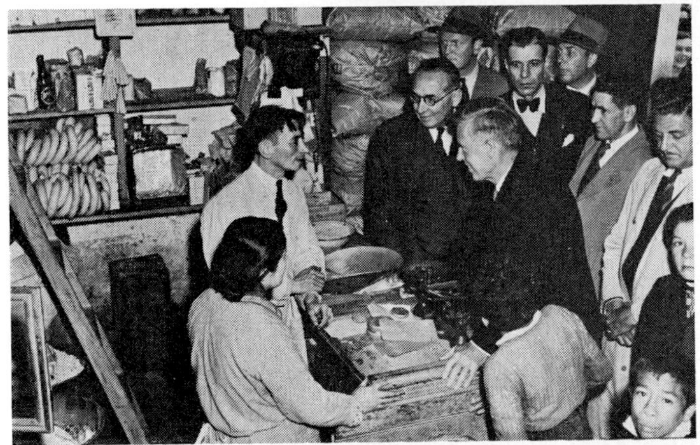

Henry Wallace visits with participants in the 1943 Regional Fair of Chiriqui Province in Panama *(above)*. He is accompanied by Governor Revilla and Minister of Agriculture Fabrega. *Courtesy University of Iowa)*

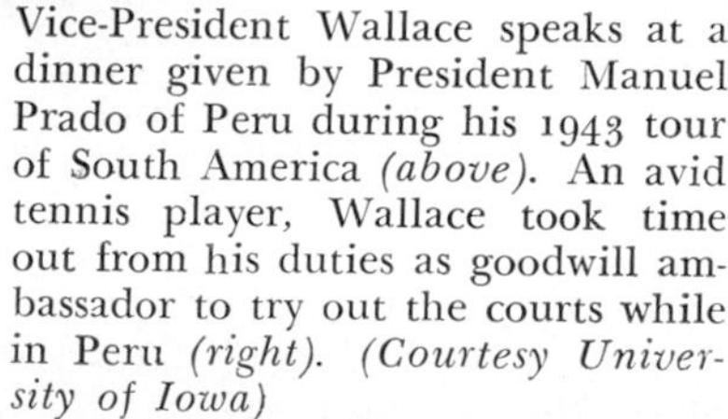

Vice-President Wallace speaks at a dinner given by President Manuel Prado of Peru during his 1943 tour of South America *(above)*. An avid tennis player, Wallace took time out from his duties as goodwill ambassador to try out the courts while in Peru *(right)*. *(Courtesy University of Iowa)*

President Roosevelt sent his Vice-President on a sensitive mission to Russia and China in 1944. This visit was later used by Wallace's political foes to support their claims of his Communist leanings. Wallace and members of his Soviet-China mission pose on the steps of party headquarters in Seimchan, Siberia *(above)*. While on this tour, he was photographed with war aces Ilya P. Mazuruk and Colonel Richard T. Knight *(right)* and as he shook hands with Russian miners at the Kolyma gold fields of Dalstroi, Northeast Siberia *(below)*. *(Courtesy University of Iowa)*

Henry Wallace was offered the post of Secretary of Comerce as consolation for being ousted as Vice-President in 1944. Here he faces a hostile Senate committee *(above)* as he testifies on his own behalf in 1945. Committee members are (left to right): Senators Guy Cordon, Oregon; Edward V. Robertson, Wyoming; Alexander Wiley, Wisconsin; Harold Burton, Ohio; and Josiah Bailey, North Carolina, Chairman (standing). Jesse Jones *(right)* testifies against confirmation as Secretary of Commerce of his former BEW adversary. Jones left government service in ill-disguised anger when Wallace was appointed to his former Cabinet post. *(Courtesy University of Iowa)*

Henry Wallace leaves the White House after talking with President Truman on September 18, 1946. Charles Ross, presidential press secretary is in the background. Truman hoped to retain Wallace in his cabinet in return for a promise of silence on matters of American foreign policy. *(Courtesy University of Iowa)*

Henry Wallace, campaigning for the presidency in 1948 as the candidate of the Progressive Party, spoke at a rally in Nashua, New Hampshire, where he emphasized the need for repeal of the Taft-Hartley Act. *(Courtesy University of Iowa)*

After retiring from public life and assuming the duties of an editor for *The New Republic,* Wallace made his home at Farvue Farm *(above)* in Westchester County, New York. *(Courtesy James W. Wallace)*

Although a private citizen, Wallace continued his role as a people's diplomat. He is shown here inspecting an experimental agricultural plot in Guatemala in 1964.

Retirement from politics ended years of active campaigning, but despite the turmoil and bitter disappointments Wallace displays inner serenity as he poses in his library at Farvue Farm.

Wallace received an invitation from John F. Kennedy to attend the inaugural ceremonies on January 20, 1961; this courtesy had not been extended to him since 1944. He posed with eminent Democratic leaders—(left to right) former President Harry Truman, President Kennedy, Vice-President Lyndon Johnson, and Speaker of the House Sam Rayburn—and spoke at the inaugural banquet (right). *(Chase Studios Ltd., Washington, D.C.)*

Henry Wallace's final years were spent working with his favorite plant, hybrid corn, and among his beloved flowers. *(Courtesy Mrs. Henry Wallace)*

To bring Asia and the problems of postwar reconstruction to the attention of the American public, Henry Wallace prepared a short study of the Far East. *Our Job in the Pacific* was published in the spring of 1944 by the American Council of the Institute of Pacific Relations. At the outset he postulated, "The United States will be so important in the postwar Pacific that we must, in our own interest, assume the obligations that our new position entails. To discuss our 'withdrawal' from the Far East is no longer realistic, and the Open Door principle which has been the chief basis for our Far Eastern policy for a hundred years is no longer a sufficient guide to the new and complex situation which we shall face when the war is over."[25]

Wallace's contention was that the United States could not remain an oasis of plenty amid a desert of world poverty. He declared that prosperity combined with security was desired, and this made foreign aid mandatory. He argued that the United States could not prosper alone. Both trade and aid were needed. "We cannot maintain a high standard of living if it is to be undermined by the low standards of others,"he asserted. American security had to be part of a common cause for maintaining peace. A certain amount of national self-interest was thus intermingled with Wallace's idealism. War production had expanded the gross national product enormously. When pent-up consumer demand was met after the war, expanded foreign markets would be needed to sustain the upward swing of the economy. To stave off the expected slump, Wallace encouraged an elaborate apparatus to implement monetary stabilization, reciprocal trade, credit, loans, and technical assistance to potential buyers. Also in his judgment an "international government bank with appropriate guarantees for both government and private funds" might serve to stimulate investments in underdeveloped countries.[26]

One aspect of foreign aid that Wallace perceived before others became aware was the salient fact that Asian nations first had to undergo agricultural reform before they could raise living standards. The Vice-President warned in 1944 what the famous Swedish economist, Gunnar Myrdal, reiterated in 1968 (in his massive study *Asian Drama, an Inquiry into the Poverty of Nations*): "Asiatic countries must, therefore, aim not only for political equality nor only for industrial equality. They must also attain equal standards of agricultural efficiency."[27] Wallace was of the opinion that foreign students coming to the United States should not spend four years at a college or university, but should receive training in agricultural and technical skills for periods not to exceed six months. He feared, and correctly so, that too many years spent in America discouraged such trainees from returning to villages or small communities in their homelands, thus contributing nothing to rural reform there.

Knowing that the war in Europe had loosened the hold of colonial powers on their possessions, Wallace desired to see the United States take its stand with the emerging nations of the world. Economic aid must assist liberated areas, not abet their enslavement. "The thing we must avoid at all costs is any type of new imperialism," he counseled, "We must resist any temptation toward the imperialistic use of our air power."[28] Wallace presumed the airplane would be the successor to the gunboat and battleship, which constituted the means of European subjugation of Asia. Without apology Wallace literally held the Four Freedoms and the Atlantic Charter as absolute principles to be upheld. These epitomized to him the end of the old system of western colonialism in Asia.

Since he attributed the causes of war to economic imperialism and to military machinations of the old balance of power system, he cautioned against reviving these practices. Japan was not to be balanced off against China or the Soviet Union. The defeated Nipponese were to be converted into an "Asiatic Sweden," and China (the Nationalist government) would be brought into the fraternity of major nations. What about the Soviet Union? He earnestly believed that "Russian-American friendship must be one of the main pillars of the century of the common man." He claimed, and here Wallace guessed wrong, "Russian interest in the Far East is not likely to be that of territorial expansion." Actually Stalin was eager to regain what the Czar had lost to Japan in the Russo-Japanese War (1905) and was also intent upon absorbing Outer Mongolia into the Soviet Union. Instead of viewing the Soviets as a rival or assuming they would fill the vacuum left by China's weakness and Japan's defeat, Vice-President Wallace believed it was possible to get along with Stalin. With a friendly attitude, trade, and tourism he felt sure Soviet suspicions of the West could be dissipated. "There are things for us to learn from the Russians," he contended, ". . . such as the development of the Arctic and sub-Arctic, together with the many contemporary Russian scientific advances in medicine, agriculture, and the study of soils." Nationalistic aggrandizement on the part of the United States was to be forsworn, so that international cooperation might prevail. "Our methods must harmonize with our objectives," he emphasized. "If our interests are linked with the interests of others, our foreign policy must be one of participation and association with other nations."[29] Wallace continually presumed that the Soviet Union intended to follow a similar course after the war.

Criticisms of these foreign policy objectives were soon to be heard. John W. Bricker, governor of Ohio and Thomas E. Dewey's running mate in 1944, called Wallace a "wild radical, a visionary idealist, and a merchant of globaloney."[30] William P. Witherow, once president of the National Association of Manufacturers, dubbed Wallace's foreign aid proposals as being the equivalent of providing "a quart of milk for every Hottentot."[31] Senator Hugh Butler of Nebraska toured Latin America and promptly labeled U.S. expenditures there a "hemispheric handout that is neither good nor neighborly."[32] Conservatives challenged the spending of huge sums to help other countries, and neoisolationists questioned the wisdom of prolonged involvement in either Europe or Asia.

When President Roosevelt asked Henry Wallace to undertake another diplomatic journey for him in 1944, this gave the Vice-President an opportunity to visit both the Soviet Union and China. He was always glad to serve F.D.R. and the trip also provided him with the opportunity to see firsthand two countries that would play an important role in the postwar era. People-to-people diplomacy had scored a triumph during his South American tour, and he was eager once again to represent the interests of the common man.

CHAPTER 7

PEOPLE'S DIPLOMAT: THE SOVIET TOUR AND AN

IN MARCH of 1944 when President Roosevelt brought up the possibility of a diplomatic mission to China, Wallace's immediate reaction was favorable. He felt such a trip would provide him with an excellent opportunity to tour parts of the Soviet Union and India in addition.

F.D.R. was sorely worried about internal conditions in China. Chiang Kai-shek was not pressing the war against Japan and, in fact, appeared to be floundering amid total confusion. Because of Chiang's personal feud with the crusty American commander General Joseph W. Stilwell, military operations on the entire China-India-Burma front were bogged down and ineffective. Chinese Communists under the leadership of Mao Tse-tung (self-styled Chairman of the Peoples Republic of China) fought their own war against Japan without coordination or cooperation with Nationalist troops. Chiang sought frantically to maintain sovereignty over territory occupied by the Red Chinese, but to no avail. The Generalissimo was riding a dying dragon that was being strangled by corruption, inefficient administration, and military bungling. A diplomatic genius would have been required to

They have taught their tongues to speak lies. . . .
JEREMIAH 9:5

INEFFECTUAL MISSION TO CHINA

prescribe a remedy for this hopeless situation. In the final analysis no solution was workable, unless the United States was willing to commit huge resources to bolster the economy of Nationalist China.

Arrangements were quickly made for Henry Wallace to embark upon this most difficult mission. He was to leave the United States on May 20, 1944, and arrive in Chungking some time in mid-June. The Vice-President would fly over Siberia and make several stops in Soviet territory. He was to rendezvous en route with W. Averell Harriman, U.S. ambassador to the Soviet Union, for a briefing on Sino-Soviet relations. Time did not permit Wallace to go to Moscow or to make goodwill stops in India. His primary assignment was to see if he could resolve the many problems existing in China.

Wallace made no pretense of being an expert on Chinese or Russian affairs. In reply to his request for assistance, Cordell Hull had the Vice-President briefed by such specialists as Charles Bohlen, Joseph Ballantine, Owen Lattimore, and John Carter Vincent.[1] The latter, who was head of the Division of Chinese Affairs in the State Department, had also prepared a series of position papers on China, and these were passed on to Wallace by Presidential Assistant Lauchlin Currie. They are particularly interesting in view of later events. One of the papers criticized Winston Churchill for his alleged policies: "(1) Conservation of British manpower . . . ; (2) Repossessing of those portions of the Empire in the Mediterranean areas and Asia . . . ; (3) Preventing China from developing into a major power . . . ; (4) Reducing Russia's strength as a major power by delaying the opening of an effective second front against Germany. . . ."[2]

Another report titled "Chiang Kai-shek and China" claimed, "The Generalissimo seeks to dominate because he has no appreciation of what genuine democracy means." The most misleading memorandum of all was that which dealt with "The American Stakes in Chinese Unity: Proposals for Preliminary American Action." It declared, "Foreign observers (including Americans) who have recently visited the Communist area [claim] . . . that the Communist regime in present policy and practice is far removed from orthodox Communism; that it is administratively remarkably honest; that popular elections are held; that individual economic freedom is relatively uncurbed; that the regime appears to have strong popular support and that it is described less accurately as Communist than as agrarian democratic."[3]

Although Wallace was to make his own decisions regarding matters in China and the Soviet Union, such roseate appraisals of Red China and the negative evaluation of British policy must have had some influence upon his thinking. He understandably could be led astray on certain matters concerning both China and Russia, when the experts who were to counsel him did not themselves fully comprehend the true nature of the Communist movement of either Mao Tse-tung or Joseph Stalin.

Newspaper speculation was rife concerning F.D.R.'s motives for sending the Vice-President on this long journey, since it would take Wallace out of the country just before the Democratic National Convention would convene. Was Roosevelt exiling Wallace as the first step in dropping him from the ticket in 1944? Friends warned the Vice-President that his absence prior to the convention would seriously jeopardize his chances for renomination. Secretary of Labor Frances Perkins literally begged him not to go, but Wallace detected no guile in the President's request.[4] Having no doubt that his prolonged mission would deprive him of an opportunity to seek delegate strength, he nevertheless felt his political fortunes were in good hands. He trusted F.D.R.; and during his absence Harold Young, his special assistant, was to conduct a vigorous campaign on his behalf for delegate support.[5] When Wallace prepared a press release on the eve of his departure, he jested with Stephen Early about the rumors connected with his assignment. He told the White House press secretary that F.D.R. "would get a good laugh out of the first sentence of the last paragraph." It read: "For the time being nothing more can be said of certain aspects of the Vice-President's trip."[6]

The diplomatic entourage accompanying Henry Wallace was very small. His companions included John Carter Vincent, chief of the Division of Chinese Affairs; Owen Lattimore, deputy director of the overseas branch, Office of War Information; John Hazard, chief liaison officer, Division for Soviet Supply of the Foreign Economic Administration; and Captain Kennith Knowles, military observer and secretary. Carrying Wallace and his party was a C-54 Skymaster flown by Colonel Richard T. Kent, the same pilot who transported Wendell Willkie on his *One World* journey in 1942. By keeping a diary, Wallace was able later to publish an account of his experience under the title of *Soviet Asia Mission*.

Henry Wallace was eager to stop at various places in the Soviet Union so that he might meet and talk with the common people of Russia. He had been studying the Russian language and now made use of it. Although he gave several speeches in Russian, the Vice-President had to rely on John Hazard as a translator when conversational difficulties arose. Wallace was a great believer in the efficacy of popular diplomacy. As often as possible he made contact with average Russians so that they would get to know an American.

Approximately every 800 miles the air force plane would touch down in Siberia for refueling, and Wallace would visit a town or city in the vast expanses of this sparsely settled area. Innumerable sightseeing tours enchanted him. As one knowledgeable in botany, he was fascinated with the flora of this region. Obviously anything pertaining to agriculture intrigued him, especially the collective farms (which he had never considered appropriate for America). Russian officials paid deference to him and seemed eager to show the Vice-President anything he desired to inspect. The potential of this land was enormous, and the inhabitants seemed hospitable beyond imagination. Wallace honestly felt, as he recorded his personal reactions in a diary, "I am sure that no farm-raised person in the United States could become as well acquainted with the ordinary people of Russia as we did without having a deep admiration for them."[7]

The first major address given by Wallace to a Russian audience was at Irkutsk. This Siberian city of 230,000 was located near Lake Baikol and constituted the starting point for the Trans-Siberian Railroad. It was an arduous 1,500-mile journey to the end of the line at Vladivostok for those traveling overland. This city and surrounding environs contained farms, factories, mines, a university, and the Yaktusk Museum. Surprised by the expertise of their agricultural research, Wallace praised his hosts for their accomplishments. Everywhere the Vice-President went he witnessed energetic building and a dynamic quality pervading the populace. All these sights prompted him to tell a Russian audience, "It was with deep emotion that I set foot upon your soil last week." He went on, in this official ceremony at the City Dramatic Theater, to laud their achievements. Speaking slowly in Russian, Wallace exclaimed, "There exist no other two countries more alike than the Soviet Union and the United States. The vast expanses of your country, her virgin forests, wide rivers, and large lakes, all kinds of climate—from tropical to polar—her inexhaustible wealth, remind me of my homeland."[8]

He told the Russian people that once the Nazi invader was expelled the time would come for reconstruction of war-torn areas. With deep emotion a theme dear to his heart was stressed anew: "Now that the early dawn of the future postwar peace slowly rises on the horizon it becomes quite clear that only the full collaboration of our two great countries and their allies can insure to the world a stable and true development." He called for continued Russian-American friendship. Interchange of "information, seeds and the best breeds of cattle with the Soviet Union, Canada and the United States may considerably raise the productivity of all these districts." Reiterating his hope for a new era to come, the Vice-President closed by predicting, "The great masses of people everywhere who lived through all the horrors of common and personal disasters believe that their suffering and sacrifices were not in vain, and that the horrible days of war will be followed by bright days of peace and justice, and of plenty for every man."[9]

The Soviet news bureau Tass covered this speech, and it was faithfully printed in Moscow papers. Another of Wallace's talks, given on June 11 at the Novo-Sibirsk Opera House, also received wide circulation within the Soviet Union. The Vice-President again addressed townspeople who received his words with enthusiasm. Advances in Soviet science and technology were lauded, a plea for continued Soviet-American friendship was repeated, and a call for future cooperation was issued. Since the second front had started and the successful Allied landing at Normandy heralded the approach to total victory, Wallace spoke optimistically of things to come, "When the present war has ended with the victory of the United States, in which your country and mine are allied, and the hateful enemy is beaten, the entire world will have to turn swords into ploughshares and return once more to peaceful labor, rebuilding devastated areas, creating the best possible living conditions for all liberated people."[10]

Ambassador W. Averell Harriman helped arrange Wallace's itinerary and was pleased with Moscow coverage of the trip. The American ambassador met with Joseph Stalin on June 10, 1944, to discuss issues pertaining to Soviet participation in the war against Japan and future Russian dealings with China. Four days later Harriman joined the Vice-President at Tashkent to brief him on the status of Sino-Soviet relations. Those accompanying Harriman included Llewellyn E. Thompson, Jr., second secretary and counselor of the embassy; Fu Ping-Sheung, Chinese ambassador to Russia; and Luis Quintanilla, Mexican ambassador to Russia. The latter came at the special invitation of Henry Wallace who wanted to emphasize United States–Latin American solidarity.

The Vice-President conferred with Harriman for three days. These conferences were interspersed with tours of Tashkent, a metropolis of 1,100,000, and the nearby city of Alma-Ata. With amazement, Wallace noted irrigation projects for growing cotton and much scientific activity at the Academy of Sciences at Uzbekistan. Large deposits of radium and uranium existed in the area, and Russian scientists were busy mapping them. They displayed knowledge about such technical topics as solar radiation, atmospheric ionization, atomic fission, and magnetic fields in central Asia. Since Wallace had helped initiate America's A-bomb program, he understood the long-range implications of such scientific research. This increased his desire for promoting amicable relations between the Soviet Union and United States, lest they become rivals armed with new weapons. The point was driven home to him that Russian scientists were equal in skill to their American counterparts. This made it seem imperative that technology should serve to unite rather than to divide the peoples of the United States and the Soviet Union.

Following the consultations, Harriman returned to Moscow, and Wallace departed for China. The American ambassador carried with him a personal letter from Wallace addressed to Joseph Stalin. It thanked the Russian leader for many courtesies that had been extended to the vice-presidential party and commended all those who had served as hospitable hosts. He had only praise for the energy and accomplishments of the Russian masses. Stalin was complimented for carrying out a "policy of the Government of the U.S.S.R. which has made this progress and these achievements possible. . . ." Not missing a golden opportunity, Wallace appealed to Stalin for continued friendship after the war so that his country might cooperate with America in working for the benefit of all humanity. His letter to Stalin closed with the solicitous request: "May our two great nations working in close harmony make their contribution to the cause of the prosperity of the whole world by the same abundant production in peacetime as was achieved by them during the war."[11]

A final message to the Russian people was in the form of a press conference in Alma-Ata, just before crossing the border into China. In the spirit of warm friendship Henry Wallace exclaimed, "I must say that my personal impressions surpass all my expectations. I am enraptured by the scope of building and the great achievement." The Vice-President announced, "While our approach to the satisfaction of the common man's needs may differ, our ultimate objectives are identical." As if to bridge the ideological gap by his own nomenclature, Wallace explained that these two different methods of obtaining social justice must not "lessen our deep mutual sympathy or stand in the way of close collaboration for the benefit of all freedom-loving humanity." Speaking as a world diplomat representing all peoples, he bade farewell by saying, "My present journey has given me an opportunity to become acquainted with the culture of the peoples of the Soviet Union. Soon I shall become acquainted also with the culture of the Chinese people. The only sure guarantee of prolonged world peace, after this war has been won, is continued close collaboration between various peoples representing these four cultures—Anglo-Saxon, Latin, Soviet, and Chinese."[12]

From Moscow, Ambassador Harriman sent the U.S. State Department a series of reports verifying the popular success of Wallace's goodwill tour. The Vice-President had been given excellent press coverage and had been "greeted by the Soviet officials and agriculturalists with great cordiality and respect, and with enthusiasm on the part of the Russian audiences at the theaters he attended." Struck by Wallace's keen "interest in and knowledge of agriculture," Harriman also noticed that "Russian agriculturalists were obviously impressed with the Vice-President's knowledge of scientific agriculture, and the Soviet officials by his friendliness and sincerity. . . ." The Ambassador concluded, "I believe his visit has made a substantial contribution to good Soviet-American relations."[13] This optimism seemed verified when Eric A. Johnston, representing American business, also toured Russia in 1944 and he too was well received.

Amid the cordial atmosphere of wartime camaraderie neither Willkie, Wallace, nor Johnston looked for ulterior motives in the fine treatment extended to them while traveling inside Russia. All three were presumably shown whatever they desired to see. The usual secretiveness of Soviet officials appeared to dissolve, and thus all these men came away with good impressions of the Russians. However, Wallace did not know that his reception had been well planned by the Soviets and he saw only what they wanted him to see. For instance at Magadan, a far-north Pacific port city which the Vice-President visited briefly, labor camps existed for political prisoners. Watchtowers had been dismantled and all signs of prison labor disguised, so that Wallace was unaware of their actual presence. Writing in 1952, Henry Wallace confessed, "I had not the slightest idea when I visited Magadan that this . . . center of a vast, sub-artic gold field—was also the center for administering the labor of both criminals and those suspected of political disloyalty." Commenting on how he and Willkie were deceived, Wallace wrote in *This Week Magazine*, "As I look back on my trip across Soviet Asia to China, I can see after reading accounts by former slave laborers who escaped from Siberia that I was altogether too much impressed by the show put on by high Russian officials, who as human beings seemed just like typical capitalistic 'go-getters.' "[14]

As Henry Wallace crossed over the Soviet border into China in mid-June of 1944, little did he know he was becoming even more deeply embroiled in an affair which would haunt him for many years thereafter. President Roosevelt had instructed the Vice-President to work for the attainment of four basic objectives in China: first, to induce Chiang Kai-shek to coordinate his military efforts with the Chinese Communists; second, to get the Nationalists to step up offensive operations against the Japanese; third, to impress on Chinese officials the necessity for arriving at satisfactory agreements with the Soviet Union relative to matters in the Far East; and fourth, to secure permission for American air units to be stationed in Communist territory. At this stage F.D.R. seemed preoccupied with military matters, although he did envision Nationalist China as one of the Big Four who would ultimately keep peace in the world. Yet all his instructions pertained to winning the war against Japan, none on strengthening Chiang's government against the Communists.

Uppermost in Wallace's mind was the problem of achieving military unification for China. He did not know that the hatred and antagonism existing between Nationalists and Communists precluded all cooperation nor was he fully aware of the disintegration taking place within the Kuomintang. For all intent and purposes a Red China under Mao Tse-tung had already been established, and Chiang was impotent to do anything about it. His own support was crumbling, and inability (or unwillingness) to initiate reforms soon eroded whatever loyalty remained among the masses. Henry Wallace was the first of many, including Patrick J. Hurley, Albert C. Wedemeyer, and George C. Marshall, to become ensnared in the China tangle. After 1948, with the hysterical anti-Communist atmosphere then prevailing, all those involved in trying to resolve China's enormous problems were carelessly indicted by the China lobby for allegedly selling out Chiang Kai-shek to the Communists. The situation in 1944 was far different, however, from that portrayed later. Nationalist China was teetering on the brink of disaster, while the United States simply did not have the moral, military, or economic means to rescue the Kuomintang regime from itself or its adversaries.

The Vice-President was struck by the startling contrast between Soviet Asia and China. Chinese peasants did not display the energetic desire shown by Russians nor did they possess adequate tools or machinery needed to produce ample supplies of food. Writing in his diary, Wallace made the observation: "Obviously a strong China must have a more efficient agriculture. It is dangerous to think too much of industrialization without realizing the ways in which efficient industrialization depends on improved agriculture. In solving her agrarian problems, China can learn much from the American farmer and the farmers of neighboring Soviet Asia."[15]

Another problem soon became evident, and it troubled him. The Vice-President no sooner had landed at the frontier town of Tihwa (also known as Uraumchi) than he detected a feeling of hostility toward Russia. Soviet control of Outer Mongolia was resented, and border incidents were not uncommon. Wallace met Shen Shih-tsai, the governor of Sinkiang Province, and discovered to his dismay that the official was in reality a Chinese warlord. Wallace began to feel the situation was far worse in China than Roosevelt had ever realized. His pessimistic feeling was reinforced when he talked to American military personnel after his plane was forced by bad weather to land at a B-29 base near Chengtu. To a man, these air force officers reviled Nationalist Chinese officials. They scored Chiang's failure to supply them with either weather information or intelligence reports on Japanese positions. These complaints gave Wallace more to ponder as he continued his flight to Chungking.

Soon after arrival at the Chinese capital serious talks began between Wallace and Chiang Kai-shek. They met privately at times, with only an interpreter present (usually Madame Chiang or Dr. T. V. Soong), and on other occasions a large group assembled, including John Carter Vincent, Owen Lattimore, John Hazard, and Dr. Wang Shih-chieh. The Vice-President took time out to confer with Clarence E. Gauss, American ambassador to China, and made it a point to see Madame Sun Yat-sen and Dr. Sun Fo (the wife and son of the famous founder of modern China). Wallace was no expert on China; therefore, he sought advice and counsel from every source available. With the information he possessed, he sought to fulfill the objectives of his mission.

The initial conference on June 21, 1944, lasted a little over an hour. A second session with a larger group present was much longer. Chiang Kai-shek took the initiative by blaming the military reverses in China on the Big Three. By altering the Cairo decision at Teheran, they had decided against sending larger numbers of troops and war material to him, thus hampering his efforts to defeat the Japanese. Consequences of this, he contended, were economic difficulties and poor morale among his soldiers. Chiang released a bitter tirade against General Joseph Stilwell, whom he regarded as *persona non grata.* The Generalissimo's deepest hatred was vented against the Chinese Communists. Remonstrating at length, he claimed they were taking their orders from the Third International and were openly trying to subvert his government. When Wallace tried to assuage Chiang's fears by reminding him the Third International had been dissolved and the American Communist party gave patriotic support in winning the war, the Nationalist leader only repeated his charge that Mao's followers were neither agrarian reformers nor loyal supporters of the legitimate government. Chiang reported that negotiations between Wang Shih-chieh, representing him, and Lin Tzu-han, speaking for the Communists, were stalled because the Red Chinese would not acknowledge Nationalist sovereignty over all China.

Neither Wallace nor Roosevelt had been fully aware of the nature of the split between Nationalists and Communists. From U.S. experience and taking Stalin at his word concerning the cessation of international revolutionary activity, the Vice-President did not quite comprehend why Chiang Kai-shek and Mao Tse-tung could not get together to wage war against Japan. At the third meeting Wallace tried to make it clear that America was not interested in aiding the Communists as such but merely wanted all Chinese forces to unify their efforts in repelling the Japanese invaders. He brought up the matter of poor intelligence and lack of weather reports for American B-29 groups and inquired whether it was possible for U.S. personnel to be stationed in territory occupied by the Communists. Chiang agreed to allow an American military team into the area if they went under the auspices of his government. A definite understanding was reached that U.S. observers could enter North China. This was to be the only concrete agreement achieved during Wallace's stay in Chungking.

The Vice-President informed Chiang that the Soviet Union desired a warm-water port in the Far East and indicated President Roosevelt thought Dairen might be suitable for this purpose. Chiang did not react negatively but emphasized this could be arranged easily enough if Chinese sovereignty were not jeopardized. He agreed with Wallace that Sino-Soviet relations must be kept amicable. The Nationalist leader pressed for an assurance that Roosevelt would act as an intermediary between his country and Russia, possibly even sponsoring a diplomatic meeting. Without instructions to commit the President to this course of action, Wallace demurred. However, he did take upon himself to lecture Chiang on the vital necessity for instigating internal reforms. Status of the peasants, high rents, poor farming techniques, and general inflation were glaring weaknesses, Wallace pointed out. Without quick changes the loyalty of the people would wane and the war effort collapse. Generalissimo Chiang Kai-shek promised reforms would be inaugurated along the lines suggested, and the last formal session closed on a cordial note. Before leaving, the Vice-President presented Chiang with a scroll from President Roosevelt.

On the way to the airport, Chiang Kai-shek (with Madame Chiang acting as interpreter) presented a list of items for Wallace to bring to Roosevelt's attention. He wanted to thank the President for his action in securing abrogation of Open Door treaties. These so-called unequal treaties had allowed European nations (and the United States) to have extraterritorial rights in China. The Generalissimo said he accepted decisions made by the Big Three to press the war in Europe to a conclusion before concentrating on Japan. He reaffirmed his faith in Roosevelt and trusted that sufficient aid would come to prevent China from falling prey to Japan. Everything in his power would be done to establish friendly relations with the Soviet Union, Chiang assured Wallace; but he again stated his belief that Mao's Communists were disloyal and untrustworthy. Feeling his request to have General Stilwell relieved of his command would be denied, he asked that General Claire L. Chennault be appointed as liaison between himself and President Roosevelt. And finally, the Nationalist leader reiterated his desire to initiate reforms. After the war, land holdings would be broken up and interest rates for farmers would be reduced to 10 percent.[16]

The emissary that boarded his plane on June 24 for the flight home was not a happy one. From first-hand experience Wallace realized conditions were deteriorating, with prospects of chaos ensuing in short order. The Vice-President discussed at length with John Carter Vincent what measures might be adopted to aid China; and when the plane stopped for fuel at Kunming, he also had an opportunity to talk with Joseph Alsop (who was on the staff of General Claire Chennault). Because of the gravity of the situation, Wallace wired a preliminary report to Roosevelt. Sent from New Delhi, it summarized Chiang's position and warned the President of dire things to come if Chiang's government were not bolstered. He told the President it would be wise to appoint someone other than Stilwell as a liaison between himself and Chiang, so that closer military coordination might be established. He recommended General Albert C. Wedemeyer for the post. After this brief message, the Vice-President boarded the plane to return to America. With many hours to reflect on what he had seen and heard, he drafted an outline of final recommendations to be made to Roosevelt.[17]

His written report to the President recited in detail the dismal state of affairs in China. "Chiang showed himself so prejudiced against the Communists," wrote Wallace, "that there seemed little prospect of satisfactory or enduring settlement as a result of the negotiations now under way in Chungking." The Vice-President emphasized the immediate "need for reform in China, particularly agrarian reform, to which Chiang agreed without much indication of personal interest." Reciting still more dismal news, he related a sad story of decay and disintegration. "Economic hardship and uninspiring leadership have induced something akin to physical and spiritual anemia," his findings disclosed, thus causing "widespread dislike for the Kuomintang government." While conceding there "seems to be no alternative to the support of Chiang," he warned nevertheless that "Chiang, at best, is a short-term investment." Wallace predicted that unless a "new coalition" were formed within the Nationalist government, revolution could not be prevented. The Vice-President desired to see liberal and progressive Chinese, particularly western-trained men of stature, included in a revitalized coalition. Needed in China were leaders "whose outlook is not limited to perpetuation of the old, landlord-dominated rural society of China. . . ." A reform-minded Nationalist government "could be aided by the manner of allotting both American military aid and economic aid, and by the formulation and statement of American political aims and sympathies both in China and in regions adjacent to China."[18]

F.D.R. received Wallace's report with interest but did not appear to follow any of its recommendations. The President appointed General Patrick J. Hurley as liaison officer to Chiang Kai-shek and persisted in trying to get the Generalissimo to collaborate with the Communists. Roosevelt applied pressure by suggesting his role as intermediary between China and Russia would be easier if all Chinese groups united their military efforts. Roosevelt thanked Chiang for his message as relayed by Wallace, and then told the Nationalist leader, "It occurs to me that any such conference [between China and the Soviet Union] would be greatly facilitated if a working arrangement had been reached beforehand between the Chinese Government and the Chinese Communists for effective prosecution of the war against the Japanese in North China."[19]

Obviously Franklin D. Roosevelt did not agree with Chiang Kai-shek on the Communist issue, nor did the President take into consideration Wallace's counsel about the impossibility of such cooperation. F.D.R. persevered in his attempt to force Nationalist-Communist collaboration and ignored the Vice-President's advice about forging a new liberal coalition within the Kuomintang. Nothing was done to force reforms on Chiang and thereby initiate the only steps that could have save his faltering regime. Ambassador Clarence Gauss tended to agree with Wallace's pessimistic assessment of the situation, and General Stilwell sent repeated warnings about the total corruption and incompetence of Chiang's government. When the Nationalists ultimately lost control of the Chinese mainland, Wallace's political enemies sought to assign part of the blame to him by virtue of his 1944 mission to China. Strange as it may seem, hostile critics tried to claim that the Vice-President advocated that Chiang should form a coalition government with the Communists.[20]

Henry Wallace knew little of what lay ahead when his plane reached Seattle, Washington. After seven weeks and 12,000 miles of exhaustive travel, he paused on July 9 to deliver a radio address to the nation. He told his American audience that an "Era of the Pacific" was in the making. Explaining what he meant, Wallace claimed, "The rapid agricultural and industrial development of this great area means so much to the peace and prosperity of the postwar world that I am glad on my return to America to give my impressions of the manifest destiny of the West of America and the East of Asia. . . ." He revealed that China "needs help" but stressed U.S. benefits to be gained by inaugurating a "vigorous two-way trade with Soviet Asia and China." Such action would "greatly increase the population and prosperity of our Northwest." Mutual benefits could be derived from reciprocal air traffic, cultural exchanges, and cooperation in science and technology. Future "causes of war can be removed," the Vice-President vowed, by being "friends with both Russia and China and . . . [exchanging] with them the goods and information which will raise the standard of living of all our peoples." After military victory over Japan, America should attempt to rectify the long-standing grievances that Asia harbored against the western world. "Here are vast resources of minerals and manpower to be developed by democratic, peaceful methods–not the methods of exploitation but, on the contrary, the more profitable method of creating higher living standards for hundreds of millions of people."[21]

American newspapers had given the Wallace trip widespread coverage. Considerable expectation was aroused that future cooperation with Russia was assured, and public opinion jumped to the conclusion that China's internal dissension would soon be settled. Of necessity Wallace remained silent on the secret details of his mission, the result being that the American people were not made fully aware of the precarious position of Chiang Kai-shek's government. Outwardly things seemed bright. The Normandy invasion was successful, and Russian overtures for friendship appeared genuine. All indications made it apparent the Grand Alliance would retain its solidarity after hostilities terminated. Americans looked forward to the presidential elections with an intention of ratifying Roosevelt's wartime leadership. Implicit in their trust was a belief that F.D.R. would also win the peace.

The C-54 Skymaster carrying Wallace finally landed in the

nation's capital on July 10. Waiting to greet him were presidential assistant Samuel Rosenman and Interior Secretary Harold Ickes.[22] They were bearers of bad news. Roosevelt, they informed the Vice-President, had decided not to press for his retention on the Democratic ticket. Wallace was in no mood to talk about his renomination or what F.D.R. had allegedly decided. He brushed aside Rosenman and Ickes, telling them he would discuss his political future with the President in person. Wallace did not believe them, and he had no intention of voluntarily stepping aside for anyone. His hopes for future peace and prosperity rested on Roosevelt's reelection and whatever assignment the President might give to him in carrying out plans for a postwar world. Wallace must now plead his own case for remaining as Vice-President, and he was prepared to do just that.

CHAPTER 8

DEFEAT AT THE DEMOCRATIC CONVENTION AND

THE Democratic National Convention was scheduled to open at Chicago on July 19—just nine days after Henry Wallace arrived home.

Much backstage maneuvering had already taken place, but on the surface it appeared as if Wallace had a good chance for renomination. His speaking tour and recent trip abroad had netted him much publicity, the Congress of Industrial Organization Political Action Committee (CIO-PAC) (headed by Sidney Hillman) backed his candidacy, liberal New Dealers worked for his retention on the ticket, and Negro leaders gave Wallace their solid support. A Gallup Poll published on July 15 revealed Wallace to be the overwhelming choice of registered Democrats. He led the field with 65 percent of the responses. Other preferences were not even close to that polled by Wallace—14 percent wanted Senator Alben Barkley, 6 percent decided for Senator Harry Byrd, and the remaining 16 percent was divided among such contenders as James F. Byrnes, Sam Rayburn, Paul Douglas, Edward R. Stettinius, and Senator Harry S. Truman.[1] In terms of general popularity the Vice-President seemed certain

Wait on the Lord: be of good courage. . . .
PSALMS 27:14

VICTORY IN THE CAMPAIGN OF 1944

by all odds to be Roosevelt's loyal running mate once again.

Harold Young, special assistant to the Vice-President, had worked constantly to mend Wallace's political fences. Young was well aware of Wallace's disdain for handling such details as soliciting delegates and building a political machine. Doing what had to be done as best he could, Young secured a considerable number of pledges from state delegations. He was sure of Washington, Oregon, Minnesota, Wisconsin, and Iowa (for which Wallace was elected chairman). Votes from New York, Georgia, and Florida were assured, as were those of some twenty other states if President Roosevelt indicated his wish to have Henry Wallace renominated.[2]

Nothing is certain in politics, and Henry Wallace was cognizant of the role F.D.R. would have to play if his retention on the ticket were to be achieved. After all, Roosevelt had forced his selection on the convention in 1940. Knowing he would have to persuade the President to keep him, the Vice-President was prepared to leave the decision to Roosevelt, once he had presented his case. Two factors made his task extremely difficult. He did not know specifically who within the Democratic party was working against him nor was he sure to what extent his chief had committed himself to another running mate.

For many months a secretive cabal had laid the groundwork for dropping Wallace from the ticket. A key figure in this stop-Wallace drive was Edwin W. Pauley,[3] a conservative oilman from California who held the post of treasurer for the Democratic National Committee. Enlisted in this intrigue to dump Wallace were other important party leaders. These included Edward Flynn of the Bronx; Mayor Edward C. Kelly of Chicago; Mayor Frank Hague of Jersey City; Robert Hannegan, chairman of the Democratic National Committee; Frank Walker, Postmaster General; George Allen, secretary to the Democratic National Committee; General Edwin C. "Pa" Watson, White House aide; presidential Press Secretary Stephen Early; and Charles Michelson, long-time speechwriter and publicity man for the Democratic party.

To beat someone in politics (or a horse race), so goes the saying, one needs a contender. The "Pauley conspiracy," as Edwin Pauley so designated his group, first sought to weaken Roosevelt's allegiance to Wallace, then they worked openly to influence the President to endorse another candidate for Vice-President. Every effort was made to see that F.D.R. became aware of anti-Wallace sentiment. By the time Vice-President Wallace returned from China, Roosevelt had decided against his renomination. Whether or not F.D.R. made up his mind independently or on the basis of advice from others cannot be fully ascertained. One thing was certain; when Wallace called on the President on July 13, he had already lost the nod. But in typical Rooseveltian fashion no successor had yet been selected.

Not knowing the finality of F.D.R.'s decision, Henry Wallace felt confident he could win White House support for his renomination bid. After conferring with Harold Young he was told at least 290 delegates had pledged their votes to him on the first ballot. When he revealed this to Roosevelt, the President exclaimed, "Well, I'll be damned!"[4] To find out where he really stood, Wallace asked point-blank whether F.D.R. had any objections to his entry into the race. If the President had indicated then and there that Wallace's withdrawal was desired, the matter would have ended; the Vice-President would have complied. But that is not what happened. Roosevelt, instead, gave his loyal colleague the go-ahead. The only qualification the President placed upon his approval was a stipulation that unlike 1940 he could not again dictate to the convention. He promised nevertheless to lend a helping hand by volunteering a letter of endorsement, so the delegates would know he preferred Wallace. With a smile and a wave, F.D.R.'s last words to the Vice-President were, "While I cannot say it in that way publicly, I hope it will be the same old team."[5]

Wallace left the White House in high spirits. He felt sure he could pull it off. While Roosevelt had declined to insist upon him, he had ostensibly removed all roadblocks to his fight for renomination. Had the Vice-President known the truth, he would not have been so jubilant. F.D.R. seldom left anything to chance in politics once he had ascertained the consensus of the party's professionals. Wallace had watched Roosevelt operate for twelve years; yet it did not occur to him that he was now the victim of political duplicity. It would have been a rare thing for the President to throw open the convention and allow it to choose whomever it desired for his running mate. His communication to the delegates would have had to spell out this course clearly, thereby rejecting anyone but Wallace for second spot on the ticket. The reverse happened. Roosevelt did pick a candidate, and his letter allegedly endorsing Wallace proved in actuality to be a renunciation. While seemingly approving the same team, his letter removed the incumbent from contention with these well-calculated words: "I personally would vote for his renomination if I were a delegate to the Convention. At the same time I do not wish to appear in any way as dictating to the Convention. Obviously the Convention must do the deciding."[6] With that kind of spurious help, Wallace was doomed to defeat.

Edwin Pauley, Robert Hannegan, and those opposing Wallace still had their jobs cut out for them. Whereas they knew Roosevelt had dropped Wallace, no one was sure of his choice of running mate. Pauley wanted Sam Rayburn and Hannegan was for Senator Truman; however, they finally agreed to push Truman's candidacy. They stressed the fine reputation this Missourian had made as chairman of the special Senate Committee to Investigate the National Defense Program, claimed he was a New Dealer, and emphasized his valuable border state residence. The President, to their dismay, kept bringing up the name of Justice William Douglas. While waiting to see Roosevelt just prior to the convention, they worked closely with Mayor Kelly to organize things so that Wallace could not win on a first-ballot blitz. A Willkie-type stampede was the one thing they feared, where party regulars were overridden by an emotional surge of popularity.

At long last a dinner appointment was scheduled for July 19. Those in attendance were Pauley, Hannegan, Allen, Kelly, and Walker—all anti-Wallace in their sentiment. They were all eager to get Roosevelt committed to Truman. The President seemed in no hurry. He engaged in small talk, told jokes, and went through his cocktail-mixing routine with relish. No man seemed to enjoy the subtle display of power more than F.D.R. Through dinner he kept the conversation away from political subjects and finally, with tension high among his guests, he asked all to retire with him to the study. Everyone was surprised when the President's son-in-law, John Boettiger, joined the gathering. Finally the discussion focused on what they had come to decide; namely, who would be the 1944 vice-presidential candidate.

Franklin D. Roosevelt astonished the group by bringing up the name of John Winant, the U.S. ambassador to Great Britain, and frightened them by once more extolling the virtues of Supreme Court Justice William O. Douglas. The President assured the group that Bill Douglas's youth and liberalism were fine qualifications, but no one in the room except John Boettiger seemed convinced. Robert Hannegan and others kept up a constant flow of pro-Truman talk, countering every argument F.D.R. put up against him. Roosevelt finally yielded by telling Hannegan, "Bob, I think you and everyone else want Truman." That was the understatement of the evening. Before anyone could voice concurrence, his concession to them was made complete. "If that's the case, it's Truman." Sensing a reluctance on Roosevelt's part and being a sharp politician, Hannegan sought and received a written commitment of the President's endorsement of Harry Truman. Upon departing, Pauley and Hannegan smiled when the Chief Executive announced jauntily, "I know this makes you boys happy, and you are the ones I am counting on to win this election. But I still think Douglas would have the greater public appeal."[7]

The two political figures most in the dark about what had transpired at the White House were Henry Wallace and Harry Truman. Presuming he had a clear field, the Vice-President expected to win the nomination in an open convention; believing himself no real contender, Senator Truman had come to Chicago to nominate his friend James F. Byrnes. Frank Walker broke the news to Byrnes, who really thought he would be tapped for second spot, and Robert Hannegan informed Truman of his good fortune. The man from Missouri would not believe he had been selected until it was confirmed by Roosevelt via telephone. At Wallace's headquarters the report about Truman getting the President's nod was dismissed as a false rumor. Henry Wallace not only was certain he was the popular choice but that F.D.R. would keep hands off until the vice-presidential balloting was completed. Optimism ran high as his Hotel Sherman suite swarmed with such supporters as CIO-PAC people, labor leaders, representatives of New York's Liberal party, long-time New Dealers, Washington officialdom, and important Negro leaders. When asked by newsmen if he would withdraw in favor of Truman, Wallace remarked unhesitatingly, "I wish to say that I am in this fight to the finish."[8]

Mayor Kelly had taken the utmost precautions at the convention to prevent Wallace forces from gaining control. Hannegan and Pauley also believed it prudent to secure another statement from Roosevelt, designating Truman as the President's personal choice. This they did when F.D.R.'s train paused at Chicago on its way to San Diego, California. The first inkling Henry Wallace had of the backstage maneuvering came when he was preparing to second Alben Barkley's nominating speech. The Vice-President was in a favorable position to be able to appear before the convention to second Roosevelt's nomination before a vice-presidential nominee would be selected. Wallace, accompanied by his assistant Harold Young, proceeded to the small office under the platform to wait until the demonstration for President Roosevelt subsided. He also wanted to glance over the text of his speech. Upon entering this private chamber, he heard Edwin Pauley talking on the telephone. Before he could excuse himself or leave the room, Wallace was aware that Pauley was speaking with F.D.R. From what Wallace could hear over the roar of the crowd, the topic of conversation centered on Harry Truman. When Pauley noticed Wallace and Young, he felt embarrassed. After a few moments of awkward silence and not knowing how much they had overheard, he confessed bluntly, "Well, at least you've heard it play-by-play." The Vice-President's only retort was, "This is my campaign speech," as he tapped his briefcase, "this is the one that will do it."[9]

In his capacity as chairman of the Iowa delegation, Henry Wallace mounted the rostrum, not just to second Roosevelt's nomination, but to commit the Democratic party to a set of liberal principles. By so doing he hoped to make himself indispensable to the party, as one qualified to help implement its program for the postwar period. It was without a doubt the most dynamic speech he ever gave. In a moment of rare charisma and without pulling punches or yielding an inch to his political adversaries, he announced his unequivocal support for Roosevelt and presented his own platform for domestic and international reforms.

"The name Roosevelt is revered in the remotest corners of the earth," explained Wallace, "the name Roosevelt is cursed only by Germans, Japs, and certain American troglodytes." Following roars of approval, he continued to praise the President by insisting, "The first issue which transcends all others is that complete victory be won quickly. Roosevelt, in a world sense, is the most experienced military strategist who has ever been President of the United States. Roosevelt is the only person in the United States who can meet on even terms the other great leaders in discussion of war and peace. The voice of our New World liberalism must carry on." This lavish extolment evoked more cheers. Then, delivering his bombshell, the Vice-President proclaimed loudly, "The future belongs to those who go down the line unswervingly for the liberal principles of both political and economic democracy regardless of race, color, or religion. In a political, educational, and economic sense there must be no inferior races. The poll tax must go. Equal educational opportunities must come. The future must bring equal wages for equal work regardless of sex or race."[10]

The galleries, packed by the PAC, screamed their approval, while southern delegates looked at each other in silent disbelief. Even hardened newsmen could hardly believe their ears. They fully expected the Vice-President to be conciliatory and conventional in his quest for delegate support. No one seeking high office had ever before spoken so openly about civil rights. Such courage and candor awed even those who violently disagreed with Wallace. "The Democratic party in convention assembled is about to demonstrate that it is not only a free party but a liberal party," shouted Wallace; "the Democratic party cannot long survive as a conservative party." Again deafening applause greeted his remark. He linked Roosevelt to the liberal cause by asserting vehemently, "By nominating Franklin Roosevelt the Democratic party is again declaring its faith in liberalism. Roosevelt is a greater liberal today than he ever has been. His soul is pure. The high quality of Roosevelt liberalism will become more apparent as the war emergency passes. The only question ever in Roosevelt's mind is how to serve the cause of liberalism. He thinks big. He sees far."

Wallace's high-pitched voice rang with emotion as he spoke of the reasons why President Roosevelt's reelection was so important for all mankind: "With the spirit of Woodrow Wilson but avoiding the pitfalls which beset that great statesman, Roosevelt can and will lead the United States in cooperation with the rest of the world toward that type of peace which will prevent World War Number 3. It is this peace for which mothers and fathers of America hope and work."[11]

The afternoon session ended in tumult, with everyone talking about Wallace's amazing address. With a presidential nominee already chosen by acclaim, the convention reconvened for an evening of nominating speeches for the vice-presidency. Robert Hannegan displayed his letter from Roosevelt to heads of key delegations. It undercut Wallace's candidacy by stating, "You have written me about Harry Truman and Bill Douglas. I should, of course, be very glad to run with either of them and believe that either one of them would bring real strength to the ticket."[12] Despite this presidential interdiction, enthusiasm for the Vice-President was high. After his name had been placed in nomination, a loud and boisterous demonstration took place. Much time elapsed, however, as the names of many favorite sons were presented to the convention. Hannegan and Pauley were fearful the emotion engendered by Wallace's stirring speech might set off a first-ballot renomination. They implored Mayor Kelly to force a recess by any means possible. He used the subterfuge about fire regulations being violated to ask the chair to entertain a request for adjournment till the next day. David Lawrence of Pennsylvania presented the formal motion for a recess and Senator Samuel D. Jackson, permanent chairman, called for a vote. A bandwagon atmosphere existed, with the galleries chanting in unison, "We want Wallace!" When the voice vote was finally taken, a cry of "no" from the floor was ignored.[13] With parliamentary skill Senator Jackson killed the Wallace threat by arbitrarily proclaiming the ayes prevailed, and the delegates were dismissed until the next day.

After being saved by the gavel, Hannegan and his forces went to work during the night. They buttonholed chairmen of state delegations and showed them Roosevelt's letter. Pro-Wallace people within various delegations tried to counter the pressure being exerted by various bosses, as they dubbed Hannegan and his cohorts, by claiming F.D.R. wanted an open convention. When the clerk began calling the roll, anti-Wallace leaders believed they had persuaded enough delegations to hold back their votes to assure Truman a second-ballot victory. Senator Jackson read President Roosevelt's communication regarding Wallace to the convention. Newspaper columnists had already spread its contents the day before; but this supposed endorsement, if anything, bolstered Hannegan's efforts to thwart Wallace on the first ballot. As the roll call proceeded, it became evident Henry Wallace was displaying considerable strength from the floor. At one point his vote total reached 480. The 48 votes of Illinois could have assured him the nomination, but Mayor Kelly held them for Truman by casting them for favorite son Senator Scott W. Lucas. A final tally, after some delegations changed their votes, was 429½ for Henry Wallace, 319½ for Harry Truman, 98 for Senator John Bankhead, and 49 for Senator Alben Barkley. All remaining candidates drew a total of 280 votes.[14]

The PAC's Sidney Hillman and Philip Murray of the CIO worked furiously to put Wallace over on the second ballot. Hannegan depended upon urban and southern leaders to swing the nomination to Truman. Senator Bankhead stymied this by not allowing Alabama to withdraw his name, but Governor O'Conor of Maryland and Senator Robert Kerr of Oklahoma (a favorite son) started the Truman bandwagon rolling. Maryland's 18 and Oklahoma's 22 votes (voting under the unit rule) started things off well. Enough favorite sons held their votes hoping for a deadlock. This forced a third ballot in which the tide definitely began to swing to Truman. The relatively unknown Missourian won on the final count by a margin of 1,031 to 105.[15] Senator Truman seemed as surprised by the results as the general public. With a grin on his face and looking rather small-townish in his wrinkled white suit, Roosevelt's new running mate stammered through his acceptance speech with little aplomb. To those who had worked so hard for Wallace, this usurper did not seem to measure up to the man who was still Vice-President.

Failure to regain renomination made Wallace both sad and angry. He blamed his defeat on the machinations of Hannegan, Pauley, Kelly, Flynn, and Hague. Did he not think F.D.R. shared a portion of the responsibility? The Vice-President simply could not bring himself to admit that Roosevelt shared in the guilt. Instead, Wallace absolved the President by rationalizing deftly that his chief had been beguiled by the lying tongues of schemers. He looked up to and admired Franklin D. Roosevelt too much to acknowledge any Machiavellian motives on the part of the President.[16] Any tinge of bitterness that lingered dissolved upon receiving a wire from Roosevelt congratulating him for his "magnificent fight." The President's telegram included the comment, "Please tell Ilo [Wallace's wife] not to make any plans for leaving Washington in January."[17] This at least signaled to Wallace an indication that Roosevelt intended to keep him in the new administration if the electorate responded with a fourth term.

If Wallace was not aware of all the ramifications of his Chicago defeat, they were brought to his attention by the many postmortems offered by political observers. Even before the convention met, Mark Sullivan bluntly pointed out that too much of Wallace's support came from "radicals and other left-wingers."[18] Many conservatives and even moderates within the Democratic party felt the CIO-PAC possessed inordinate power in high councils. Wallace's cause was not helped by being so closely identified with New York's Liberal party and, above all, the praise of the *Daily Worker* was anathema to conservatives. Because of the Vice-President's advocacy of Soviet-American friendship, the Communist press lauded him. But when Wallace championed civil rights, it was all too easy for southerners to claim that this too demonstrated his radical, un-American views. Senator Harry Byrd charged openly at the Democratic state convention that Henry Wallace was a "convert to doctrines and ideologies foreign to the faith and tradition of Virginia."[19] Senator Ellison D. "Cotton Ed" Smith, addressing as he put it the "white Democrats of South Carolina who believe in States rights, white supremacy and constitutional government," alleged, "Wallace's principles are identical with those who advocate him and it might be said that the Communists, the radicals and the misfits are all supporting him."[20]

Democrats from south of the Mason-Dixon line were not alone in condemning Wallace for his stand against discrimination and poll taxes. The issue of minority rights was fraught with political dynamite, and many Democrats would rather not have it become a major plank. Senator Theodore Green of Rhode Island admitted the Vice-President was "sincere, able, . . . [and] a great liberal," but he criticized Wallace's seconding speech as "tactless" and devoid of "good judgment." Renomination was a sure thing, he reasoned, had Wallace only been conciliatory to the South.[21] When a reporter asked the Vice-President why he did not placate southerners by avoiding the race question, his answer was uncomplicated and clear. "I just said what I thought."[22] That was the only answer he gave.

The question remained as to why leaders of urban Democratic organizations opposed Wallace when the Vice-President obviously appealed to city voters. Labor and minority groups, an important segment of the New Deal coalition, were outspoken supporters of Wallace. Despite this strength in urban-industrial areas, the so-called city bosses distrusted idealists, ideologues, and those committed to principles of reform rather than to practical politics. Men such as Flynn, Kelly, and Hague did not understand Henry Wallace. He mystified them with his crusading rhetoric and lofty ideals. The Vice-President was not interested in precincts, patronage, or municipal problems. These professional politicians, on the other hand, got along well with F.D.R. Having come up through New York politics, Roosevelt understood their concerns and favored them with flattery and favors. Their machines, in turn, got out the huge votes that assured victory. This same group looked upon Harry Truman as one who understood machine politics. He had been associated with the Pendergast organization of Kansas City, and this in their eyes qualified him eminently for a spot that would place him in line of succession to Franklin D. Roosevelt.

A city hall politician does not speculate about humanity or metaphysical explanations; he deals with specific people about concrete problems. This might involve anything from fixing a parking ticket to repairing a hole in the street. Every time Henry Wallace spoke on behalf of all mankind or about the need for international reforms, the Kellys and Flynns and Hagues failed to comprehend what was involved. They disdained talk about abstractions or promises of a pending earthly Elysium. Their concerns revolved around such specifics as federal grants to cities, war contracts, and priorities for material needed in municipal construction. When the war ended, their wants would shift to such things as patronage, power, and political favors.

Henry Wallace was very much interested in seeing that metropolitan areas prospered, but his view was much broader—encompassing not only the U.S. economy but that of the world. In a Chicago address honoring Marshall Field, Wallace tried to explain what he meant: "We may face the future with the greatest confidence provided both the newspapers and the larger businessmen discern clearly the signs of the times and work harmoniously with government in the revising of tax laws for risk capital, in drawing up plans for the sale of self-liquidating exports of heavy goods to so-called backward nations, and in the provision for adequate and prompt large-scale government work on highways, airports, river valley authorities and the like."[23]

Reference to the Deity and bits of religious verbiage have always been taken for granted in the world of politics, but Henry Wallace differed from other political figures in his absolute sincerity and dedication to spiritual ideals. From his religioeconomic interpretation of past events, Wallace averred, "Christianity is not star-gazing or foolish idealism. Applied on a worldwide scale, it is intensely practical." Working for "peace and the general welfare" was for him merely implementing the "Sermon on the Mount."[24] In carrying out this injunction, the spiritual and material well-being of all involved were enhanced. Social justice, brotherhood of man, and the blessedness of universal peace were principles stressed in the Old and New Testaments. It was from these sources that Wallace received his inspiration for sociopolitical action aimed at helping all mankind.

Sophisticates or secular scoffers tended to dismiss the Vice-President either as a religious eccentric or as being incredibly naive. Hence the labels mystic or dreamer became common adjectival derogations attached to Wallace's name. Samuel Rosenman, a long-time aide and confidant to President Roosevelt, contended in his memoirs that Wallace incurred the distrust of party leaders primarily because of his lack of "tact" and the widespread belief that he was something of a "mystic and supernaturalist." In Rosenman's judgment the Vice-President helped create this image of himself by making "unfortunately phrased speeches" which distorted his ideas into "statements of readiness to embark on crackbrained and unrealistic projects of worldwide charity handouts."[25]

Unfortunately for Wallace his Christian idealism was so misconstrued, and it happened repeatedly. Harold Young once reprimanded Lynn Landrum of the Dallas *News* for making similar charges. Young, a Texan, wrote angrily, "Mr. Wallace and those working to win this war are not crackpots."[26] Politically speaking, one is in trouble when such a denial even seems necessary. Obviously F.D.R. heard these rumors. In fact Pauley and his fellow conspirators made sure the President did hear about them. This adverse publicity, plus Wallace's feud with Jesse Jones, may well have made Roosevelt receptive to suggestions for changing running mates. Some of Wallace's intimate friends felt the President viewed Wallace as a rival, not for the presidency, but as spokesman for world liberalism. Thus, according to this unverified version, F.D.R. played his cynical spider-and-fly game at the convention in order to make it appear as if Wallace were being given a chance to win the nomination on his own. F.D.R. was the star of his administration and as such was jealous of his prerogatives. Eleanor Roosevelt, many years later, gave this unadorned explanation for her husband's behavior: "Franklin's faith in Wallace was shaken . . . he said that Wallace had had a chance to make his mark, and since he had not been able to convince the party leaders that he was the right person for the job, it was not possible to dictate again who was to be the candidate."[27]

Failure to regain nomination as Roosevelt's running mate shocked liberals and pro-New Dealers who looked to Wallace for leadership. Walter Reuther, President of the United Automobile Workers Union (CIO), praised him for his "uncompromising devotion to the true principles of American liberalism."[28] Radio commentator William Shirer wrote him that if the "liberals had not come out for Roosevelt so strongly in advance they might have gained a few more concessions."[29] Sumner Welles wrote assuringly, "You have seemed to me the man best fitted to replace him [F.D.R.] as the leader of . . . [the liberal] forces when the time comes that he steps aside."[30] The secretary of the Negro Alliance of America, James W. Lucas, also voiced confidence that Wallace's "attitudes and ideals" would ultimately elevate him "to a still higher office in years to come."[31] Upton Sinclair vowed: "Don't worry for a moment. Your time will come—and soon!"[32]

Paul de Kruif, author and lecturer and close friend, advised Wallace to get busy "organizing the new American common man's party for 1948."[33] Rudolph M. Evans, onetime AAA administrator, indicated to his old friend that the "finger of destiny points your way for a long time pull."[34] Another agrarian colleague from the Agriculture Department, James D. LeCron, wrote, "Who knows what the next four years will bring forth?"[35] Under Secretary of the Interior Abe Fortas wanted the Vice-President to know, "I greatly admire the splendid fight which you have made."[36] New Mexico's Senator Carl Hatch counseled Wallace to "keep on fighting."[37] Liberal columnist Max Lerner commented, "No fight is lost which has leaders like yourself."[38] Robert Nathan, labor economist and union adviser, seconded the idea that although defeated the Vice-President should continue his role as leader of the liberals. "In the past few days, I have spoken with a number of liberals and every one of them is convinced that you can and should become the leader of a strong and vigorous liberal movement in this country."[39] U.S. Supreme Court Justice Felix Frankfurter sought to comfort Wallace by lauding his "far-visioned" seconding speech. He called it a "most enduring contribution to the educational process which the convention serves." The Vice-President felt a sense of pride when Frankfurter quoted from a note sent to him by the great Louis Brandeis on October 7, 1934. It stated, "Read Wallace's *New Frontiers*. He may err in economics. But he is intelligent, thinking and in many respects well-read—he is a great exalted possession for America."[40]

Much of the correspondence received by Henry Wallace commended him for his bold courage in speaking his mind. Coordinator of Inter-American Affairs Nelson Rockefeller commended the Vice-President in these words, "Your integrity and fearlessness in support of liberalism will remain an inspiration to the people of this country for years to come."[41] His former Bureau of Economic Warfare cohort, Milo Perkins (now no longer in government service), described the convention defeat as reflecting both "glory" and "tragedy." He consoled his former chief by writing: "There will be other periods and what is more important, there is a period of every day in which each of us must determine for himself whether he is going to live like a fountain or give up to a whirlpool kind of defeatism."[42] Archibald MacLeish, the head of the Library of Congress, asserted, "That was a brave and noble speech of yours."[43] Pollster Elmo Roper said he admired the "sheer courage" of Wallace's convention address, calling it "one of the most outstanding public speeches which I have heard in the last 20 years."[44] University of North Carolina President Frank P. Graham telegrammed, "Wish to second your magnificent second of Roosevelt."[45] Encouragement came also from David E. Lilienthal, chairman of the TVA, who penned these sentiments: "Yours is not the first case, nor will it be the last, in which a man of integrity found his leadership confirmed and his ideas confirmed by what the papers of the day described as a defeat or set-back."[46]

A most rewarding communication came from Chicago *Daily News* reporter Nancy McInery. She had been on the floor of the convention while Wallace was delivering his seconding speech. The reaction was tremendous, she related, and one female delegate in the Louisiana delegation was overheard to say, "That man is honest. I don't agree with him because I don't want my children to go to school with niggers, but I admire his integrity."[47] Senator James Mead of New York, who stuck with Wallace all of the way, maintained his fight in Chicago was a "contest that was worthy of my support."[48] And William L. Batt of the War Production Board confided: "I hate to see you fail to receive adequate appreciation for what you are. You have been a devoted and unselfish public servant, and I believe history will record that fact."[49]

If Henry Wallace had had a desire to leave politics, there

were many job offers awaiting him. His old friend and colleague Dr. Henry C. Taylor, who knew him from the days when Wallace's father was Secretary of Agriculture, wanted him to accept a position as a college or university president. Mordecai Ezekiel and other agricultural cohorts urged him to become the head of the proposed Food and Agricultural Organization of the United Nations. Both Marshall Field, publisher of *PM,* and Ernest Kirschter, editorial editor for the St. Louis *Star-Times,* offered Wallace an opportunity to be a columnist for their respective papers, while Bruce Bliven sought him as an editor of *The New Republic.* None of these proposals really interested him at this time. He revealed his future intentions to William Agar, executive vice-president of Freedom House, by informing him, "I am going to do what I can to re-elect the President. After the election is over, I hope we can make the Democratic party into a genuinely liberal party."[50] To Dr. George S. Counts, one of the founders of the Liberal party of New York, Wallace confided, "I think the lesson of the convention is that liberals will have to do everything possible to make a truly progressive party out of the Democratic party."[51] What influence he would now have on Roosevelt was something he had to consider. Wallace divulged his uneasiness to the noted author Franklin P. Adams by writing, "I am very hopeful that the President will follow a definitely liberal course after he is re-elected."[52] He definitely saw his duty in terms of staying in politics and working to keep the Democrats liberally oriented. His disquietude was assuaged to some extent by the influx of mail which (he claimed in a letter to former U.S. ambassador to Mexico Josephus Daniels) "tells me there is a stronger liberal spirit among the people than I had thought."[53]

Immediately after the Chicago convention Wallace spent a short time in Des Moines recovering from his arduous trip and taking time to think about his political future. Once he had rested and reflected on recent events, the ordeal receded into the background. He returned to Washington, D.C., to ascertain his role in the coming campaign. After a short meeting with F.D.R. he felt assured the President would offer him an important position in the new administration. Nothing specific was mentioned, but hints were dropped that Wallace would play an important role in postwar affairs. Roosevelt suggested that he feel out the public pulse and mend some of his political fences before the official campaign was launched. This he did by touring the country and making special visits to the South and New England. His respective hosts in these areas were Governor Ellis Arnall of Georgia and Governor Howard J. McGrath of Rhode Island.

Starting in October and going strong until election day, Henry Wallace devoted all his energy to the campaign to get Roosevelt reelected. In a major speaking trip he covered Ohio, Indiana, Iowa, Nebraska, Minnesota, Wisconsin, Michigan, Missouri, Illinois, and New York. All during his tour he assailed the Republican nominees, Governor Thomas E. Dewey of New York and Governor John W. Bricker of Ohio. But one of the most interesting aspects of his one-man campaign, for he had not consulted the Democratic National Committee and never once contacted Harry Truman, was his strong advocacy of civil rights. Wallace became an outspoken crusader for minorities, especially Negroes, when few politicians of national stature championed their cause. He deliberately attended an interracial cocktail party in the nation's capital, at a time when it was still segregated, as a symbol of his goodwill to black Americans. It was he who first addressed Negro citizens in Harlem and Chicago. Wallace visited the ghettoes when other political leaders of both parties ignored these blighted areas. Flanked by congressmen William L. Dawson and Adam Clayton Powell, the Vice-President told Chicago Negroes that the Democratic party must be both liberal and national in scope. He discussed the enlightened attitude of such southerners as Ellis Arnall of Georgia, Lister Hill of Alabama, Claude Pepper of Florida, and Frank P. Graham of North Carolina. "The South is very important to the cause of liberalism throughout the nation," Wallace insisted, "if we are to have a great liberal party in this country. . . ."[54]

All during the presidential campaign of 1944 Henry Wallace continued to denounce racial prejudice and segregation, while preaching the need for social integration and equal opportunities for minorities. Almost alone he made civil rights an important issue. In one of his most hard-hitting speeches, given at Madison Square Garden in New York City, the Vice-President presented a program for legislative action to insure an end to discrimination. The Vice-President opened his address by defining what he meant by a liberal: "A liberal is a person who in all his actions is continuously asking, 'What is best for all the people—not merely what is best for me personally?' " From this premise, he reasoned, "Christ was the greatest liberal of all when he put life before things—when he said to seek the Kingdom of Heaven first and things would take care of themselves." Only by a "rebirth of liberalism" could the general welfare be served. The "new liberalism," pointed out Wallace, meant "permanent peace and maximum jobs." It imposed upon each individual the soul-searching imperative to ask how he could serve humanity, and it demanded that government concern itself with the material and political needs of every citizen in the nation. Without equivocating, Wallace asserted, "I want specifically to include the Negro and every other minority group. If that means a permanent Fair Employment Practices Committee patterned after the committee already established by the President, then we must have it. If that means Federal aid to education such as was killed in this Congress by the Republicans, then we must have it. If that means abolition of the Poll Tax, then the Poll Tax must go. I repeat what I have said before and shall always believe—in an economic, educational, and political sense, there must be no inferior races."[55]

Out of the wormwood and ashes of war would come a transformed international community. For this to come to fruition, however, a world leader was needed, and this man was Franklin D. Roosevelt. Over and over again the Vice-President implored voters to reelect Roosevelt to insure peace and prosperity in the postwar world. Indelibly etched on Wallace's memory were the terrible mistakes of the post-World-War-I era. Denouncing the domestic and international policies of Harding, Coolidge, and Hoover for bringing on depression and war, he ascribed a large share of the responsibility for economic isolationism, high tariffs, laissez-faire practices, and business selfishness to their policies. His fellow Iowan, both as Secretary of Commerce and President, had in his estimation set the stage for the decline of world democracy. Whereas Thomas Dewey was no Hoover, Wallace nevertheless equated a G.O.P. victory with a return to the mistakes of the past.

When the last speech was over and the ballots were counted, President Roosevelt's mandate was renewed by a popular vote of 25,602,505 to 22,006,278. Thomas E. Dewey had done his best, but he could not overcome either the people's lack of confidence in his own party or the reluctance of an electorate to turn out a war President before hostilities ended. Roosevelt and Truman drew 432 votes in the electoral column to 99 for the Dewey-Bricker combination. Henry Wallace was elated over election results despite his absence from the ticket. Political observers noted that he had seldom mentioned Truman by name except in a perfunctory manner. This was true, since Wallace did not really know Truman nor did he particularly regard the Missourian as an important liberal. His loyalty to the ticket focused on Roosevelt, not Harry Truman. F.D.R. acknowledged his gratitude by telegraphing Wallace after his Madison Square Garden address, "If your prediction that I'll win by 100 electoral votes comes true, then I'll make my prediction of 60,000,000 jobs come true, and don't forget that I'll have one important job for you."[56] It did not go unnoticed by reporters that Jesse Jones, in contrast to Wallace's stellar performance, delivered only one rather lethargic campaign speech for Roosevelt. Newsmen also seemed to think Jones was largely responsible for the so-called "Texas revolt." This maneuver, in which his two nephews were prominently involved, sought to free presidential electors in Texas from casting their votes for Franklin D. Roosevelt no matter what popular vote was recorded in the Lone Star state. This type of manifest disloyalty did not enamor F.D.R. of his Secretary of Commerce.

Speculation was rife after the election as to what position the President would offer Henry Wallace in his new administration. Long-time friend Addison M. Parker was so bold as to suggest, "Your efforts on behalf of Roosevelt were, I think, one of the main contributions to his reelection."[57] The Vice-President drew large audiences in postelection appearances also, particularly at labor meetings or with organizations representing minority groups. In Chicago when he addressed the CIO National Convention, Wallace's speech was interrupted repeatedly with loud applause. On several occasions over two thousand delegates chanted in unison, "Wallace in '48!" Editorial comments in leading dailies conceded that Wallace had made a brilliant comeback from his defeat at the Democratic convention. Rumors circulated about various positions which might be offered him. Jay G. Hayden, writing in the Detroit *News* and representing organized labor's viewpoint, claimed, "Wallace, even more than the President, has become a symbol of the New Deal . . . nothing less than a first-rate appointment for him will do."[58] One press report, a leak credited to Governor Ellis Arnall, indicated the President had offered him a choice of any cabinet spot excepting that of Secretary of State. *Wall Street Journal* columnist George B. Bryant claimed, "Mr. Wallace is the left-wing candidate for the Commerce Department."[59] A much more acute observation was made by Radford E. Mobley of the Akron *Beacon Journal.* He commented: "If Wallace takes over the post as Secretary of Commerce he will not only come out the victor in the old running fight between him and Jesse Jones, he will also place himself in a position to guide domestic commerce during this period. Further, he will have a direct hand in shaping world commerce at a time when it must be rebuilt brick by brick. . . . Finally, Wallace will be in a position to advance his chances for election to the presidency in 1948."[60]

President Roosevelt had indeed asked Wallace to join his cabinet again. Instead of returning to his former post as Secretary of Agriculture, Wallace asked for the appointment of Commerce Secretary. From the experience of his father, who was Secretary of Agriculture in the Harding-Coolidge era while Hoover was Secretary of Commerce, he felt more influence could be exerted on economic policies from the latter office. If Wallace were to be Secretary of Commerce, F.D.R. would have to ask Jesse Jones to resign. This the President did on January 20, 1945. He dictated a message to his secretary Grace Tully and told her to have it delivered to Jones at once. When she demurred, thinking it was too curt and indiscreet, he insisted it be sent without delay.[61] The letter to Jesse Jones read, "Henry Wallace deserves almost any service which he believes he can satisfactorily perform. I told him this at the end of the campaign, in which he displayed the utmost devotion to our cause, traveling almost incessantly and working for the success of the ticket in a great many parts of the country. Though not on the ticket himself, he gave of his utmost toward the victory which ensued. He told me he thought he could do the greatest amount of good in the Department of Commerce, for which he is fully suited, and I feel, therefore, that the Vice-President should have this post in the administration."[62]

The deposed Secretary of Commerce was offered the ambassadorship to either France or Italy as a consolation prize, which was declined; even after F.D.R. asked him to be chairman of the board of governors of the Federal Reserve System, Jones refused to have anything to do with the new administration. With great anger and deep resentment toward his successor, Jesse Jones resigned in a huff. Writing to Roosevelt in an undisguised, insolent tone (and making the letter public), the strong-willed Texan argued, "You state that Henry Wallace thinks he could do the greatest amount of good in the Department of Commerce, and that you consider him fully suited for the post. With all due respect, Mr. President, while I must accede to your decision, I cannot agree with either of you."[63] By severing his relationship with the Roosevelt administration, Jones ended his long career as a public servant. It was, after a fashion, a belated victory for Wallace who regarded him as a holdover from the days of Hoover.

When the nomination of Henry Wallace for Secretary of Commerce was sent to the Senate for its advice and consent, conservative Republicans and southern Democrats served notice they intended to oppose confirmation. Since Roosevelt was about to depart for the Crimea to meet with Churchill and Stalin at Yalta, the task of getting the nomination approved fell to the new Vice-President. Since Harry S. Truman was a former senator, it was supposed that he could help break up the coalition lined up to vote against approval. Battle lines formed for a fight of major proportion. There was to be no surcease of controversy as Henry Wallace began a new phase of his turbulent career.

CHAPTER 9

THE COMMERCE DEPARTMENT: PLANS FOR POSTWAR

INSTEAD of the usual grand ceremony in front of the Capitol, Franklin D. Roosevelt's fourth inaugural took place on the south portico of the White House.

The abbreviated and austere affair symbolized in a strange way the brief tenure of his final term as President. Only a few of the perceptive guests noticed how the crushing burdens of office had taken their toll. Insiders were generally lulled into believing his physical condition was excellent because they did not notice the gradual erosion of his strength and vibrancy. Political leaders who saw Roosevelt infrequently were often shocked to see the gaunt and tired face of a man who was slowly dying.

Two days after he took his last oath of office, President Roosevelt departed for the Crimea. There he would participate in his last Big Three summit conference. His intent was to make Yalta the capstone to military victory in Europe and Asia, while simultaneously using it as the cornerstone for the foundation of future Soviet-American cooperation. In reality this conference signaled the climax and ultimate demise of wartime harmony and collaboration between Russia and the United States. Drawn together by

Behold, I . . . will reveal unto them the abundance of peace and truth.
JEREMIAH 33:6

PROSPERITY

a common goal, the conquest of Nazi Germany, each nation's self-interest paralleled that of the other for a brief span. With Hitler's defeat imminent, the bonds of the temporary alliance loosened noticeably. According to purely military appraisals by the American Joint Chiefs of Staff, Soviet participation in the war against Japan was highly desirable from a strategic point of view. This placed Joseph Stalin in a position where he could bargain for territorial concessions; and he did not hesitate to do so, even while Roosevelt and Churchill were themselves seeking military advantages in the Far East for their respective countries. Submerged differences now rose to the surface, and despite an unwarranted optimism on the part of many American policy makers future relations with the Soviet Union were not filled with bright prospects even at this early date.

While F.D.R. crossed the ocean to parley with Stalin, Henry Wallace was left at home to face a hostile Senate. His nomination for Secretary of Commerce had been sent as a matter of routine to the Commerce Committee headed by Georgia's Senator Walter F. George. Trouble developed when dissident Democrats and distressed Republicans murmured in disgust at the prospect of their old nemesis occupying the former chair of Jesse Jones. Almost immediately a penumbra of hate enveloped the confirmation proceedings, as personal and ideological differences fed the fires of discontent.

Complicating matters even more, party discipline totally disintegrated during the extended debate over Wallace's confirmation. Senator George led the conservative assault by introducing a bill to remove the Federal Loan Administration from Commerce Department jurisdiction. This stratagem was to prevent Henry Wallace from gaining control of any money-lending agencies, even if he were confirmed as a cabinet member. Whereas Jones had been allowed this privilege, it was to be denied to Wallace. Hostile opponents sought to prove Wallace irresponsible and incapable of handling such huge sums of government money. Jesse Jones was more than eager to testify to this fact and consequently denounced the nominee as a man without business experience as well as one who indulged in "careless experimentation." Disagreeing vehemently with Wallace's liberal political philosophies, the Texan denounced them as being at variance with those principles that had "made our country great." When Senator Claude Pepper tried to trick Jones into answering affirmatively the question of whether one administrator could handle several agencies (which indeed he had done), the former cabinet member gave the bellicose reply, "If you are trying to ask me if Henry Wallace is qualified for both jobs, I will say 'no'."[1]

Always eager for a congressional donnybrook, reporters jampacked the committee room when Wallace made his appearance. Expediency would have dictated a conciliatory approach, but he did not seek to curry the committee's favor with rhetorical blandishments. Getting right down to the crux of his opponent's arguments, Wallace stated forthrightly, "You know and I know that it is not a question of my 'lack of experience.' Rather, it is a case of not liking the experience I have." Then with a calm, yet vibrant voice he emphasized that the real issue at stake was whether he as Commerce Secretary would use his powers to advance the general welfare. Keeping the initiative, Wallace insisted important postwar problems had to be resolved. Most important was the task of finding 60 million jobs when war production ceased. Aiding small businessmen in adjusting to postwar needs was another major consideration also. In a straightforward manner he told the committee it was no secret that he favored "planned . . . Federal, state, and local projects" to prevent mass unemployment, if they were needed during reconversion. Furthermore, he informed them of his support for such measures as guaranteed minimum wages, crop insurance, federal housing, health insurance, broadening old age benefits, destruction of monopolies, and governmental action to promote full employment. If he were given authority over the Federal Loan Administration, which he greatly desired, Wallace promised to "use its power in the interests of all the American people." His only concession, and this was realistic in the face of sure congressional action to strip his office, was a disclosure that if he were in fact deprived of authority over the lending agencies in question, he would nonetheless "carry on the job of Secretary of Commerce until the war ends."[2]

During the lengthy hearings before this committee, hitherto unknown facts were brought to the attention of an interested public, many of which were quite favorable to Wallace's reputation. It was established that the former Secretary of Agriculture and Vice-President was in all respects a sound administrator. As Secretary of Agriculture he had supervised agencies that made loans totaling some $6 billion with no record of maladministration. Included in this category were the Commodity Credit Corporation, Farm Credit Administration, Rural Electrification Administration, and Farm Security Administration. Through answers elicited by Senator Claude Pepper's friendly questions, attention was also focused on his business acumen. It was not general public knowledge that Wallace had successfully founded the first company to produce and distribute hybrid seed corn on a commercial basis. Started in 1926, the Pioneer Hi-Bred Corn Company had grown rapidly into a multimillion dollar enterprise by 1945, thus reflecting favorably upon Wallace, its first president and mentor. He relinquished his control over the venture in 1933 upon entering government and thereafter served as a scientific consultant only. In 1942 the company also began to market hybrid chickens under the trade name Hy-Line. This too was an area where Wallace had been a pioneer in genetic experimentation. No one thought of Wallace as a businessman, yet profits from his enterprises made him independently wealthy. At the time of his death in 1965 the estate of Henry Wallace was valued at $840,000.

Debate in the Senate over the George resolution (S. 375) revealed a close-knit alliance between southern Democrats and Republicans. Walter George and Harry Byrd led the southerners, while Robert A. Taft of Ohio rallied fellow G.O.P. conservatives in the stratagem of first seeking to remove the Reconstruction Finance Corporation from Commerce Department jurisdiction and then if possible blocking the nomination itself. Florida Democrat Claude Pepper tried vainly to secure party solidarity against the initial maneuver, but his efforts were futile. Consequently the Senate voted to remove control of federal lending activities from the Commerce Department by a vote of 72 to 12 despite the existence of a nineteen-man majority by members of the Democratic party.

The legislative fight in the House of Representatives was just as fierce, but the results were the same—albeit much closer. Congressman Chet Holifield (D-California) challenged Wallace's opponents to "attack his ideas and not the man."[3] This did not forestall a host of malicious accusations. One such charge was made by New York's Leonard Hall, who claimed Wallace acted as if he had "received a call to change the New Deal to the New Communism."[4] Liberals and administration supporters almost thwarted approval of the George Bill when a motion to recommit the measure to committee lost by a close vote of 204 to 196. Following this defeat by pro-Wallace forces, House passage followed by an overwhelming margin of 400 to 2.

A last-minute appeal was made by Eleanor Roosevelt to her husband, who was still at sea, to intervene in this struggle.[5] The President, however, decided to accept this compromise solution, assuming correctly that Wallace's confirmation would then be approved. Wallace foes were able to get a negative vote in the Commerce committee of 15 to 5 against confirmation, but this recommendation was quickly overturned on March 1, 1945, when the entire Senate approved Wallace's nomination as Secretary of Commerce by a vote of 56 to 32. Shortly thereafter Fred Vinson was appointed and confirmed as the new federal loan administrator.

Despite the loss of some of his power, Wallace nevertheless felt optimistic about what he could accomplish as Secretary of Commerce. He was convinced F.D.R. wanted him to implement his plans relative to postwar needs, since F.D.R. had written him after the campaign, "I am grateful to you, not only for what you did but also for what you are in the meaning of my administration and its purpose for the people." The President expressed these added sentiments: "There will be men who will explain—and explain away—the reasons for our successes at the polls. You and I know that we won only because we have stood and must stand for those things closest to the hearts of the people. They voted, I think, for a faith in the confidence that we would carry that faith forward to full victory for freedom on this earth and to the use of our full powers for plenty here at home. We can be proud of the manner in which we have advanced the stakes of human dignity and security in the past. We must recognize the imperative in the continuing advance to which people have assigned us."[6]

Henry Wallace interpreted this eloquent statement of gratitude as an investiture of authority to proceed with plans to implement the President's "Economic Bill of Rights." Roosevelt would of necessity be involved for some time to come in matters of military and foreign policy. Thus the Commerce Secretary took as his directive the President's State of the Union Message of January 6, 1944. Its twin themes were the attainment of a "people's peace" and practical achievement of a "second Bill of Rights under which a new basis of security and prosperity can be established for all—regardless of station, race, or creed."[7]

Henry Wallace did not consider either the Four Freedoms or this Economic Bill of Rights as mere flowery rhetoric but as an agenda for action. Since the principles implied in each proclamation were those he had been advocating since the war began, he meant to use his new office to make them come true. At a testimonial given in his behalf while the Senate confirmation struggle was going on, Wallace told his friends, "There are two issues in this fight. The first is jobs for all after the postwar boom is over. And the second is like unto it. The common man of America can and therefore must be better off in time of peace than he was in time of war."[8]

Resolute and determined to forge the foundations of a prosperous and peaceful America, Secretary Wallace solemnly entered upon his new duties. To his chagrin he found the Department of Commerce a sprawling bureau with no centralized direction or administrative guidance. His predecessor Jesse Jones had been interested primarily in RFC matters and paid little attention to various service agencies making up the Commerce Department. In his typical administrative style Wallace immediately began to reorganize his department so that it would function effectively. He wanted to coordinate the multifarious activities of Commerce into an efficient unit of action. While he was engaged in this preliminary work, news of the Yalta Conference began to filter back to the United States. Wallace's hopes and expectations rose when preliminary reports to the public gave the impression all was going well.

Immediately upon the President's return Henry Wallace sent his chief the following message of commendation: "The picture of the three at Yalta [Stalin, Roosevelt, and Churchill] is such an obvious demonstration of the fact that America furnished the dominant spiritual note. I wish to congratulate you wholeheartedly on having carried the world forward another step under very trying circumstances."[9] The picture of the Big Three triumvirate to which Wallace made reference depicted President Roosevelt in a state of extreme exhaustion. But the Secretary of Commerce saw in the picture only Roosevelt's symbolic role as peacemaker of the world and arbiter between Churchill and Stalin.

In obvious need of rest President Roosevelt went to his favorite retreat in Warm Springs, Georgia. Henry Wallace was sitting in a dentist's chair at 4:35 P.M. on that fateful day of April 12, 1945, when the report of Franklin D. Roosevelt's death came over the radio. Stunned beyond belief, Wallace had to fight back the tears. He remembered that last photograph of F.D.R. at Yalta. It captured for posterity (as Winston Churchill described it so aptly) the fact that Roosevelt's "face had a transparency, an air of purification, and . . . a far-away look in his eyes."[10] With cape spread loosely on his shoulders and his eyes gazing into the distance, as if looking at some far-off vision, the President personified the fond longings of millions of Americans. As Wallace conceived it, Roosevelt like Moses had quite literally led his people to the Promised Land only to be denied entrance himself. This mental picture of F.D.R. as the noble leader giving his life for humanity's benefit never dimmed nor diminished with time. When present at the interment of his beloved leader in the rose garden at Hyde Park, Wallace could not help remembering he had first met F.D.R. at this same Hudson manor home in 1932. They had fought many political battles together and now, like Joshua of old, Wallace felt he was left to carry on alone.

After Harry Truman's succession to the presidency, Henry Wallace believed it necessary for him to commit the new administration irrevocably to a program that would fulfill the plans which Roosevelt had commissioned him to devise. In 1945, Secretary Wallace wrote a book to explain just what measures were needed to promote full employment and peace. Using a title representing the number suggested by F.D.R., in *Sixty Million Jobs* he spelled out a series of legislative proposals for attaining a "people's peace" as well as a "peace of abundance." The heart of the book was his view of federal authority: "My interpretation of the responsibility of government is that in the early postwar years, action should be taken to check the decline in employment, by stimulating opportunities for business activity and the demand for workers in private industry—and government should be authorized to initiate its own supplementary programs if such stimulation fails to do the job."[11]

In addition, he proposed "that the President . . . be directed by law to submit to Congress a national full-employment budget each year."[12] This procedure, he reasoned, would force government officials to think in terms of balancing the economy and not the budget. It would entail long-range planning to expand the gross national product, thus ensuring an economy of abundance and economic sufficiency for all segments of the American population.

Another important aspect of Wallace's economic thinking revolved around the interrelationship of poverty with racial inequality. Without an expanding economy and full employment, he realized all policies to promote integration would be well-nigh impossible to implement. Segregation was both morally wrong and a dangerous cancer on the body politic. He believed it could be alleviated, in a practical sense, through a thriving economy that would provide enough jobs to absorb less skilled workers. He deemed it incumbent upon government not only to ensure protection of civil liberties but to provide economic opportunity by eliminating chronic unemployment among minority groups. From wartime experiences he perceived clearly the connection between an abundance of jobs and a high rate of Negro employment. His fear of the future related to the time when a decreased number of available positions would again force black Americans into idleness and permanent ghetto poverty. Hence his hope was that by prompt action the government could prevent a return to the prewar pattern of job discrimination.[13]

Since the Secretary of Commerce was cognizant of recent scientific breakthroughs, especially the secret work on atomic energy during the war, he correctly anticipated that "technology has become a concern of statecraft."[14] Discerning the formation of an elaborate technostructure in which the application of scientific research became an integral part of managerial know-how, Wallace wanted those dividends applied to the general welfare. The spinoff from atomic research should be made available to all businessmen, not just giant corporations. Experience with war mobilization made him aware that 90 percent of the government contracts went to big industrial firms. Some of these same firms, however, had been guilty of suppressing prewar inventions because of their affiliations with domestic monopolies or international cartels; thus he counseled the establishment of a federal agency to coordinate the increasing activities of the government in scientific fields. Information gained from wartime research and enemy patents seized by the alien property custodian were to be made accessible to small businesses as well as large ones. Obviously his primary concern was to see that the little operator received a helping hand to increase competition and provide more jobs.

Sixty Million Jobs was an extension of a revitalized New Deal, but it barely mentioned the new President. Harry Truman did acknowledge the work, however, with a friendly note commenting: "Why don't you autograph a copy of the sixty million jobs for me. I have been reading the reviews and they seem to have really gone to town on the book."[15] Liberals of all persuasions hailed this publication as a basic statement of their party's legislative program. Dr. Alvin H. Hansen of Harvard University, a noted exponent of Keynesian economics, described Wallace's work as "an education in applied economics" valuable enough to be "read and reread by every voter."[16] Although it would not have occurred to President Truman to consider a full employment program as one carrying out "social ideas of the Sermon on the Mount,"[17] as Wallace did, he did see considerable merit in the broad proposals advocated by his Commerce Secretary.

Henry Wallace not only sought to influence the course of domestic policy he also intended to help guide the direction of his country's future relations with the Soviet Union. Having become accustomed to great latitude in the Roosevelt administration, commenting on foreign policy did not seem out of line to him. As the recipient of the Churchman Award of the year, he used this occasion to comment on international affairs. Speaking at the Waldorf Astoria Hotel ballroom on June 4, 1945, Wallace tried to prevent the resurgence of an anti-Communist movement in America now that the war was nearing its end. Assuming that wartime collaboration should (and could) continue, he warned, "These enemies of peace are those who are deliberately trying to stir up trouble between the United States and Russia. . . . Before the blood of our boys is dry on the field of battle these enemies of peace try to lay the foundations for World War III. They proclaim that because the ideologies of the United States and Russia are different, war between the two is inevitable. They seize upon every minor discord to fan the flames of hatred. . . . We must offset their poison by following the policies of Roosevelt in cultivating the friendship of Russia in peace as well as in war. I know this is the policy of President Truman."[18]

While Henry Wallace envisioned the dawn of a new era in postwar relations, George Kennan assessed things differently from Moscow. As counselor of the American Embassy, he had prepared an incisive memorandum detailing precisely what diplomatic maneuvers might be expected from the Soviet Union. In Kennan's words, "It is entirely agreeable to Moscow that Americans should be indulged in a series of illusions which lead them to put pressure on their government to accomplish the impossible and to go always one step further in pursuit of the illusive favor of the Soviet Government. They observe with gratification that in this way a great people can be led, like an ever-hopeful suitor, to perform one act of ingratiation after the other without ever reaching the goal which would satisfy its ardor and allay its generosity."[19]

On the domestic scene one of the first major legislative proposals of the Truman administration to go before the Congress was the Full Employment Bill (S. 380). Sponsored by Senator James E. Murray (D-Montana), it embraced many ideas long advocated by Henry Wallace. This specific measure was the outgrowth of a reconversion bill submitted earlier by Senator Harley M. Kilgore (D-West Virginia). It also represented positive contributions of the Committee for Economic Development, whose chairman was Paul Hoffmann of Studebaker, and the individual contributions of Bertram Gross, Alvin Hansen, Leon Kyserling, Robert Nathan, Louis H. Bean, and Beardsley Ruml. These were people with whom Wallace had considerable contact and who collectively represented the New Deal–new economics mode of thought.[20]

When the Full Employment Bill was dropped into the legislative hopper, it immediately aroused a storm of strong opposition. A G.O.P.–southern Democrat coalition formed to kill or modify what conservatives regarded as a measure to bring socialism to America. Robert A. Taft (R-Ohio), Bourke B. Hickenlooper (R-Iowa), and George Radcliffe (D-Maryland) were members of the Senate Banking and Currency Committee; from this vantage point they worked incessantly to emasculate the measure. In the House of Representatives such stalwart defenders of old-time laissez-faire capitalism as Clare Hoffman (R-Michigan) and Carter Manasco (D-Alabama) attacked the proposal as one detrimental to free enterprise. President Truman placed his influence squarely behind the Full Employment Bill and Democrats began to rally to its support. Speaker Sam Rayburn and Senate Majority Leader Alben Barkley led the legislative battle flanked by such vigorous supporters as Robert Wagner (D-New York), Joseph C. O'Mahoney (D-Wyoming), Glen Taylor (D-Idaho), Charles Tobey (R-New Hampshire), Wright Patman (D-Texas), and John J. Cochran (D-Wyoming).[21]

Denying the Full Employment Bill was socialistic in character or even any type of insidious statism, these proponents sought only to commit the federal government to a policy of sustaining full employment. This in itself could hardly be socialism, they argued, since no one suggested government ownership of means of production. They wanted private enterprise to sustain the economy, but did point out that some overall management was needed. The President was to submit a "National Production and Employment Budget" which offered guidelines by taking into consideration all economic factors and recommended federal action only in those sectors needing attention. Congress, in turn, was to establish a Joint Committee on the National Budget to keep itself abreast of deficiencies or soft spots that might develop in the national economy. This bill would formally commit the government to what it already had been doing since the advent of the New Deal, namely, providing for constant monitoring and maintenance of a healthy and viable economy.[22]

Appearing before the Senate Committee on Banking and Currency on August 28, 1945, Henry Wallace testified, "I am wholeheartedly in favor of the passage of this bill." Enthusiastically he explained, "Under this measure, the Federal Government would, for the first time, recognize its overall responsibility for assuring opportunity of employment to all who are able and willing to work." Wallace repeatedly assured the committee of his opposition to a so-called "planned economy" used by socialist countries; he carefully differentiated between that form of statism and "intelligent planning to keep our American economic system competitively free and vigorous." In other words Wallace distinguished sharply between rational, democratic allocation of resources and the totalitarian type of five-year plans used by Russia. Absence of any planning or refusal to use governmental powers in maintaining economic stability would be tantamount to returning to the "boom and bust" cycles of laissez-faire capitalism. "We stand at the crossroads of history," argued Wallace, therefore "we must not enter the era of atomic energy without recognizing that continued cooperation of business, agriculture, labor and government is imperative to meet the challenge of full production and full employment in peace."[23]

After a prolonged national debate the Full Employment Bill

emerged as the Employment Act of 1946. In the final compromise form all provisions for mandatory government action were eliminated in favor of specific recommendations for federal intervention when economic conditions warranted it. The Seventy-ninth Congress thus formally enacted into law the Progressive–New Deal concept of positive government. Of great significance was the new institutional contrivance called for by the act. The establishment of a Council of Economic Advisers (CEA) and a Joint Committee on the Economic Report was authorized; the former ensured the President expert counsel and the latter, Congressional response to presidential proposals. Edwin G. Nourse, first chairman of the CEA, stated that this monumental piece of legislation established the machinery for "mobilizing all our organizational resources, public and private, within our system of free enterprise, for a sustained high level of national production and the correspondingly high level of national income."[24]

Apart from his expertise in economics, Henry Wallace was always acutely aware of the importance of science and technology. Typical of his desire to upgrade the caliber of the Commerce Department in this area was the appointment of Dr. Edward U. Condon as director of the National Bureau of Standards. Also on December 4, 1945, Secretary Wallace sent the President a memorandum titled, "Proposed Importation of German Scientists for U.S. Science and Industry Benefit." Truman was thereby advised of the value of recruiting renowned German scientists displaced by the war. Wallace suggested the following scientists be induced to come to America: W. J. Reppe, chemist; Hellmuth Hertz, physicist; Georg Joos, expert in optics; O. Graff, engineer (designed the *Autobahn*); and Otto Hahn, former director of the Kaiser Wilhelm Institute für Chemie. Time was of the essence, the Secretary informed President Truman, since "in recent weeks the movement of German scientific personnel from American control to zones under control of our allies, especially the U.S.S.R., has increased markedly. It is evident that many of the outstanding German scientists will not longer be available unless a decision is made quickly to permit their importation to this country."[25] Once again on February 6, 1946, Wallace warned the President that "Russia and other countries are rapidly taking these men."[26] The Secretary did not know that an Operation Paperclip was already in progress, but this recruitment program was aimed primarily at satisfying military demands for scientists, engineers, and technicians in rocketry.

Wallace fervently hoped that whatever scientific knowledge

emerged from the war might be harnessed to help all humanity. He desperately wanted technological innovation to assist man to be his brother's keeper, not his killer. Because this was especially true in the realm of atomic physics, the Secretary took the initiative to have nuclear energy applied to peaceful uses. To do this he recommended to Truman on January 22, 1946, that administration approval be given "to the joint acquisition and operation of a uranium pile and laboratory by the National Bureau of Standards and the National Institute of Health for the purpose of applied and fundamental research in medicine, biology and physics."[27] Estimated costs would involve an initial expenditure of $6 million with annual appropriations of several million for operating costs. In approving the plan in principle, the President reminded Wallace, "No steps in this direction can be taken until Congress acts on the control of atomic energy. Since the Senate has gone on strike there is no telling when this will take place."[28]

Three bills were then pending in the Senate. They all dealt in one way or another with federal financing of scientific research and facilitating the exchange of information on an international level. Their authors were Harley M. Kilgore (S. 1297), Warren Magnuson (S. 1285), and J. William Fulbright (S. 1248). Appearing before joint Senate hearings held by two subcommittees of the Commerce Committee and a subcommittee of the Military Affairs Committee, Henry Wallace strongly supported the dual propositions embodied in this trio of bills. "I unqualifiedly endorse Federal support of scientific research activity, including the social sciences, and of technological development," he testified. "This would tend to equalize opportunities for small and large business, prevent monopoly, preserve free enterprise and stimulate economic progress." Along with his testimony he included a caveat. Acquisition and dissemination of scientific knowledge could not proceed under the shroud of "rigid regulations and secrecy requirements of war." Since in his opinion free inquiry would be hampered by unnecessary interference with intellectual and academic freedom, he declared, "The maintenance under conditions of peace, of security regulations and secrecy in any sphere of scientific research, including nuclear physics or atomic research (not industrial know-how of military value), would retard progress, would fail in its objective of preventing the scientists of other nations of the world from obtaining similar information, and would as one prominent scientist recently put it, give us the false security of a 'scientific Maginot Line.' "[29]

In an article intended for publication in *Reader's Digest* but never published, Wallace revealed how deeply he was committed to the idea that the advent of the atomic age made it necessary for mankind to completely reorient its thinking. "As long as the United States makes atomic bombs," he wrote, "she will be looked upon as the world's outstanding aggressor nation and the United Nations Organization cannot function as it was designed to function at San Francisco." To him the atomic era signaled the "golden age of abundance." It was as if "God was saying to us, 'Enter now into the land of abundance and enjoy all its fruits sharing joyously with one another of the riches which are there for everyone.' " This new marvelous source of power convinced him that "armies and navies as we have known them in the past are completely outmoded. And so also is Communism because with atomic power appropriately developed we shall have a 20-hour week and no proletariat. All the 'isms lose their old meaning."[30]

Without doubt Henry Wallace placed much more emphasis upon aiding small business than any of his predecessors. He transferred his preference for family-owned farms in agriculture to smaller operators in the commercial arena. His strong stand in favor of federally financed research was in part motivated by a desire to see the fruits of such endeavors freely accessible to small businesses. Addressing a regional meeting of the Agricultural Adjustment Administration in St. Paul, Minnesota, on January 10, 1946, Secretary Wallace averred, "The independent farmer and the independent businessman must remain the seedbed of our free enterprise system."[31] Fearing the industrial-military complex created by the war would foster corporate collectivism to the extent that all competition would be extinguished, he subsequently told a Select Committee of the House to Investigate and Study Small Business, "There is no more effective means of combating the evils of monopoly than the promotion of new, small enterprises whose primary interest is to innovate, compete and expand, rather than to restrict production and protect a vested interest."[32] Wallace could not forget the retrenchment mentality displayed by American business during the recession of 1937–38 and the fact that the RFC had built most of the nation's defense plants. To increase Commerce Department services to these little companies, Wallace expanded the existing Small Business Unit into a more effective Office of Small Business. By placing this new office under the jurisdiction of Under Secretary of Commerce

Alfred Schindler, he insured its status and importance within his department.

It did not take long before the personnel in the sprawling Department of Commerce realized their chief was an imaginative and dynamic administrator. Morale rose dramatically. Old-timers in the department had never before witnessed such enthusiasm and eagerness to get things done. Every time Wallace appeared before a congressional committee, he sought to explain broad policy and thereby justify appropriations for the services his department would render to the nation. In defending a proposed budget figure of $163 million, he told a subcommittee of the House Appropriations Committee, "The Department of Commerce is in some respects a unique government department in that it has practically no functions of a regulatory or control character. Its operations can be described almost entirely in terms of various services: scientific, technological, aeronautical, statistical and economic, which it provides for the business community in the public interest. . . . The dividends can be expected to be many times the sum total of the investment; and will take the form of increased volume of business activity, foreign and domestic, and of the protection of the property, health and safety of the people of the United States."[33]

Slowly but surely Henry Wallace was proving to be an asset to the Truman administration. His rejuvenated department began to win the grudging respect of some businessmen. Many of his economic ideas would certainly have been much more palatable to conservatives in the long run had they not been identified so closely with New Deal liberalism or his foreign policy views that ran contrary to those of the business community. Certainly most of the Secretary's recommendations to Truman were sound, and a number of important business leaders began to understand this. His support for enlarging foreign trade, for instance, appealed directly to large industrialists who were seeking expanded overseas markets.

Wallace urged the President to back a Senate bill (S. 1181) for increasing the Export-Import Bank's lending authority. He also endorsed the $4 billion loan to Great Britain. Speaking at the annual National Farm Institute in Des Moines, Wallace informed farmers, "The nations that make up the British Empire are our best customers and also our main source of supply for much of what we import." Stressing the fact that money advanced to Britain was not a giveaway program, thus seeking to counter an all too common criticism of foreign aid, Secretary Wallace maintained, "Unless we realize that we are a part of the world market—unless we lift up our eyes from our immediate domestic concerns, and see the whole economic situation, across the United States and around the world, we are going to find ourselves again in the condition of the twenties and thirties."[34]

Lest businessmen think exclusively in terms of retrenchment, Wallace preached the need for a bold expansion of the economy. He advised broadening the reciprocal trade program, argued for government subsidization of airports to spur commercial intercourse with foreign countries, and pushed for construction of the St. Lawrence Waterway to increase trade in the Great Lakes region of the United States. Before the subcommittee of the Senate Foreign Relations Committee he reasoned: "Opening up of the St. Lawrence Waterway would contribute both to the achievement of a larger volume of trade and to our ability to handle it. . . ."[35]

With midterm elections nearing, Secretary Wallace prepared to campaign for the return of a liberal-oriented Congress. His efforts in 1946 were aimed predominantly at getting progressive Democrats elected. He felt President Truman was sincerely trying to carry out the domestic program F.D.R. outlined before his death. Without any hesitation Wallace on his own initiative also spoke out on the necessity for advancing the cause of civil rights.

Choosing Tuskegee Institute in Alabama, where his friend George Washington Carver had made many of his discoveries, the Secretary proclaimed resolutely, "There is no inferior race in the United States." He told the largely Negro audience in attendance at the Founders' Day ceremony, "Given good health, education, and opportunity the color of a man's skin is no handicap." Artificial barriers of racial prejudice did exist, but they could be overcome. Proposing the following ways to end discrimination, he said, "Many Negroes who are well prepared by education for good jobs are unable to secure them because they are black. . . . This condition can be improved to some extent by a permanent Fair Employment Practices Committee. It can be helped by abolishing the poll tax. It can be aided by educating the people. A revival of religion in the hearts of people will help. . . . When full employment is achieved, when the fear of insecurity is gone, all of the races which make up this great country can dwell together in peace." Wallace's counsel was not heeded at the time, and subsequent events have shown that the ignoring of these issues was a mistake.[36]

Had Henry Wallace limited his participation in the Truman

administration entirely to domestic issues, he might well have held office until 1952. But inexorably he became involved in matters impinging on foreign policy. This began with his interest in seeing the fruits of secret wartime atomic research universalized and made available everywhere in the world. Shortly after V-J Day Congress began deliberations on several proposals for peacetime control of atomic energy. The May-Johnson Bill called for retention of stringent secrecy and quasi-military supervision of atomic energy. Senator Brien McMahon, chairman of the Special Committee on Atomic Energy, sponsored a rival measure to ensure civilian supremacy.

President Truman supported the McMahon Bill (S. 1717), as did Henry Wallace. Their positions were not identical, however, since the Secretary wanted atomic energy developed solely "by private enterprise rather than by government monopoly." Stating his position to the Senate committee, he claimed such a procedure would guarantee "free international exchange of basic scientific information, and for exchange of technical information when international arrangements make that possible." Wallace frankly feared that if a "military clique" kept control of atomic matters, it could "use this fearful new power to impose new and more terrible forms of authoritarianism and imperialism." Cautioning against letting "international suspicions" serve as a barrier against "prompt harnessing of this new source of energy for the benefit of mankind," he found himself for the first time running contrary to Truman's desires.[37] The President believed government supervision and licensing were necessary and felt sharing of information was not feasible until stringent international controls had been established.

Because of the havoc wrought by the atomic bombs dropped on Hiroshima and Nagasaki, Wallace was convinced this terrible weapon must be outlawed. Over a CBS radio program he predicted, "We shall see the beginning of . . . [a] new international morality as soon as peoples and political leaders devote themselves to the scientist's ideal of an ever-growing truth instead of appealing to an ever-darkening ignorance." Once the bomb was banned, he explained, "the United Nations should have a scientific inspection force to make it absolutely certain that international commitments are kept and that no group anywhere is planning atomic skullduggery of any kind." Most nuclear physicists agreed with Wallace, including the famous Albert Einstein. But the Commerce Secretary wanted to go even further to ensure permanent peace, and that meant making "war itself impossible and unthinkable." He called for a "moral and psychic revolution." Elaborating, Wallace exhorted, "Some of us say that the Golden Rule is a beautiful ideal, but not very practical. I say that Christian morality, not as practiced during the last nineteen hundred years, but as Jesus himself taught it, has finally become the most practical thing in the world. It has become so practical that all nations in the world must practice it or there will no longer be a human race to worry about."[38]

President Truman was not oblivious to the moral and political implications of this issue and had instructed Secretary of State James Byrnes to initiate departmental studies dealing with the feasibility of international control. Two groups began to formulate plans for this purpose. One committee was headed by Under Secretary of State Dean Acheson and another by Tennessee Valley Authority director David E. Lilienthal. When merged, their proposals became the Acheson-Lilienthal Plan. Henry Wallace liked this approach, since it recommended that the United Nations set up an international commission to regulate atomic energy. But later when this emerged as the Baruch Plan with a strict inspection system, he came out against it. Wallace felt the latter proposal would unnecessarily antagonize the Soviet Union and thus impede international cooperation. He claimed it would instead trigger an atomic arms race with Russia.

Before Bernard Baruch presented his plan to the UN, President Truman had considered all aspects of the problem. A memorandum from Secretary of War Henry L. Stimson prompted him to ponder seriously the advisability of allowing a free exchange of information on nuclear physics. On September 11, 1945, the aged Stimson recommended that a "direct and forthright approach" to the Soviet Union on atomic matters might clear the air for future cooperation. By offering them an arrangement to limit the use of the bomb, such negotiations would not become embroiled in a "general international scheme" or become part of a series of "expressed or implied threats" to their security. Stimson couched his counsel in careful language, "My idea of an approach to the Soviets would be a direct proposal after discussion with the British that we be prepared in effect to enter an arrangement with the Russians, the general purpose of which would be to control and limit the use of the atomic bomb as an instrument of war and so far as possible to direct and encourage the development of atomic power for peaceful and humanitarian purpose."[39]

President Truman announced to his cabinet that its September 21st meeting would be devoted exclusively to a discussion of the atomic question. That appointed day happened to be the seventy-eighth birthday of Henry L. Stimson, who had served three presidents and was making his final cabinet appearance. Truman respected the judgment of the retiring Secretary of War as a senior statesman and asked him to open the discussion. Speaking extemporaneously, Stimson explained to all present what he had in mind. He told them all aspects of the problem had been considered, and after consulting with General George Marshall and giving thought to Russian actions at Potsdam, he still came to the conclusion that a direct agreement with the Soviets on atomic control might well be the best solution. It would allay Russian suspicions and forestall an arms race for nuclear weapons; humanity would be the benefactor from such a settlement.[40]

Truman listened in silence without indicating either approval or disapproval. Henry Wallace spoke in favor of Stimson's plan and agreed that it was the wisest course to pursue for guaranteeing peace. Others present who indicated a general concurrence with Stimson's views were Dean Acheson, sitting in for James F. Byrnes who was in London; Abe Fortas, representing Harold Ickes; Under Secretary of War Robert Patterson, who was to succeed Stimson; Robert Hannegan, the Postmaster General; and Leo Crowley, the foreign economic administrator. Secretary of Labor Lewis B. Schwellenbach, who was absent from this particular meeting, later voiced his agreement with Stimson's proposal. After being contacted for their views, Dr. Vannevar Bush, director of the Office of Scientific Research, and Major General Philip B. Fleming, head of the Federal Works Agency, joined in support of Stimson's proposal.

Those members of the cabinet registering opposition or serious reservations included James Forrestal, Secretary of the Navy; Clinton P. Anderson, Secretary of Agriculture; Tom Clark, Attorney General; Fred M. Vinson, Secretary of the Treasury; Director of Reconversion John Snyder; and Senator Kenneth McKellar the Senate president pro tem, who was present because there was no Vice-President at the time. The agenda of this important gathering was limited to an exchange of open and frank opinions about the advisability of seeking direct collaboration with Soviet leaders concerning the future of atomic energy. No decision was made, but Truman thanked all participants for their candid judgments on this vital issue.[41]

All had gone well in this closed-door session of the cabinet. Argumentation was spirited but amicable, and Truman received the consultation he so desired. After this meeting the inevitable rumors began circulating as to what actually had transpired. Stories were soon circulating that Henry Wallace had made a sensational proposal to provide the Soviet Union with all data concerning atomic weaponry. Although Wallace did not even play a key role in the discussions except to second what Stimson had said, he was nevertheless maligned with gossip about something that had never happened. Was it his old foe Senator Kenneth McKellar who had leaked false information to the press? No one knew for sure. Many years later in 1951 when *The Forrestal Diaries* were published, one entry related to this famous cabinet session. It claimed Wallace was "completely, everlastingly and wholeheartedly in favor of giving it [the A-bomb secret] to the Russians."[42] This charge was branded a lie by Wallace, but since James Forrestal was dead no retraction could ever be made.

Another episode in 1951, during the high tide of "McCarthyism," caused Wallace much emotional anguish. An Associated Press representative asked him to make a comment on what Leo Crowley had allegedly said in a speech to the Holy Name Society of Milwaukee. The allegation made was that both Henry Wallace and Dean Acheson favored giving the secret of the atom bomb to Russia. Wallace wrote Crowley, then chairman of the board of the Chicago, Milwaukee, and St. Paul Railroad, to protest the false accusation. Bristling with indignation, the letter sought to correct the record about the now famous cabinet meeting: "Dean Acheson spoke very briefly and agreed with Stimson. You also in the main agreed with Stimson as did many others in the cabinet. I knew that at least one person thought you were in 1945 . . . [what] I called the 'lyingleaker' of the cabinet meeting. I never thought so and still find it hard to believe."[43]

Whereas President Truman's decision to press for international control of atomic energy through the auspices of the UN coincided originally with Wallace's view, the alterations of the Acheson-Lilienthal Plan were not acceptable to him. On the domestic scene Truman supported civilian over military control but of necessity compromised with the proposal sponsored by Senator Arthur Vandenberg (R-Michigan). The Atomic Energy Act as finally passed established a five-man civilian Atomic Energy Commission, provided for a Division of Military Application, and set up a Military Liaison Committee. Exchange of information on atomic energy with other nations was expressly forbidden unless approved by a joint resolution of the Congress.

Wallace was extremely disappointed with this act for its failure to ensure immediate dissemination of atomic technology for peaceful uses. Essentially Wallace felt U.S. atomic policy was needlessly harming good relations with the Soviet Union, particularly since their scientists would soon discover the secrets of the atom anyway.

The Secretary of Commerce was becoming inextricably involved in foreign policy issues. Thinking that he represented the Roosevelt tradition in statecraft, he could not refrain from speaking out publicly on the status of Soviet-American relations. His overwhelming fear was that his country and Russia were on a collision course unless policy changes were inaugurated immediately. Russian attitudes were hardening into an inflexible anti-American position, while Truman was improvising a "get-tough" policy. Contours of the Cold War were being molded amid a rising tide of war hysteria. Within this murky milieu of fear and hostility Henry Wallace initiated his personal crusade for peace. The mirror of history refracts different images to different eyes, and to Wallace the world was doomed if it pursued what appeared to be a mad course to World War III. In the face of such a pending disaster, according to his evaluation, he could not remain silent on decisions of such lasting significance though it might be more politic to do so.

CHAPTER 10

COLD WAR CRITIC: THE CABINET CRISIS OF 1946

AXIOMATICALLY, wartime alliances resemble the desperate behavior of wildlife in a dangerous forest fire. Hunter and hunted may hover together momentarily for mutual protection until the conflagration passes, but the predator instinct returns once again when all is normal.

Similarly during World War II the American eagle and Russian bear collaborated in a common cause until the peril which united them no longer existed. Since subordination of national self-interest to foster international cooperation merely for its own sake has never been the usual pattern of diplomatic relations, U.S. leaders might well have anticipated a drastic change in the nature of Soviet-American collaboration once the Third Reich had been crushed. Certainly there was relatively little tangible evidence available that friendship would continue on the mere strength of prolonged goodwill or other altruistic motives.

Even before President Roosevelt's death there were definite intimations that Soviet intentions were actually running contrary to those of Britain and the United States. Revelations of the Katyn massacre, Kremlin coolness toward the Polish Government

They shall beat their swords into plowshares, and . . .
nation shall not lift sword against nation. . . .
ISAIAH 2:4

in Exile (with headquarters in London), and the establishment of the puppet Lublin Committee as a provisional ruling body over liberated Poland all signified ominous Soviet designs on Eastern Europe. Pledges made at Yalta regarding free elections, by Anglo-American standards, were words without substance when it came to implementation. Stalin's failure to live up to such political agreements was augmented by new outbursts of anti-Western propaganda not heard during the war years. *Red Star* solemnly warned Russian soldiers in its September 26, 1944, issue, "The front now runs through territory outside our borders. To find his way about in these new conditions, a Communist needs sound ideological equipment more than ever."[1] In other words, comrades in uniform were cautioned against being corrupted by contact with Americans of the capitalist world.

After V-J Day, Americans looked forward with high hopes to the formation of a United Nations Organization. It appeared to all that the founding of the UN at San Francisco would usher a new era into existence. On the assumption he need only continue the Roosevelt foreign policy, Truman launched the UN; but to his amazement, he had also to deal with the increasing recalcitrance of the Russians. Public opinion was not prepared for any sudden shift in official attitude toward the Soviet Union, yet the President and his close advisers were becoming convinced, albeit reluctantly, that agreements made at Yalta were not being honored by Joseph Stalin.

It was obvious from the outset of his presidency that Harry Truman's style was quite different from Roosevelt's. He spoke bluntly and never couched his ideas in grandiose prose. Concrete details, not abstract principles, moved him; he always preferred to play power politics with a trump up his sleeve. For this reason Truman rejected Secretary Stimson's proposal either to ban the bomb or to unilaterally share information on atomic energy freely with Russia. The atom bomb was his ace in the hole in any future diplomatic poker game with Stalin. When the Missourian thought he detected a doublecross, he reacted instinctively to put pressure on the Soviet Union. Thus a tougher approach gradually came into existence, not by design, but because of day-to-day improvisations.

All presidents are to some extent prisoners of the advice they receive. Harry Truman paid deference to the hawkish hardliners, yet he did not cease listening to the opposing views of those desiring conciliation and concessions to the Soviets as a means of continuing wartime cooperation. This accounted for the President's decision to send Harry Hopkins on a special mission to see Stalin and his reversal of a previous order cutting off lend-lease supplies.[2] Henry Wallace knew Truman had not yet fully made up his mind to abandon the wartime policy of collaboration; therefore, he tried to rally those still favoring this position. Wallace thus became the leader of those idealists who desired concessions to ensure continuance of Soviet cooperation. To help him convince the President to continue what he believed to be F.D.R.'s policy of internationalism, Wallace had former Under Secretary of State Sumner Welles prepare a written statement containing broad foreign policy suggestions. Although addressed to Wallace, the document was meant to influence Truman. The Commerce Secretary sent the memorandum to President Truman with the comment, "It is worth reading because, as you know, he enjoyed the confidence of President Roosevelt with regard to the good neighbor policy and world organization." Welles stressed the need for maintaining postwar unity among the Big Three powers, especially Russia, so that the UN might get off to a good start. Consequently he advised temporary acceptance of the veto power in the Security Council with the idea it could be modified in favor of a three-fifths vote at some later date (perhaps some seven to ten years). In addition he stressed the imperative need for regaining "moral leadership" of world opinion so that U.S. efforts within the UN could be devoted "to further the realization of the four freedoms."[3]

Right at the time that Truman appointed General Walter Bedell Smith to replace Harriman as U.S. ambassador to the Soviet Union, Henry Wallace again made a strong effort to dissuade the President from launching a hard-line policy against the Russians. In a long letter to Truman, dated March 14, 1946, Secretary Wallace deemed it opportune to try what he called a "new approach" to peace. He therefore advised Truman to make an all-out attempt to "disabuse the Soviet mind and strengthen the faith of the Soviets in our sincere devotion to the cause of peace by proving to them that we want to trade with them and to cement our economic relations with them." Suggesting that a trade commission be sent to Moscow and intimating he would like to be a member of it, Wallace argued, "We know that much of the recent Soviet behavior which has caused us concern has been the result of their dire economic needs and of their disturbed sense of security. The events of the past months have thrown the Soviets back to their pre-1939 fears of 'capitalistic enslavement' and to their erroneous belief that the Western World, including the U.S.A., is invariably and unanimously hostile."[4]

General Walter Bedell Smith also desired postwar cooperation with the Soviets, but he found the Russians extremely uncooperative, even to the extent of refusing him permission to keep an airplane (with its crew) stationed in their country.[5] Eisenhower's former Chief of Staff soon discovered the war time camaraderie was gone, and he was treated with stiff formality instead of the cordiality of an ally.

Distraught over the continued deterioration in Soviet-American relations, Henry Wallace began to draft a still lengthier statement to send to President Truman. As it circulated among Commerce Department associates for comment and criticism, Richard H. Hippelheuser pointed out some weaknesses that were later to add to the furor which resulted in Wallace's forced resignation from the cabinet (after the confidential memorandum was leaked to the press). Addressing his remarks to Philip M. Hauser, who was also aiding Wallace in preparing this document, Hippleheuser noted the position paper "devotes too much space to the means for allaying Soviet distrust while slighting the grounds for American distrust of the Russians."[6]

On July 23, 1946, this memorandum was sent as a letter to the President. Wallace once more contended that U.S. actions were needlessly provoking harsh responses from Russian leaders. Examples of such incitement were the atomic bomb tests at Bikini, continued B-29 production with plans to build the B-32, construction of U.S. air bases all over the world, a $28 billion budget for national defense, and persistent talk of the need for a preventive war. Wallace was also highly critical of the Baruch Plan regarding international control of atomic energy. Due to Baruch's insistence, and with Truman's approval, the proposal presented to the UN called for rigid inspection within the Soviet Union and disclosure of information on all fissionable materials. A proposition of that type, claimed the Commerce Secretary, was the same as "telling the Russians that if they are 'good boys' we may eventually turn over our knowledge of atomic energy to them and to the other nations." This approach, he predicted, would only motivate the Soviets to "redouble their efforts to manufacture bombs, and they may also decide to expand their 'security zone' in a serious way."[7]

In the realm of atomic energy more than anywhere else, Wallace believed the United States should demonstrate its peaceful intent to Russia. The Secretary's break with administration foreign policy began basically with his opposition to the premise that scientific secrecy and military restrictions were necessary to preserve American security. Wallace viewed such repressive measures as self-defeating. They would not, in his view, deter the Soviet Union from developing its own atomic bomb but would only serve to prevent international development of nuclear power for peaceful purposes. Within this frame of reference the Commerce Secretary was echoing the opinion of a significant segment of the scientific community.[8]

Bernard Baruch, on the other hand, altered the initial Acheson-Lilienthal Plan to make it more foolproof in operation. Baruch, who personally headed the American delegation to the UN Atomic Energy Commission, certainly wanted international control of fissionable materials *but* with specific safeguards that would ensure honest compliance. Dramatizing the need for some form of worldwide check on atomic weapons, the elder statesman of American politics presented the stern warning, "We are here to make a choice between the quick and the dead." Continuing the solemnity of his June 14, 1946, address to the UN delegates, he admitted, "Science, which gave us this dread power, shows that it can be a giant help to humanity, but science does not show us how to prevent its baleful use."[9]

Furthermore Baruch insisted not only upon an inspection system but upon provisions for instigating strict sanctions or meting out immediate punishment to those violating international regulations. Also, no Security Council veto could be used to circumvent UN authority or to protect transgressors. Only after effective controls were operative would the United States cease manufacturing atomic weapons or destroy its stockpile of A-bombs. Harry Truman backed this procedure. The President had written to Baruch just before his presentation to the UN, "We must have assurance that the raw materials from which atomic energy can be released are controlled at the source and I am of the opinion that we should not under any circumstances throw away our gun until we are sure the rest of the world can't arm against us. I think we understand each other on this subject."[10]

At the UN, a counterproposal was announced by Andrei Gromyko. He made it plain the Soviet Union was opposed to internal inspection of any kind or abrogation of the veto power for any reason. He demanded immediate cessation of all A-bomb production and destruction forthwith of any stockpiles existing in the United States. Gromyko would not budge from his unilateral position, nor would Baruch concede inspection. President Truman felt he could not in clear conscience yield up the American atomic monopoly (for the brief period we had had it) without provisions for UN observation teams to conduct inspection tours. On the other hand, Joseph Stalin would not under any circumstances permit outsiders to check on Soviet endeavors in scientific research. Quite naturally the United States wanted a *quid pro quo*, a not too unusual procedure in international negotiations, but Kremlin fears of inspection by foreigners precluded any settlement for genuine international control of nuclear power.[11]

Within Truman's cabinet Henry Wallace fought a losing battle. Stimson, the man who first suggested the sharing of atomic knowledge with Russia, had now retired because of ill health. Other members of the Truman administration, particularly Senator Tom Connally of the Foreign Relations Committee, began to feel Soviet objection to the U.S. version of international atomic control was but another aspect of their overall belligerence toward the West. The senator from Texas had accompanied Secretary Byrnes to frustrating sessions of the Council of Foreign Ministers, and he sincerely felt the Russians were deliberately obstructing all avenues of the peacemaking process.[12] The venerable Winston Churchill agreed substantially with this assessment—so much so that he wanted to arouse the American public. On March 5, 1946, the former prime minister took advantage of an invitation from Westminster College at Fulton, Missouri, to deliver his famous Iron Curtain speech. With President Truman on the same platform, Churchill uttered his Cassandralike warning, "From Stettin in the Baltic to Trieste in the Adriatic, an iron curtain has descended across the Continent."[13]

Whereas Truman did not officially underwrite Churchill's words, Wallace interpreted the President's physical presence as an overt step toward forging an Anglo-American alliance against Russia. Because he thought such action would only cause further deterioration in Soviet-American relations, Secretary Wallace lashed out bitterly against what he believed was a resurgence of British imperialism. One specific event he had in mind stemming from the war was British occupation of Greece and support of Greek monarchists. Indeed, Britain's policy had been to prop up the rule of Constantine Tsaldaris until such time as a plebiscite could be held to determine the future status of the monarchy. This intervention was also carried on by the Labor government which succeeded Churchill's wartime coalition. British policy was to prevent both Greece and Turkey from falling prey to Communist insurgency.

When a full-scale peace conference was finally scheduled to meet in Paris in July of 1946, its agenda was crowded—ensuring sessions until well into the winter. To be taken up were such urgent matters as peace treaties with Austria and Italy; resolution of the Italian-Yugoslav dispute over Trieste; postwar boundaries of Hungary, Bulgaria, and Czechoslovakia; navigation rights on the Danube River; reparations; coordination of regulations governing the occupied zones of Germany; and questions dealing with Germany and Poland. Confronting one another would be James Byrnes, accompanied by senators Tom Connally and Arthur Vandenberg; Vyacheslav Molotov of the Soviet Union; French Foreign Minister Georges Bidault; and British Foreign Minister Ernest Bevin.[14]

Prior to the convening of the Paris Conference Henry Wallace began his own campaign to influence the American position. At a testimonial dinner for Mrs. Eleanor Roosevelt in honor of her recent appointment as a U.S. delegate to the UN, Wallace said of the former First Lady, "She will use all of her influence to see that the United States mediates between the British and the Russians, instead of ganging up with the British against the Russians, or with the Russians against the British."[15]

In response to a question on an ABC radio program regarding the probability of an atom bomb being developed by the

Soviets, the Commerce Secretary replied, "Whether or not we do have an atomic bomb race with Russia is very largely up to us. We can either prevent such a race from taking place, or we can cause it to happen. If we go ahead with an attitude of hostility and antagonism, and if we entrust the whole area of development and use of atomic power to our military people, there will be such a race."[16]

Not oblivious to this rising undercurrent of distrust evinced by the American people, Wallace set about to explain Russian behavior to skeptical audiences. In an address to the American Society for Russian Relief, a group honoring W. Averell Harriman for his many years of service as U.S. ambassador to the Soviet Union, Henry Wallace reiterated reasons why Russian actions seemed so obstinate to the West. Using historical arguments to establish the authenticity of Soviet fears, he reasoned, "The Soviet Union knows what the leading capitalist nations, especially Great Britain, tried to do to it from 1919 to 1921. They know what certain of the military in the capitalist nations are thinking and saying today. And just as some military men profess that the only road to peace is atomic bombs, bases, huge appropriations for armaments and arctic expeditions, so the Soviets may feel the only road to peace and security is for them to give the capitalistic nations tit for tat." Disregarding evidence to the contrary, Wallace asserted flatly, "The Soviet Government and its leaders disclaim aggressive intentions and any desire for world dominion."[17]

When President Ávila Camacho invited Wallace to visit Mexico in the fall of 1946, the Commerce Secretary took advantage of the occasion to link the Roosevelt good-neighbor policy with his cold-war views. Therefore he proceeded to tell the Mexicans that all Americans, those living in the North and South, were "allies of humanity." Appearing before the Mexican Labor Organization on September 5, he elaborated by defining democracy as the "political expression of Christian thought." As such, Wallace explained, "It is a belief and faith in the goodness of man. Only those who do not believe in the common man are able to accept totalitarian doctrines. We, the democrats of America, have no faith in the elite, nor in a superior man, nor in a so-called superior race. But we do believe in the common man. We do believe in the people. . . . We do say that if all men are equal before God, they ought also to be equal before man. We believe that in democracy, properly understood, sovereignty comes directly from the people, and therefore a good government is one which will serve the interests of the people." Commending Latin labor leaders for their attainments in securing a modicum of economic democracy for Mexican workers, he counseled them to "beware of the false democrats—fanatically devoted to freedom but systematically indifferent to justice." Hailing Mexico's "noble revolutionary tradition," Wallace praised their history by saying, "Here you have fought with heroism for justice and liberty."[18]

In many ways Henry Wallace equated the Russian revolution to the one that had taken place in Mexico. Both were underdeveloped countries and both had thrown off old regimes. In their initial stages the accent was on social justice, while political democracy developed more slowly as an aftermath of revolution. By using this analogy, Wallace found himself in the more tenable position of defending the temporary undemocratic features of the Communist ruling body. While some vague historical parallels existed, it was not an altogether convincing comparison. The dictatorial way in which Stalin ruled, the long-standing Russian expansionist tendencies existing whether the country was run by czars or commissars, and an ideological fanaticism parading first as Pan-Slavism and then as Communism all joined together to make Soviet history quite unlike that of Mexico. Whereas Wallace regarded the Bolshevik revolution as a manifestation of the common people's drive for economic and political democracy, it was in reality a revolt led by a small, disciplined minority. Its use of totalitarian methods such as secret police, purges, and suppression of all opposition made Soviet democracy a farce in terms of western traditions. While Wallace acknowledged Russia's shortcomings in the realm of political liberties, he fully expected an evolution of democratic institutions within the Soviet Union. The massive gap between what existed and what he presumed would happen often made him appear as an apologist for Communist tyranny.

Henry Wallace did not intend to be a spokesman for any foreign nation, but his attacks on America's shortcomings were often interpreted as assaults on his own country. At a Jackson Day meeting in Los Angeles sponsored by the Democratic National Committee, Secretary Wallace bluntly informed Californians, "We do not have political democracy in the United States as long as the poll tax disenfranchises millions of voters. We do not have economic democracy in the United States as long as people are discriminated against in their jobs because of color or race or religion or sex." Calling for victory in the November elections, he vowed, "We must keep the Democratic party the party of the people's progress—both in national and international affairs." President Truman received praise from him at this time for his "steadfast adherence to the New Deal philosophy."[19]

While touring Pennsylvania, Wallace gave hearty support to Senator Joseph Guffey's reelection bid, in Boston he attacked the Republicans for allowing price controls to lapse, and to organized labor in Detroit he lashed out at the selfishness of the National Association of Manufacturers. Business leaders were scored for their opposition to renewal of the Office of Price Administration. In reply to the G.O.P. slogan, "Had enough?" he retorted, "In our country, just as throughout the world, the Four Horsemen of the Apocalypse of our day still are riding hard. These are the Horsemen of Greed and Want, Fear and War. Given a free rein, they would ride roughshod over the hopes of mankind everywhere."[20]

Accepting an invitation to address the American Labor party of New York City, Henry Wallace took time out to speak in favor of the reelection of Vito Marcantonio and Adam Clayton Powell, since both fought for civil rights and Soviet-American cooperation. Powell, a Democrat, was one of the few Negro representatives in Congress; and Marcantonio, although a self-designated independent, openly accepted Communist party support. Even while endorsing this third-party candidate for Congress, Henry Wallace advised Harlem's Negro and Puerto Rican residents to work for the election of liberal Democrats by telling them, "I believe in the two-party system. I want the party I belong to—the Democratic Party—to be the progressive party. The American Labor Party cannot, of course, elect delegates to Democratic conventions. This lessens your influence. Any progressive party which attempts to operate on the national scale will find, because of the laws in most states, that it will guarantee a reactionary victory by dividing the votes of progressives."[21]

Because many liberals of all persuasions had honestly become disenchanted with Harry Truman, there were many rumors about the need for forming a third party by 1948. Ostensibly it would be New Deal–oriented on domestic issues and pro-UN internationally. Trying hard to discourage such a venture, Wallace repeatedly spoke out against such a course. Speaking in Truman's home state at a rally sponsored jointly by the Liberal Voters League and the St. Louis Political Action Committee, Wallace once more sought to discredit this ill-advised endeavor. "Now let us analyze this talk bluntly and realistically," he said. "It is time for third party advocates to stop kidding themselves," because "even if they were thinking of 1952 instead of 1948, I believe it is unrealistic to expect that they could bring about a change in the election laws in enough states to build a really effective national organization. And so far as 1948 is concerned, a third party effort would insure beyond all doubt the election of a reactionary Republican—give him the name of Bricker or whatever name you want." His final charge, and it was sound advice that he was to disregard in the not too distant future, was the statement, "I say, in all sincerity, that the progressive forces of this country have no basis today for disillusionment in the Democratic party as an instrument of national progress."[22]

To safeguard the election of James M. Mead and Herbert Lehman, a massive rally was to be staged at Madison Square Garden under the joint auspices of the National Citizens Political Action Committee and the Independent Citizens Committee of the Arts, Sciences, and Professions. Mead was trying to dislodge Governor Thomas E. Dewey from his Albany post, while Lehman was vying with Republican Irving M. Ives for the vacated Senate seat. By receiving the backing of both the Liberal party and American Labor party (ALP), these two Democrats seemed assured of attracting a huge metropolitan vote in New York City. The two independent parties were much more to the left in political orientation than most Democrats, with the ALP being the most radical of all even to the point of attracting support from Communists. Neither party, however, had much power outside the five boroughs of New York. One of the reasons Henry Wallace was asked to be the featured speaker was to guarantee an enthusiastic voter turnout in metropolitan areas, so as to counter expected G.O.P. strength in upstate regions.[23]

One of the key promoters of the Madison Square Garden rally was Calvin B. Baldwin, the CIO director of the Political Action Committee. He urged that a major statement on foreign affairs be made and advised an outright attack upon the American warmongers who used anti-Communism as a shield for making profits from the cold war. Wallace had known "Beanie" Baldwin from the days of his service in the Agriculture Department and during the time the latter headed the Farm Security Administration (1940 to 1943). Naturally the Secretary saw Baldwin frequently and generally sympathized with his efforts to remedy the problem of rural poverty. After Baldwin became active in the CIO-PAC Wallace continued to see him. They both agreed on the need for social justice, racial integration, and world harmony based on Soviet-American cooperation within the UN. Not so clear to Wallace was Baldwin's feeling that a Popular Front type of left-wing coalition against an incipient fascism was needed to promote universal peace.[24]

With the intention of presenting a reasonable and balanced speech, Secretary Wallace prepared a text that criticized the failure of both major powers to arrive at amicable solutions to outstanding problems. Instead of merely sending the prepared text to the White House for routine clearance, the usual procedure in these matters, Secretary Wallace decided to see Truman personally. He met with the President for about thirty minutes on September 10, 1946. Placing a copy of his address on Truman's desk while holding one himself, Wallace read certain excerpts aloud. As he went over the entire text, the Commerce Secretary periodically interjected explanations relative to the meaning of significant statements. On the surface his proposed talk, while stringent in style, seemed to be fair in its overall outlook; therefore President Truman gave it his approval. Knowing that his Secretary of Commerce could attract many votes for Democrats among the various liberal elements in New York, he even went so far as to say it represented the thinking of the administration. Insofar as Truman was trying to placate all wings of his party, it seemed good political strategy to keep the extreme left satisfied. Had Truman allowed one of his advisers to read the speech, he would have received a contrary evaluation of its effect on the general public. The President's off-hand endorsement of this address set the stage for a cabinet crisis of major proportions.[25]

Meantime in Paris the American delegation was mired down in a series of most difficult negotiations with Soviet representatives. James Byrnes, with the wholehearted backing of Connally and Vandenberg, took a firm stand and pressed the Russians for military withdrawal from their Eastern European satellites. To underscore U.S. determination to stop any possible Soviet domination of the entire European continent, Secretary of State Byrnes scheduled a special speech of his own for September 5. Talking to a German audience at the Stuttgart State Opera House, Byrnes dramatically announced that whereas the United States would continue its de-Nazification program it did "not want Germany to become a satellite of any power." Flanked by Connally and Vandenberg, with General Joseph T. McNarney and Ambassador Robert Murphy also present on the stage, Secretary Byrnes declared it was the intention of his country to help occupied Germany "win their way back to an honorable place among the free and peace loving nations."[26]

Truman's trouble began even before Henry Wallace actually

delivered his Madison Square Garden speech. Since the text had been released prior to the evening rally, newsmen were able to ask President Truman about it during an afternoon press conference. What started as a routine White House session with reporters ended by making even more headlines. An immediate question was raised to a specific quotation from Wallace's speech, namely, the sentence, "When President Truman read these words, he said they represented the policy of this administration." Without hesitating Truman replied, "That is correct." This led to another inquiry, "Does that apply just to that paragraph, or to the whole speech?" Again, without delay, the President answered, "I approved the whole speech." Inevitably someone asked the Chief Executive whether he regarded Wallace's pronouncements as constituting a "departure from Byrnes' policy." Truman retorted quickly, "I do not." A quick query came back, "Toward Russia?" Responding immediately, the President shot from the hip, "They are exactly in line."[27]

In the State Department William L. Clayton, the acting secretary in the absence of Byrnes and Acheson (the latter was on vacation), took an extremely dim view of Wallace's proposed speech. Clayton, along with James W. Riddleberger (acting head of the Division of European Affairs) and Loy W. Henderson (head of the Division of Near and Middle Eastern Affairs) scrutinized an advance copy of the address, and all came to the conclusion it should not be given. It seemed to them a clear repudiation of the position Byrnes had taken vis-à-vis the Russian stand. Phoning Press Secretary Charles G. Ross, Clayton urged him to influence Truman to rescind his public endorsement. Without waiting to discover what Ross would do, he immediately cabled Byrnes in Paris and told him what had happened. With no word from Charles Ross to indicate a presidential repudiation of the speech nor any attempt to have it altered, many State Department officials waited anxiously to see what would happen after Henry Wallace actually delivered it.[28]

Some twenty thousand people jammed into the old Madison Square Garden arena to hear Wallace. The ALP and the Liberal party had dutifully gotten out their faithful followers, as did the Independent Citizens Committee of the Arts, Sciences, and Professions. Leaders of the rally had also seen advance copies of Wallace's text, and they specifically did not like some of the unfavorable references to the Soviet Union. Deleted before air time were the passages: "The Russians should stop conniving against us in certain areas of the world just as we should stop scheming against them in other parts of the world" and "Meanwhile, the Russians should stop teaching [that] their form of Communism must, by force if necessary, ultimately triumph over democratic capitalism."[29]

Once Wallace began his speech, radio listeners at home were amazed to hear boos, catcalls, and angry shouts whenever even mild criticisms were spoken about Russian actions. Whether intimidated by this reaction or pressed for time because of the interruptions, he made more cuts in the original text and this added to the confusion. One person who was present at this weird performance recalled picking up a newspaper version and found to his dismay: "All the way through, sections had been left out which might have given offense to the audience."[30] Because Wallace did this, for whatever reason, the remaining parts of the speech seemed disproportionately critical of U.S. foreign policy.

Standing in bold relief was the curt warning that Americans "must not let British balance of power manipulations determine whether and when the United States gets into war." Decrying the continuing existence of British imperialism, Henry Wallace vehemently opposed those advocating "an alliance of mutual defense with Great Britain as the key to our foreign policy." The way to "prevent war and insure our survival in a stable world," he insisted, was to "look abroad through our own American eyes and not through the eyes of either the British foreign office or a pro-British or anti-Russian press." Having said this and in view of the missing sections of his speech, Wallace really placed Truman on the spot when he declared, "In this connection, I want one thing clearly understood. I am neither anti-British nor pro-British—neither anti-Russian nor pro-Russian. And just two days ago, when President Truman read these words, he said they represented the policy of his administration."[31]

Because most condemnations of Soviet foreign policy had been deleted, the Commerce Secretary's attempt to rationalize Russian attitudes and actions seemed like a long and labored apologia for Communistic imperialism. Wallace rehearsed once more the historical reasons why the Soviet Union desired friendly neighbors purely for security purposes. This explanation, which had some validity, placed him in the paradoxical position of defending the existence of a Soviet sphere (albeit allegedly for national defense) while criticizing Great Britain for trying to regain control of her Mediterranean lifeline (as if Britain did not also have to think of friendly countries astride her traditional seaways). Furthermore, he made himself sound pro-Communist when he readily conceded, "We may not like what Russia does in Eastern Europe" and even admitting, "Her type of land reform, industrial expropriation, and suppression of basic liberties offends the great majority of people of the United States." Sounding like a harsh realist, Wallace ackowledged they would "socialize their sphere of influence just as we try to democratize our sphere of influence." Heretofore, and indeed later, he had never sanctioned such diplomatic practices. Then as if to justify the polarization of the world into Communist and non-Communist blocs, he predicted, "Russian ideas of social-economic justice are going to govern nearly a third of the world, . . . [while] our ideas of free enterprise democracy will govern much of the rest."[32]

Completely submerged if not totally lost were his views that this two-world arrangement was to be only a temporary expedient because of undue Soviet fears of encirclement. Wallace was not condoning a permanent Russian sphere nor was he underwriting the spread of Communism. What he failed to communicate in this context was his firm conviction that only through American patience and conciliation could a "one world" ever evolve. Actually, he wanted international cooperation, not a globe bifurcated permanently into hostile halves. The avoidance of this eventuality was precisely what he had intended to stress, but it never came through. He had nevertheless proposed coexistence as the first step toward ultimate world federation. "We should close our ears to those among us who would have us believe that Russian Communism and our free enterprise system cannot live, one with another, in a profitable and productive peace," averred Wallace. "Under friendly, peaceful competition, the Russian world and the American world will gradually become more alike," he predicted, because inevitably "the Russians will be forced to grant more and more of the personal freedoms; and we shall become more and more absorbed with the problems of social-economic justice." Despite the existence of "practical regional political reservations," the Commerce Secretary foresaw dissipation of these spheres of influence as soon as "both British and Russians discover the futility of their methods."[33]

Because of the flood of inquiries from newsmen who had heard Truman repeatedly affirm his endorsement of the address before its delivery at Madison Square Garden, a White House press conference was scheduled on quick notice. Surrounded by reporters in his office, the President read a prepared statement to the assembled gathering. There had obviously been a "natural understanding," he asserted, of his approval for Wallace's speech.

Claiming his assent was not meant to convey endorsement or agreement with it "as constituting a statement of the foreign policy of this country," he continued, "It was my intention to express the thought that I approved the right of the Secretary to deliver the speech." Then with a grim face Truman closed his terse announcement with the final disclaimer: "There has been no change in the established foreign policy of our Government."[34]

Harry Truman's flat disavowal of responsibility for the contents of this controversial address by no means ended the public debate it aroused. Editorial pages and articles by columnists asked the President repeatedly for clarification of his stand on key issues of American foreign policy. Wallace had his defenders—and detractors—as did Truman, who was also criticized for his ineptitude. If the President expected his Commerce Secretary to accept the hastily contrived repudiation given to newsmen, he certainly misjudged the one remaining Roosevelt holdover in his cabinet. Reporters flocked to Wallace's office on Monday (September 16) for his version of the story. He issued the following statement: "I stand upon my New York speech. It was interesting to find that both the extreme right and the extreme left disagreed with the views I expressed. Feeling as I do however that most Americans are concerned about, and willing to work for peace, I intend to continue my efforts for a just and lasting peace and I shall, within the near future, speak on this subject again."[35] The news media hardly considered this a humble recantation and neither did the American delegation in Paris.

The tempest began to blow even harder overseas as the European press printed news of the Truman-Wallace mixup. Senator Tom Connally tried to pour oil on the troubled waters by calling for unity and insisting there be "no division behind the lines."[36] His Senate cohort, the G.O.P.'s Arthur Vandenberg, announced that if a bipartisan foreign policy were to succeed, he had to be able to deal with only "one Secretary of State at a time."[37] For the time being James Byrnes decided to remain silent.

When it appeared the President was not going to discharge Wallace immediately, someone in the State Department sent columnist Drew Pearson excerpts from Wallace's July 23rd letter to Truman. The strategy was to cause more anti-Wallace sentiment, thus forcing President Truman to fire his Commerce Secretary. Pearson let his friend know of the breach in secrecy, which prompted Wallace to telephone Charles Ross advising him he was immediately releasing the entire text of his July 23rd private message to Truman. On September 17 Henry Wallace issued a public statement which read: "In view of the fact that a copy of Secretary Wallace's letter of July 23, 1946 to the President was filched from the files and is in the hands of a newspaper columnist, the Secretary of Commerce is today releasing this copy of the letter."[38] Whereas this action prevented quotes from being used out of context, this further revelation now had Harry Truman against the wall with no elbow room for political maneuvering.

Another flurry of headlines and news bulletins told the world all about the Wallace versus Truman contest over foreign policy. In Europe James Byrnes, now boiling with rage, took advantage of the public furor to tell Truman the Wallace affair had damaged his "prestige here at the Paris Conference." With ultimatumlike insistence the Secretary of State asserted, "If it is not possible for you, for any reason, to keep Mr. Wallace, as a member of your Cabinet, from speaking on foreign affairs, it would be a grave mistake from every point of view for me to continue in office, even temporarily. Therefore, if it is not completely clear in your own mind that Mr. Wallace should be asked to refrain from criticizing the foreign policy of the United States while he is a member of your Cabinet, I must ask you to accept my resignation immediately."[39]

By placating the Wallace faction, Truman had jeopardized his broad support for a bipartisan foreign policy. Now out of sheer frustration Truman dashed off a sharply worded message to Wallace that was a real gem in its use of earthy expressions. The Commerce Secretary was so shocked by its army barracks tone his first reaction was to call the White House to find out if it was genuinely the handiwork of Harry Truman. When the President would not speak to him, Wallace read the contents of this hot letter to Charles Ross. To the press secretary's utter surprise, he offered to return the offensive memorandum. Ross took advantage of this generous act and promptly retrieved this intemperate s.o.b.-type letter.[40]

Once his temper had cooled, the President decided to have a long talk with Wallace. Wanting very much to retain him in his cabinet as a political expedient for keeping liberal and left-wing support but desiring an understanding whereby the Commerce Secretary would cease from commenting on matters of foreign policy, Truman was in a compromising mood. Political loyalty was a two-way street with Truman, however, and he was willing to keep Wallace in the cabinet only in return for a promise of silence on issues touching American diplomacy. On September

18, the same day he received Byrnes' cable from Paris, President Truman met with Wallace for two and one-half hours. Reporters waited anxiously at the White House for a news break. The announcement they received was from Wallace who said he had agreed to refrain from foreign policy pronouncements until October 15 at which time the Paris Conference would terminate.

Harry Truman thought he had weathered the storm, but the tempest was not yet over. He might not have considered any further action for the time being but for the loud complaints of Byrnes and Baruch. Because he was head of the American delegation dealing with UN control of atomic energy, Bernard Baruch asked for permission to answer Wallace's arguments contained in the published letter of July 23. Secretary of State James Byrnes. was even more persistent and lost no time in contacting the President via teletype to protest bitterly against having Wallace remain in the administration. What he had taken fifteen months to do, remonstrated Byrnes, "Wallace destroyed . . . in a day."[41] Truman promptly told his Secretary of State, "The situation will be made perfectly clear tomorrow." For added emphasis the President repeated assuringly, "There will be no misunderstanding."[42]

Back at his desk where he faced the plaque with the inscription, "The buck stops here," Harry Truman tried to get things clear in his own mind. Writing diary-style, the President penned a long memorandum to himself analyzing Henry Wallace's position. As if trying to convince himself of the need to fire his Commerce Secretary, this September 19th document was filled with many derogatory statements. "I am not sure he is as fundamentally sound, intellectually as I had thought," he wrote. The man seemed like a "pacifist 100 per cent" went another notation. His final conclusion was no doubt meant as a final indictment for the record: "He wants us to disband our armed forces, give Russia our atomic secrets and trust a bunch of adventurers in the Kremlin Politburo. I do not understand a dreamer like that. The German-American Bund under Fritz Kuhn was not half so dangerous. The Reds, phonies and the 'parlor pinks' seem to be banded together and are becoming a national disgrace."[43]

By stating his case, albeit in exaggerated and oversimplified terms, the President convinced himself he must discharge Henry Wallace regardless of the political repercussions. On the next day, September 20, Harry Truman phoned Wallace and announced calmly, "Henry, I am sorry, but I have reached the conclusion that it will be best that I ask for your resignation."[44] These words caught Secretary Wallace by surprise. Forcing himself to answer with considerable self-composure, he stated politely, "Why, yes, Mr. President, if that is your wish; certainly!"[45] Some thirty minutes later Truman received a communication that had been typed personally by Henry Wallace. It read: "As you requested, here is my resignation. I shall continue to fight for peace. I am sure that you will join me in that great endeavor."[46]

At a 10:30 A.M. news conference the President made a formal announcement of what had transpired. There was an audible reaction of astonishment among the reporters present when Truman related how he had asked Secretary Wallace for his resignation. "Mr. Wallace will be happier in the exercise of his right to present his views as a private citizen," said the President with a tone of finality. In order to appear as master of the situation, Truman declared firmly, "Mr. Byrnes consults with me often, and the policies which guide him and his delegation have my full endorsement."[47]

Breathing more easily now that the ordeal was over, Truman wrote a breezy letter to his mother and sister telling them how really he "hated to do it." While praising Wallace as the best Secretary of Agriculture the nation ever had, he nevertheless penned the observation, "Henry is the most peculiar fellow I ever came in contact with." Yet in a moment of regret he confided that Wallace "was so nice about it I almost backed out!" But with his irrepressible cocksureness, after the hassle was over, he added the biting comment, "Well, now he's out, and the crackpots are having conniption fits. I'm glad they are. It convinces me I'm right. . . ."[48]

When offered free radio time to present his version of what happened, the former Commerce Secretary was eager to take advantage of it to speak his mind to the American public. Without rancor and in no way engaging in a tirade against the President, Wallace offered a straightforward explanation for his behavior: "Winning the peace is more important than high office. It is more important than any consideration of party politics." Speaking with great moral earnestness he declared, "I feel that our present foreign policy does not recognize the basic realities which led to two world wars and which now threaten another war—this time an atomic war." His farewell speech said nothing about withdrawal from politics. To the contrary, he asserted, "I intend to carry on the fight for peace."[49]

CHAPTER 11

"THE NEW REPUBLIC" AND THE FIGHT FOR PEACE

AFTER his sudden departure from the Truman administration, Henry Wallace was counseled by such old agrarian friends as Mordecai Ezekiel and Henry C. Taylor to return to the field of agriculture either as head of the UN's Food and Agriculture Organization or by becoming president or dean of an agricultural college. He ultimately accepted a proposal from Michael Straight to join the editorial staff of *The New Republic.*

That Wallace should be considered for such a post was quite compatible with his background. Before joining the Roosevelt administration in 1933, he had acquired a notable reputation throughout the entire Midwest as a fighting farm editor. From 1924 until he became Secretary of Agriculture in 1933, he had been editor of *Wallaces' Farmer.*

When the former Commerce Secretary made his decision to reenter the field of journalism, he also moved his place of legal residence to New York. He purchased a country home surrounded by 115 acres of land in South Salem, New York. This rural area was near Connecticut and only fifty miles (within commuter dis-

Thus saith the Lord; Deceive not your selves. . . .
JEREMIAH 37:9

tance) from Manhattan where the office of *The New Republic* was located. The new abode was promptly called Farvue Farm, named as a tribute to his beloved grandfather whose farmstead in Iowa had been so designated. A picture of the first Wallace occupied a featured place in H. A.'s study, and once again fond memories were the grandson's constant companions. Excited at the prospect of being able to engage in experimental work with plants once more, Wallace left Washington, D.C., with few regrets. Having purchased a small tractor from Sears and Roebuck and in anticipation of planting time, Wallace wrote his old friend Dr. Henry C. Taylor, "I am looking ahead to have a good time with it this summer."[1]

Had Henry Wallace really known what was in store for him during the next few years, he might well have made Farvue Farm a retreat from politics instead of a place for reentry. However, one really wonders whether Wallace would have deviated one iota from his course even with the foreknowledge that he would have to endure the slings and arrows of outrageous fortune. Like St. Paul after Damascus it became an obsession with him to preach the gospel of peace and goodwill to all men. He was a man driven by conscience and conviction, so much so that his concern for political realities was often obscured by the cause itself. Setting his sights for such far-off goals thus blinded him to immediate obstacles. Misplaced trust in a new coterie of advisers led him astray again and again. Needless to say, he compounded his difficulties by misreading Soviet intentions. Yet the next few years were not really the nadir of his political career, but its noblest moment. He was deeply committed to the historic traditions of liberalism and in contrast to the revolutionary tactics of the latter-day New Left, Wallace was a paragon of virtue. This intense idealist never lost faith in the democratic process, never doubted the efficacy of moral suasion, and never advocated violence nor incited his followers to use it. Though he had feet of clay, his redeeming factor was an eventual willingness to admit where he went wrong. To err is human; to admit it is to manifest genuine humility.

In 1946 Henry Wallace was not alone in opposing Truman's foreign policy. Many former New Dealers agreed with him, for they too thought the President was departing from F.D.R.'s formula for peace. Liberals were delighted that Wallace could now contest Truman openly. Supreme Court Justice Frank Murphy wrote him: "I believe *The New Republic* will offer you the forum for free expression which is the most important thing in our land, to those of high position as well as the humble. We must all feel that we are in no kind of spiritual or intellectual straitjacket."[2] Agreeing wholeheartedly with Justice Murphy, Wallace replied, "The glory of the American way of life is that we can still find ways of speaking frankly. I trust that as we exercise this God-given privilege, we shall do it on behalf of the general welfare."[3]

Just before the 1946 midterm elections which resulted in a G.O.P. sweep of both houses of Congress, Wallace had written a short booklet entitled *The Fight for Peace*. Because this widely read work also included such items as recent addresses, the controversial Madison Square Garden speech, and a full text of his July 23rd letter to Harry Truman, it represented the first challenge of the President's leadership in domestic and foreign affairs. Possessed by a fear that the world was balanced precariously on the abyss of nuclear destruction, Wallace warned, "We are now in the second year of the atomic armaments race. . . . Time passes perilously—and there is still no peace." He blamed this predicament upon Truman: "Today our press and radio are crowded with propaganda suggesting the inevitability of war with Russia;

and we are following a foreign policy in which the Golden Rule plays a smaller part than fear of the 'Red menace.' "[4]

Bernard Baruch, who had wanted to reply publicly to Wallace's criticisms while he was still Commerce Secretary, now sought a private conference with him. At a mutually agreed upon meeting Baruch endeavored to answer all questions relating to his proposal for international control of atomic energy. The so-called adviser to presidents took this step because he considered himself a personal friend of the former Secretary (even as he had been of Wallace's father). After a lengthy session with Wallace on all aspects of international atomic control, Baruch asked him to sign a joint statement to indicate agreement between the two of them. While admitting he was misinformed on certain provisions of the American proposal to the UN Atomic Energy Commission, Henry Wallace demurred for two reasons. One objection still remaining dealt with the question of "whether the United States should continue its production . . . [and] stockpiling of atomic bombs during the period of transition before international control"; and another pertained to the need for dispelling Russian fears stemming from U.S. atomic superiority. He tried to convince Baruch that the Soviet Union would refuse to acquiesce to any status quo scheme "until a plan is devised which will assure her, by deed as well as by words, of our sincere desire to pay due regard to Russian as well as American security needs during the period of transition before international control of the atom."[5]

When Wallace refused to endorse the American proposition then before the UN, Baruch became angry. It seemed incredulous to him that anyone would propose destruction of America's atomic arsenal before a foolproof system of international inspection had been devised. The financier turned elder statesman presumed an American monopoly insured national security, while Wallace claimed it would add nothing to American defense and instead would only promote a nuclear arms race. "You have no monopoly on the desire for peace," insisted Baruch to his erstwhile friend, "I have given thirty years of my life to the search for peace and there are many others whose aims have been the same." He terminated his communication with the remark, "You are as free as I am to say what you will and when you choose."[6]

Henry Wallace did just that. In a public statement he reiterated his stand that American refusal to cease stockpiling atomic bombs was the chief roadblock to progress. Wallace also claimed the veto and inspection issue could be resolved if trust replaced suspicion at the UN. One of his first editorials for *The New Re-*

public was titled "The UN and Disarmament." In it he stated confidently, "Russia really wants peace. She talks tough and takes extreme positions, but usually makes concessions." Readers were told it was the United States who was "potentially the greatest imperialist nation in history." If the military-industrial complex built up during World War II were not used for the general welfare, he feared it would tempt U.S. leaders to engage in adventuresome conquests. "The goal of the UN is to become a world federation," he vowed, "but that can never come to pass until the Anglo-Americans and the Russians understand each other. . . ."[7]

Soon after Wallace joined *The New Republic,* its circulation jumped noticeably. Michael Straight's expectations, however, were never fully realized. Presuming his new co-worker would take an interest in the overall content of the magazine as well as helping to make it a hard-hitting liberal journal, he soon discovered that while Wallace took great care in preparing a signed editorial for each edition, he never really took an interest in other matters. Wallace was not a member of a team; *The New Republic* was a vehicle for his opinons and no more. His mind and soul were involved in promoting peace and prosperity, and nothing else.[8]

Several things happened to induce Wallace to think of establishing a political organization in opposition to both Democrats and Republicans. First of all he received unexpected financial support from Mrs. Anita McCormick Blaine. This daughter of Cyrus H. McCormick and widow of Emmons Blaine (son of James G. Blaine) was a liberal philanthropist who spent huge sums for projects that sought to better the lot of mankind. Her contribution of $10,000 to Wallace allowed him to keep an office in Washington, D.C. With his former aide Harold Young in charge, a huge mailing list was sustained to insure Wallace's continued influence on public opinion.[9]

Second, the former Commerce Secretary received much support from key liberals as well as from the general public. Of the 8,000 letters he received immediately after his discharge from the Truman cabinet, over 85 percent were favorable. Encouraged by sculptor Jo Davidson and "Beanie" Baldwin to think of himself as an independent political spokesman, Wallace's loyalty to the Democratic party began to wane. He wrote to his old friend in Iowa, Democratic State Chairman Jake More, "If the Democratic party is not going to become genuinely progressive, the quicker it dies the better."[10]

A third source of inspiration was the contact from abroad. Both Donald Bruce, Labor member of Parliament, and Kingsley Martin, liberal editor of the British publication *The New Statesman and Nation,* prompted Wallace to broaden his horizons and think of founding an international peace movement.[11] Huge crowds at home and invitations to speak overseas fostered a hope that he might be able to alter the course of events despite his exodus from Washington officialdom.

Talk among various liberal groups about the need of dumping Truman in 1948 increased after the debacle of Wallace's forced resignation from the Cabinet. Certain avant garde organizations among radically liberal circles called a meeting for September 28, 1946, in Chicago to initiate some activity along this line. In the forefront of this strategy session were the National Citizens Political Action Committee (NC-PAC) and the Independent Citizens Committee of the Arts, Sciences, and Professions (ICC-ASP) which had sponsored the political rally where Wallace gave his by now famous Madison Square Garden speech. Key leaders of the NC-PAC were such diverse figures as Calvin B. "Beanie" Baldwin; Frank Kingdon; Elmer Benson; and Clark Foreman, who was also chairman of the Southern Conference for Human Welfare. Jo Davidson and New Dealer Harold Ickes, Roosevelt's Secretary of Interior, were prime figures in leading the ICC-ASP. Still other significant liberals attracted to this meeting included Jack Kroll and Philip Murray of the CIO-PAC, Walter White of the NAACP, and James Patton, head of the National Farmers Union. After many spirited discussions concerning international peace and domestic prosperity, this conference of Progressives endorsed a preferred slate of candidates from both the Democratic and Republican parties for the fall election, passed a friendly resolution strongly commending Henry Wallace, and established a Continuations Committee for future action. The tone established was definitely that of independent activism within the political process.[12]

C. B. Baldwin, who was an early agitator for a distinct third party, used his influence to maneuver a merger of the NC-PAC and ICC-ASP. This came about on December 30, 1946, when the Progressive Citizens of America (PCA) was founded. With Frank Kingdon and Jo Davidson as cochairmen it became the nucleus of what ultimately developed into the Progressive party. With a clergyman and sculptor as its leaders, the PCA had an aura of moral commitment plus amateurishness about it. While the PCA was in its formative stage, Henry Wallace was invited as a speaker.

By no means did he commit himself at this early date to a third-party movement, but pointed references were made about the failure of the Democratic party to represent the common people. In no uncertain terms the assemblage of anti-Truman liberals was told, "We must continually make it clear to the Administration that we, as progressives, would prefer the election of an out-and-out reactionary like [Robert A.] Taft in 1948 to a lukewarm liberal. We want this to be a genuine two-party country, and not a country operated by a fake one-party system under the guise of a bipartisan bloc."[13]

While most PCA leaders were by this time pretty much in favor of a third party, a considerable number of New Deal-type liberals were skeptical of such a venture. Frank Kingdon, for instance, was not altogether convinced of its wisdom, nor was Robert Kenny of California. As Attorney General, Kenny had lost the gubernatorial nomination to incumbent Earl Warren when the progressive G.O.P. governor won both the Democratic and Republican primaries (cross-filing was then a common practice in the Golden State). Kenny's desire was to see Wallace enter the presidential primary in California against Harry Truman.[14] Others had thought along the lines of a third party, but he was the most energetic exponent of trying to capture the Democratic party from within. James Roosevelt, a rising star on the West Coast, liked Wallace also but took still another course by seeking to displace Truman with General Dwight D. Eisenhower.[15]

To organize those liberals still committed to a two-party system, another group, the Union for Democratic Action, called a meeting for January 4, 1947, in Washington, D.C. With Mrs. Eleanor Roosevelt as its keynote speaker, this organizational convocation gave birth to the Americans for Democratic Action (ADA). Formulating a dynamic program, they called for a continuation of New Deal reforms and U.S. support for the UN to insure world peace. The ADA took a precaution which the PCA failed to do that was to be of great significance as time went on. Without qualification, they rejected membership to Communists and their fellow travelers or to fascists and their sympathizers. Present at the founding session were such notables as Wilson Wyatt (first national chairman), Reinhold Niebuhr (key leader in the parent organization), Leon Henderson, Hubert H. Humphrey (then mayor of Minneapolis), Will Rogers, Jr., Walter Reuther, Walter White, James B. Carey, David Dubinsky, Herbert Lehman, Marquis Childs, James Wechsler, and James Loeb, Jr.

While these two major liberal factions were forming, each

reflecting ideological differences, the American Communist party (ACP) was also undergoing reorganization. Popular Front leader Earl Browder was challenged by both William Z. Foster and Eugene Dennis. The latter emerged triumphant in a power struggle, and in 1946 he issued a call for the formation of an anti-imperialist third party. New York's *Daily Worker* began to sing the praises of Henry Wallace, touting him as the one to lead such a venture against the warmongers of the world. If a major blunder can be ascribed to Wallace, it was his failure to quickly renounce ACP support. Leadership of the PCA was much too tolerant of Communists (no doubt there were from the beginning a few crypto-Communists and undetected fellow travelers in its midst), the result being that Wallace was advised not to scorn their political assistance. Wallace, a midwesterner, should have realized that New York City was not representative of the rest of the nation. In Brooklyn, the Bronx, or Harlem the Liberal party and American Labor party had long associated with Communists. Many PCA leaders saw no need to renounce ACP aid, since their political aims seemed similar. Being "unequally yoked together with unbelievers," as the Biblical saying went, was a fatal mistake for a moralist like Wallace. From its inception the Progressive party never could erase the Red label it unnecessarily acquired. It goes without saying that Henry Wallace, who never ascribed to ACP principles and did not agree with the Communist philosophy, was hurt the most. Myopic as it seemed, he did not repudiate the Communists and only later admitted his error; but this came too late insofar as his political career was concerned. If there was any one thing that tended to taint his reputation for the rest of his life it was the constant charge that he was a Communist sympathizer (or as some critics falsely charged, an outright Communist).

Some of Wallace's closest friends were apprehensive lest the former Secretary's burning desire to advance the prospects of world peace lead him to make a horrendous mistake. Paul de Kruif, a well-known writer and humanitarian who admired Henry Wallace tremendously, warned Harold Young that the Wallace supporters "*seem* to be so heavily represented by the CIO-PAC and other definitely leftie groups."[16] None of his associates doubted his loyalty or sincerity, least of all such a lifelong friend as de Kruif, but it was evident to them and others that Wallace was unduly influenced by those seeking to make him their exclusive candidate. Aubrey Williams, an old agrarian comrade-in-arms and publisher of the *Southern Farmer,* also felt Wallace was being pressured into taking over leadership of a political movement doomed to certain defeat.[17] When one pursues a cause so passionately, slight aberration seems worth the price to him—but not to the onlooker who is not so emotionally involved.

In his self-designated role as spokesman for the millions of silent little people all over the world, Wallace viewed any peace movement as an alliance of common folk everywhere. Consistent with his political philosophy, he had always wanted to unite all those seeking to promote peace and universal social justice. Therefore he consciously decided not to exclude any group expressing such aims and objectives. This made him very susceptible to counselors advising him not to engage in Red-baiting but to close ranks and unite all peace-loving groups into one mass movement. Wallace forgot that Communists seldom participated in political movements unless they gained control of them for their own purposes. Perhaps Wallace's dislike of Truman blinded him to this reality. Deep in his subconscious mind there may have lingered the festering notion that he, not Truman, should be President. It would have been inconsistent with human nature to have felt otherwise.

Right at this time the international scene was further complicated when British officials notified Harry Truman they were unable to carry on the struggle against Communist insurgents in Greece. Quickly the President decided the United States must intervene and accept former British obligations in the Mediterranean. Appearing before Congress on March 12, 1947, President Truman urgently asked for appropriations and authorization to render military and economic aid to Greece and Turkey. With it the Truman Doctrine was promulgated; namely, the United States would assist free nations in their attempt to resist domination by the Soviet Union. To Wallace this proposal seemed equivalent to declaring war on Russia. Editorializing in *The New Republic,* he pleaded for its rejection, "There is a world crisis. It is not a war crisis; the Soviet Union has made no warlike moves. . . . The program proposed by President Truman bears almost no relation to the real crisis of today and no relation to the real needs of the peoples of the world. It is a program for the purchase of mercenaries and the widening of the conflict against the Soviet Union." Insisting the Truman Doctrine made a mockery of the UN by promulgating a "global Monroe Doctrine," Wallace repeated his own formula for world concord, "There is but one hope for the hungry, one hope for reconstruction, one hope for peace—the United Nations."[18]

The chance for Wallace to make his peace movement international in scope came in the spring of 1947. In April he received an invitation to visit England from Kingsley Martin, the editor of the British Socialist journal *New Statesman.* Wallace readily accepted the opportunity provided by the offices of this sophisticated journal to make a series of speeches in London and Manchester. Included on his itinerary were stops on the continent with special speaking engagements in France, Norway, Sweden, and Denmark. His visit to Britain was well received and personally satisfying. He spoke to cheering crowds of Laborites and made use of the BBC facilities to talk to the English people in general. Jennie Lee, a Socialist member of Parliament writing in the London *Tribune,* described his reception as being very enthusiastic. Why? "He arrived here wearing the mantle of Franklin D. Roosevelt . . . and talked of support for the United Nations, and of having need to understand Russia's difficulties and to oppose the division of the world into Eastern and Western blocs." She was, however, critical of his "presentation of world affairs in which Russia is always right and the rest of the world always wrong."[19]

The Wallace tour precipitated a major furor in the United States, as could be predicted, and caused Prime Minister Clement Attlee and Foreign Minister Ernest Bevin considerable anxiety as well. Attlee and Bevin had great difficulty keeping the left-wing Laborites from nullifying the official British stand against Soviet expansionism, and Wallace's presence made their task even more burdensome. At home Harry Truman was also in a dilemma. Should he read Wallace out of the Democratic party or seek a reconciliation? Since his political fortunes were at a low ebb, he decided on the latter course. So, when asked at his April 10th press conference to comment on Henry Wallace's status as a member in "good standing of the Democratic party," the President replied without hesitation, "I have no desire to read anybody out of the Democratic party." Another inquiry followed immediately, asking whether the President's statement about not reading anyone out of the party specifically included Henry Wallace. "Certainly," Truman answered and he went on to comment, "I think . . . [he] will probably campaign for the Democratic ticket."[20]

In London, when questioned about President Truman's statements, Wallace responded in a way that left him several alternatives. He said, "I shall be campaigning in 1948 with all my power, but I will be campaigning for the ideals of the free world and the men who best express these ideals. I hope, but I cannot guarantee, that they will be on the Democratic ticket."[21] On another occasion when someone asked him about the possibility of a third party being started in the United States, Wallace dismissed the idea with the remark, "I have insistently advocated to all liberals that it would be a grave mistake to make any effort to organize a third party. . . . I expect to support and work for the Democratic nominee in the general election."[22]

After crossing the channel to visit France, *The New Republic*'s editor was feted by leaders of both Communist and non-Communist parties. No one in French politics wanted to offend Communists because of their voting strength both in Parliament and in the country at large. Two important French Communists, Marcel Cachin and Jacques Duclos, made a point of meeting Wallace at the airport. They also were with him when he addressed students at the Sorbonne. Although Wallace in no way considered his visit to be sponsored by Communists—in fact he had asked Henri Bonnet and Louis Dolivet to make arrangements for him—his associations created a bad impression at home. This was taken in stride in France but did untold harm to Wallace's reputation in the United States. American newspapers played up this joint appearance as if he were consorting with foreign Communist leaders. Anti-Communist sentiment at home vented itself on Wallace. More and more his image was being portrayed as one willingly consenting to front for the international Communist movement. In truth Wallace regarded French Marxists only as leaders of the left rather than tools of Moscow.

Every time Henry Wallace criticized his own country's foreign policy from abroad he alienated himself further from the mainstream of American public opinion. Southern and G.O.P. conservatives had never liked him; now they were given a golden opportunity to say in effect, "We told you he was a Communist all along." Representative John Rankin of Mississippi, chairman of the House Committee on Un-American Activities, called upon the Justice Department to indict Wallace under the Logan Act. This law, passed originally in 1799, forbade U.S. citizens to negotiate with foreign countries. Its application in this instance was only marginal to say the least, but it did reveal the anti-Wallace sentiment that was building up. Members of the Texas House of Representatives manifested their extreme displeasure by passing a resolution affirming the following: "Whereas, one Henry A. Wallace, an outcast from all political parties of American origin, is now in foreign lands criticizing and denouncing the President of the United States and condemning the foreign policy of this Government . . . Resolved by the House of Representatives of the State of Texas, that the people of the Lone Star state repudiate and denounce the activities and utterances of the said Wallace, and earnestly assure our President that the people of Texas are solidly behind and for him in sustaining the 'Truman Doctrine'. . . ."[23]

Senator Arthur Vandenberg, the Republican most responsible for sustaining some semblance of a bipartisan foreign policy, let it be known he would not support the administration if Truman allowed Henry Wallace to campaign for him in 1948. Writing to Attorney General Tom Clark and Secretary of the Navy James Forrestal, he confided that "the President can have me on his team in foreign affairs, or he can have Henry, but he can't have us both." The Michigan senator complained, "I think what Wallace is doing today is one of the worst things that has happened. It will confirm Molotov's notion that the country is divided on foreign policy. I looked into Molotov's face for 210 days and I know something about him."[24]

Privately Harry Truman detested what Wallace was doing, but he held his tongue and said nothing publicly. However, the lid blew off when one of his hastily composed letters again hit the headlines. This cause célèbre was the result of a reply the President made to Louis E. Starr, commander-in-chief of the Veterans of Foreign Wars. Commander Starr implored Truman to revoke Wallace's passport. The President actually defended Wallace's right "to say whatever is on his mind provided it doesn't injure his fellow countrymen." Without intending his remark to be made public, Truman added the offhand comment, "There is not very much that can be done about Henry's wild statements and if I take notice of them it only gives him more publicity. He does not represent anybody with the Government of the United States and, therefore, we can take no notice of it."[25]

Somehow Robert S. Allen, syndicated columnist of the North American Newspaper Alliance, obtained a copy of the letter and published a sensationalized if not outright garbled account of it. "The President's scorching letter is one of the utmost significance," went the highly exaggerated report. "It is the first time Mr. Truman has put himself on record assailing Mr. Wallace's publicized campaign against the administration's foreign policy, and signifies an open break between them."[26] What was meant to be a private communication on why he could not prevent Wallace from speaking as a private citizen was now converted into a public rebuke. Truman had not yet decided to break irrevocably with Wallace, although events were making such an action highly probable.

Grieved by what Wallace was doing, the aged Henry L. Stimson spoke out from retirement to lecture him through an article in *Foreign Affairs.* Roosevelt's Army Secretary offered the cogent reminder, "The world's affairs cannot be simplified by eager words." To those such as Wallace who blamed American policies for the cold war, Stimson enjoined, "I cannot too strongly express my regret that since the early spring of 1945—even before the death of Mr. Roosevelt—the Soviet Union had steadfastly pursued an obstructive and unfriendly course. It has been our hope that the Russians would choose to be our friends; it was and is our conviction that such a choice would be to their advantage. But, for the time being, at least, those who determine Russian policy have chosen otherwise, and their choice has been slavishly followed by Communists everywhere."[27]

Opposition to the Truman Doctrine, incongruous as it may have seemed, stemmed from three fundamentally different sources. This unusual alliance included liberal internationalists, former isolationists, and balance of power realists who were dismayed at the vastness of America's commitments. Henry Wallace spoke for the pro-UN internationalists desiring the establishment of strong peace-keeping machinery exclusively within a world organization. G.O.P. isolationists were led by Robert A. Taft and John Bricker of Ohio and Nebraska's Kenneth Wherry, all of whom decried the expense and commitment foreign aid imposed on the United States, not to mention the overseas involvement this implied. Old-time isolationist Senator W. Lee "Pappy" O'Daniels (D-Texas) expressed this viewpoint in simple terms when he announced, "I intend to vote against this Greece-Turkey gift-loan bill just as I voted against the British gift-loan bill."[28] Truman's foreign policy advisers were truly dismayed when the noted columnist and expert on international relations Walter Lippmann added his voice to the chorus of criticism. Steeped in the tenets of classical diplomacy, Lippmann viewed the Truman Doctrine as but another version of Wilsonian internationalism. He interpreted this massive commitment to protect free nations as dangerous globalism, i.e., a proclamation to defend democracy all over the world. Instead of either withdrawing into isolationism or venturing forth on a worldwide crusade against Communism, he exhorted U.S. policymakers to consider the following: "A diplomacy for the world as it is, which is not to expend itself in verbal declaration on the one hand, and on crusades of annihilation on the other, must deal with the balance of power and the determination of spheres of influence."[29]

On June 5, 1947, Secretary of State George C. Marshall delivered his now famous Harvard University address. Expertly dramatizing a plan for European recovery whose outlines Dean Acheson had already described in May, his speech now riveted public attention upon it. Because of the chaotic circumstances in Europe, Marshall proposed massive aid to achieve the following objectives: "It is logical that the United States should do whatever it is able to do to assist in the return of normal economic health in the world, without which there can be no political stability and no assured peace. Our policy is directed not against any country or doctrine but against hunger, poverty, desperation, and chaos. Its purpose should be the revival of a working economy in the world so as to permit the emergence of political and social conditions in which free institutions can exist."[30]

Isolationists and economy-minded Congressmen recoiled in horror at the idea of pouring more billions of American dollars into what they deemed was a bottomless pit of wasteful altruism. Henry Wallace, at least initially, reacted favorably to the proposal. He had himself previously suggested the implementation of a $50 billion reconstruction program for Europe, including a $17 billion loan to Russia. Editorially Wallace described the Marshall Plan as a great improvement over the Truman Doctrine but warned that the program should not be an anti-Russian policy disguised as relief and rehabilitation.

European leaders were delighted with this new program and assured Truman of their cooperation. British Foreign Minister Ernest Bevin challenged the Soviet Union to join the European Recovery Program or in effect tell all the world it was not really interested in the economic welfare of the continent. After due deliberation, Soviet leaders refused to cooperate in any way with the Marshall Plan. In fact Stalin forced eight East European countries to decline aid also. Under Soviet auspices a Communist Council for Mutual Economic Assistance (COMECON) was organized, and the Communist Information Bureau (cominform) was established to once again spread the doctrine of world revolution. In reality a Socialist commonwealth was being set up under the hegemony of the Soviet Union. The iron curtain was welded together with an ideological alloy that prohibited penetration—economic or political. Western Europe, to the contrary, reacted with alacrity to set up the machinery for rebuilding their wartorn economies and to lay further plans for some modicum of political unity.

Alarmed at the bipolarization that was taking place, Wallace began to have second thoughts about the Marshall Plan. In an address at Milwaukee on December 30, 1947, he asserted, "We must reaffirm our faith in the UN." This could best be achieved by making it the sole instrument for European recovery. He explained, "My plan calls for a proposal from the U.S. to the UN for the establishment of a UN Rehabilitation Fund, modeled after UNRRA [UN Relief and Rehabilitation Administration], for the rehabilitation and reconstruction of the war-devastated lands in Europe and Asia. . . ."[31]

The American public in general supported the generous and humanitarian aspects of the Marshall Plan. On the whole, most liberals now blamed the Kremlin for preventing East European nations from participating, even after those countries demonstrated their desire to join the European Recovery Program. It was obvious also that Communist parties in such countries as France and Italy seemed more intent on pleasing the Politburo than in bringing about the recovery of their own national economies. Obstructionist tactics were used to wreck Europe's chances for regaining prewar status, seemingly so that Russia might benefit from the ensuing chaos.

Even before Wallace came out against the Marshall Plan, Dr. Irving Fisher, a retired Yale University economist who had worked with him during the 1920s in the Stable Money League (an organization dedicated to monetary reform), wrote a thoughtful letter to his former colleague. Prefacing his counsel with a reminder that he was one of the original founders of the League to Enforce Peace, the parent of the League of Nations, Professor Fisher indicated frankly, "I am moved to write you suggesting that you drop your activities opposing the policies of the United States toward Russia . . . [because] continuation of this would not only be anti-American in its effects but could only react on you." Pointing out the similarity of Wallace's stand, at least in its consequences, to that of the prewar isolationists, he admonished: "You are virtually proposing what [Charles A.] Lindbergh proposed." Trying to convince Wallace of the fallacy of appeasement, Fisher concluded, "I am confirmed in my impression that you have not properly weighted the facts nor understood Russian psychology. I should hate, for your own sake, to see you become a catspaw of those who are now applauding you."[32]

Henry Wallace in this stage of his thinking had reached a point which reflected an idealism of greater dimension than that espoused by either Woodrow Wilson or Franklin D. Roosevelt. It even exceeded his earlier agrarian idealism, as that had always been tempered by his intimate day-to-day contact with the working operations of agriculture. Placing an unqualified trust in the efficacy of an untried, infant world organization to keep the peace, his faith extended beyond any expectations warranted by world conditions. Never having actually negotiated with the Russians, he lacked any firsthand knowledge of the complexities involved. Ignored were such realities as national self-interest, or even the existence of evil among men. Forgotten was the truism in international relations that "organization does not obviate force."[33] The existence of a United Nations in no way abrogated the need for each country to stand prepared to defend itself militarily.

Persuaded by Michael Straight to take a trip to Palestine in October 1947, Wallace received much inspiration from touring the Holy Land. It truly stirred his soul to walk in the footsteps of the Prince of Peace, prophets, and martyred saints. While traversing this ancient land, his moral commitment to peace was strengthened immeasurably. Humanity needed a spokesman, he mused to himself; one not afraid to enunciate the biblical ideals of universal brotherhood. On his return journey he stopped for an audience with Pope Pius XII. The message contained in the Sermon on the Mount, he was convinced more than ever after leaving the Vatican, had to be instilled in the hearts of all people. Only then would "peace and good will" come to pass among men on earth. Back in his office at *The New Republic*, Wallace revealed his deep-rooted Christian idealism with a Yuletide editorial expressing his basic beliefs:

> If the Anglo-Saxon peoples decline in importance during the last half of the twentieth century, it will be because they have failed to apply Christianity and democracy in their dealings with all the peoples of the world. . . .
>
> Isaiah, Christ, and [Thomas] Jefferson have not failed. Their principles of peace and justice between man and man are fundamental. We have failed because we have not applied their principles justly and fearlessly. . . .
>
> As long as every Foreign Office in the world is dominated by the doctrine of Machiavelli instead of the doctrines of Christ, we shall have war and the perpetuation of many kinds of dictatorship and falsehood as each of the nations prepares for war.[34]

PCA leaders C. B. Baldwin and Jo Davidson pressed continually for the establishment of a third party. Known Communists and fellow travelers also championed the plan with great enthusiasm, doubtless because of its value to Soviet foreign policy. Despite advice from close friends and certain liberals opposed to the venture, Henry Wallace was now receptive to the idea. Any resistance melted away after his return from the Middle East. After much soul-searching he made the fateful decision on December 2, 1947, and thereafter the die was cast. Since there was still sufficient time to get the third party on the various state ballots in time for the 1948 presidential election, specific arrangements were made at a meeting held in Jo Davidson's New York City apartment. Present in addition to Wallace were Baldwin, chairman of PCA; Hannah Dorner, a member of its board of directors; and Lewis Frank, Jr., of *The New Republic* staff. Leaving all the details of organization to others, Henry Wallace set his eyes on the horizon. With no promise of success and no personal rewards to be secured, he was prepared to launch a holy crusade for peace. Being a strong-willed man, once his mind was made up there was no thought of ever turning back or quitting.

His last regular editorial appeared in *The New Republic* on January 5, 1948 (although he continued to contribute articles until July 19). "I am convinced the time has come for an independent presidential candidacy." Condemning a bipartisan foreign policy, he asserted, "In peacetime one-party rule is a real threat to our democracy." As he saw it, a conservative coalition was perpetrating a "foreign policy based upon hatred and fear." This unholy alliance, he claimed, was "made of men who opposed resistance to fascism, who killed UNRRA, who attacked the heart of the United Nations in creating the Truman Doctrine, and who again bypassed the United Nations with the Marshall Plan. . . ."[35]

On the domestic scene, Wallace scored both parties for their joint failures. "Neither party puts up any effective fight against racial and religious discrimination, for the rights of the Negro people, for the elimination of restrictive covenants and anti-Semitism, for the creation of a genuine FEPC [Fair Employment Practices Committee], for the defeat of the poll tax and passage of a federal anti-lynch law." Heaping derision on Democrats and Republicans alike, he declared: "Both stand mute while freedom of speech and thought are under attack. Both cry 'Red! Communist!' at all opponents and use the Red scare to cover up their plunder of the people." Trying to remove the Red label from the third-party movement, Wallace insisted he and his followers were "not for Russia and we are not for communism, but we are for peace and for bringing real Americanism back again to the United States."[36]

Disregarding his own advice made previously about the ill-advisability of starting a third party, Wallace was caught up in his own emotional involvements and did not decide to be a presidential nominee either on the basis of realistic or rational judgment. The reformist and moralistic qualities of his makeup plus a response to a beckoning conscience committed him to a foredoomed crusade that was to become a cruel Odyssey. Like the magnificent heroes in Greek tragedies Henry Wallace embarked on his campaign with high hopes that heaven would look beneficently upon his venture of goodwill. Although the whole undertaking turned out to be a protracted disaster, in the end no man could deny that Wallace had given full measure of devotion to the cause for which he fought.

CHAPTER 12

THE PROGRESSIVE PARTY AND THE PRESIDENTIAL

POLITICAL PARTIES propelled by ideological fervor indeed have the ability to promote fanatical partisanship, but this type of zealotry possesses a peculiar vulnerability. Its sense of mission and devotion to a cause often makes it impervious to reason or reality. The ancient wisdom of Demosthenes remains valid, "Nothing is so easy as to deceive one's self, for what we wish, we readily believe." So it was with the Progressive party in 1948.

Blinded by a passionate desire to make the world conform to his preconceived notions, Henry Wallace struggled vainly to overcome superhuman obstacles. Ironically, while believing himself to be a prophet of peace, his projected portrait was that of an apologist for Russia. In the end he endured not only political defeat but a humiliation shared by few men in public life. His motives were pure, and this remained the redeeming quality for one who engendered so much bitterness during a presidential campaign.

The campaign which Henry Wallace meant to wage and the one actually conducted were not identical. In many ways the

For he put on righteousness as a breastplate,
and . . . was clad with zeal as a cloke.
ISAIAH 59:17

CAMPAIGN OF 1948

Progressive party stood for one thing and Wallace another. Actually the party organization was controlled from the outset by those representing the radical left and not liberalism per se. This made it extremely easy for Communists and fellow travelers to infiltrate into important positions within the party machinery. Once this happened, party stands began to resemble a party line. Campaign literature, speech materials, and campaign slogans sounded strangely like echoes of what Moscow wanted to hear. As if wearing moral blinkers, Wallace increasingly became an imperceptive ideologue. Words were uttered by Wallace that did not sound like him, and his performance took on a strange Jekyll and Hyde quality—one moment he was a peace protagonist and the next a propaganda parrot for the Kremlin.

Once the National Citizens Political Action Committee and the Independent Citizens Committee of Arts, Sciences, and Professions joined to form the Progressive Citizens of America, the nucleus of a political party emerged. Despite considerable difficulties encountered in getting on the ballot in many states, PCA leaders established a National Wallace for President Committee. Under its auspices a party convention was called. Everyone knew in advance Henry Wallace was to be the presidential nominee and that Senator Glen Taylor (D-Idaho) would be his running mate, but the ritual of a nominating convention was deemed necessary. Needed also were a platform, candidates for congressional seats, and a large influx of campaign workers.

When a conglomerate of Progressive party delegates gathered at Philadelphia from July 23–25, 1948, the Democrats had already renominated Harry Truman (with Senator Alben W. Barkley of Kentucky as the vice-presidential nominee); and the G.O.P. had chosen Thomas E. Dewey to lead them again, with Governor Earl Warren of California as second man on the ticket. Also in the making at the time was a States' Rights party led by South Carolina's Governor Strom Thurmond. He and other so-called Dixiecrats had bolted the Democratic party and were determined to found a southern segregationist party dedicated to the preservation of white supremacy. And not to be forgotten was the Socialist Party of America with its perennial presidential candidate Norman Thomas.

The Communist Party of America platform stated openly that "in 1948 we Communists join with millions of other Americans to support the Progressive Party ticket to help win the peace." Conceding that the new party was not anticapitalist, it was endorsed ostensibly because it deserved support to "develop as a united front" and evolve into a "broad, mass people's party." This was an obvious appeal to all liberals to form a coalition similar to the Popular Front of World War II. Though the party admittedly had "fundamental as well as tactical differences" with Henry Wallace, he was nevertheless recommended as the candidate with the best qualifications. With Marxian finality the CPA's platform declared, "The new Progressive Party is an inescapable historic necessity for millions who want a real choice now between peace and war, democracy and fascism, security and poverty."[1] Endorsement of this type was at the time the same as being patted on the back by a leper. F.D.R. never made the mistake Wallace did in neglecting to repudiate Communist support.

National press and radio coverage associated with nominating conventions (television was still quite limited) was attended with great interest by millions of Americans. Since the various parties and their candidates garnered much free air time and newspaper space during the course of these conventions, they welcomed this publicity with open arms. But the airing of the proceedings of the Progressive party, paradoxically, actually harmed its vote-getting appeal with the public. Listeners and observers were truly shocked by the ideological bickering that went on. Coupled with the obvious machinations of certain party leaders to control what went into the platform, the performance appalled even the casual onlooker. Whereas the bulk of the ordinary delegates represented sincere idealists, young people attracted to a cause, pacifists, and liberals of various radical persuasions who had come to the city of brotherly love to launch a people's party, a coterie of leaders tended to run things the way they wanted.

Trouble of all sorts began when the platform committee convened. Featuring Rexford G. Tugwell, the ex-Brain-Truster of the New Deal era, the meetings soon disintegrated into squabbles over minute ideological differences among left-wing factions. Tugwell, for instance, tussled with Vito Marcantonio over what the platform should say about Puerto Rico. Dissension again erupted over whether or not the party should go on record as favoring a homeland for Macedonians. From the floor came an amendment, the so-called "Vermont Resolution," which affirmed, "Although we are critical of the present foreign policy of the United States, it is not our intention to give blanket endorsement to the foreign policy of any nation."[2] When this rather innocuous proposal was defeated, the hammer and sickle was for all intent and purposes unfurled before an amazed gallery of onlookers.

Only later did Henry Wallace recognize what a horrendous mistake it was to have rejected the Vermont Resolution. Speaking to the second national convention of his party at Chicago on February 24, 1950, he admitted this had been a major blunder. "Enemies of progress have therefore stigmatized us as being apologists for Russia and for Communism," Wallace concede belatedly. "We inadvertently gave these enemies ammunition to shoot at us when the Progressive party turned down the Vermont Resolution at the Founding Convention."[3]

The fiasco at Philadelphia both launched and sabotaged the Progressive party. Granted that newspaper and news media were hostile, hardened professional reporters were still awed at the way in which so few dominated so many at the convention. Many of the 3,000 delegates and alternates had no say whatsoever in a party confab boasting about its open and democratic procedure. Norman Thomas, present as a journalist for the St. Louis *Post-Dispatch,* alleged the party officialdom was shot through with Communists or fellow travelers. From his own knowledge of these people, as a long-time Socialist, he claimed to have identified twenty-four on the platform committee, eleven on the rules committee, and ten on the nominating committee.[4] The very nature of the Progressive party made it susceptible to this type of infiltration and take-over. If it was not obvious to those delegates seated in Convention Hall, it certainly was to the millions who viewed the charadelike spectacle on television or via movie newsreels. This cruel caricature of a democratic convention was given its only light moment when vice-presidential nominee Senator Glen Taylor, flanked by wife and children, entertained the assemblage with old-fashioned gospel harmony.[5]

Idaho's Glen Taylor underwent much inner wrestling before he eventually decided to become the vice-presidential candidate of the Progressive party. He had been an itinerant singer and showman, and his Senate seat was the best job he had ever had. His wife begged him not to give it up. But he was willing to sacrifice everything since, to his way of looking at it, "Our cause was just and of transcendent importance to mankind." Taylor felt he was joining a "crusade to try and save mankind from extermination."[6]

Making known his decision to run with Wallace on February 23, 1948, Taylor told a radio audience, "I am happy to have the support of all those who go along with our program. But just let me say to the Communists so there will be no misunderstanding, my efforts in the future as in the past will be directed toward the goal of making our economy work so well and our way of life so attractive and our people so contented that Communism will never interest more than the infinitesimal number of our citizens who adhere to it now." Knowing his future running mate only from occasional meetings and not at all on a personal basis, he said, "I am convinced that Henry Wallace is the only leader capable of ending the cold war and reestablishing even the beginnings of international good will. He is the only leader of sufficient stature to aspire to the presidency who has not sought the cheap applause of the reactionary press by blaming all our troubles on Russia." Taylor, as one might have expected, also got the ideological sleight of hand treatment meted out to Wallace. When reprints of his speech were sent out as campaign literature, deleted was the reference he had made about things going so well that Communism would be discouraged in America.[7]

Once Henry Wallace began his frenetic speaking campaign, old friends and former agrarian colleagues were aghast at the harsh tone of his major addresses. As he no longer had the counsel and assistance of such trusted aides as Harold Young, Mordecai Ezekiel, Louis Bean, Paul Appleby, or Samuel Bledsoe, Wallace's speeches became strangely different when he began to rely on a new stable of writers. Always a hard campaigner, Wallace may not have fully realized the implications of his speeches. He certainly paid little attention to details and never inquired about the background of those who prepared speech drafts. The Alsop brothers (Stewart and Joseph) revealed the existence of a special research group financed by Frederick Vanderbilt Field which provided campaign materials for Wallace. Reporting their findings in the New York *Herald Tribune,* they concluded succinctly, "Mr. Wallace thus provides the voice. Mr. [Lewis] Frank [formerly with *The New Republic*] provides the words. But the select company to which Mr. Field plays host provides the ideas."[8]

Reporter James Wechsler of the New York *Post,* who covered the Wallace campaign intensively for ten months, was also amazed at what Wallace said at public meetings. "He was almost a caricature of an innocent, murmuring the sentence which left-wing ghosts had usually written for him and denying that ghosts existed, parroting the oldest communist clichés as if they were rare insights he had just acquired on his way to a press conference." Wechsler, once a member of the Young Communist League during the 1930s, wrote in *The Age of Suspicion* that his tour with the campaign was "a special kind of trip for me because it took me back into the left-wing precincts I had left behind a decade earlier and I saw close up the revival of the communist operation." The real man emerged only when the silver-haired, prophetlike Wallace spoke from the heart, and not from a prepared script. This was especially true during his southern swing, at which time he often spoke extemporaneously to smaller groups. Describing this phenomenon, Wechsler attested, "In his improvised performances Wallace was always far more impressive than in the great, stage-managed productions. . . . In an afternoon he might talk informally to a group of college students under a tree on a quiet campus, and in that setting he seemed almost the personification of a reasonable man."[9]

The attrition of followers from the Progressive party movement began with the departure of Harold Ickes and continued at an alarming rate until election time. Typical of this exodus was Dr. Frank Kingdon, a clergyman, who resigned as cochairman of the PCA in January, 1948. Why did he quit? He gave this reason: "The issue now is not Henry Wallace—not personal affection or loyalty—but the forces behind him and the probable results of his adventure." Claiming the Communists or their sympathizers had gained control of the movement, he nevertheless absolved Wallace from any complicity. With sadness, Kingdon made this observation: "I do not believe Henry Wallace is party to this plan. He undoubtedly believes he is fighting for peace and prosperity. . . . They will cast him aside when his usefulness to them is gone. I tried to tell him this. He would not be persuaded. The result of this refusal will be to undermine his own reputation and to imperil the aims most dear to him."[10]

Many campus activists, utopian idealists, one-world internationalists, and intellectuals also found it difficult to remain loyal to the Progressive party in the face of increasing Russian belligerency. The widely publicized attempt of Mrs. Osana Stepanova Kasenkina to escape from the Soviet consulate in New York and the crude manner in which the Russians sought to detain her rivaled methods once employed by the German Gestapo. The overt aggression of the Russians in blockading Berlin seemed crude and reckless. Also frightening was the Communist *coup d'état* in Czechoslovakia and the apparent murder of Foreign Minister Jan Masaryk. This indefensible act of subversion made the Russian bear look anything but friendly or willing to coexist. According to Wallace's public utterances (again words being put in his mouth) the whole affair was caused by the Truman Doctrine. Years later Wallace admitted candidly that his public position on the Czech crisis was, in his estimation, "my greatest mistake."[11]

By defending Soviet actions, no matter how outrageous, Henry Wallace gave his political adversaries more political ammunition than they could have possibly manufactured themselves. The Democrats found it easy to pin the Red label on Wallace. Harry Truman could simply point to the Progressive party and claim *all* the Communists were working for its success. J. Howard McGrath, chairman of the Democratic National Committee, devised the following campaign tactic: "[Americans] . . . must know that a vote for Wallace . . . is a vote for the things for which Stalin, Molotov and Vishinsky stand."[12]

Many former Wallace supporters who were running for office were grieved to discover that Progressive party candidates were opposing them. Such a one was Congresswoman Helen Gahagan Douglas. Her credentials as a liberal needed no confirmation from anyone. Yet because she voted for the Marshall Plan, the Progressives ran a candidate against her in California. "I do not seek the endorsement of the third party and I do not desire it," she announced defiantly, "I strongly support the Marshall Plan and believe the present Russian attitude in international affairs a threat to world peace."[13]

Similar occurrences took place in other states. In Illinois where Paul Douglas and Adlai Stevenson were vying against Senator Wayland "Curley" Brooks and Governor Dwight Green, Progressives put up Curtis MacDougall and Grant Oakes as their own candidates (later ruled off the ballot due to legal technicalities). This was despite the fact that Senator Brooks was considered by liberals to be the most notorious reactionary and isolationist in the nation.

As he became a political challenger to the Democrats, many of his former friends were forced to attack Wallace publicly. Senator Robert F. Wagner of New York, who had worked with him many times on important social welfare legislation, declared openly, "Henry Wallace's silence on the Soviets' aggressions, their vetoes, their deliberate falsehoods, their repression of even minimal civil rights is deafening." The unkindest cut of all was Wagner's reference to the departed F.D.R. in the following homiletic assertion, "Yes, the angels are weeping and there is a great man and good friend of Henry Wallace who, I am sure, weeps with them."[14]

This same type of political defection took place among leaders of the black community. Truman's strong convention stand on civil rights plus the Red tinge of the Progressive party were factors of prime importance. Despite his strong position for an end to racial discrimination, the only big-name Negro leaders to stick with Wallace were Paul Robeson and W. E. B. Du Bois. Conspicuously missing were Walter White of the NAACP and the long-time head of the Brotherhood of Sleeping Car Porters, A. Philip Randolph. The latter, an old-line Socialist, withdrew his endorsement of the new party with the announcement, "So far as Wallace and his Progressive Party are concerned, he is the wrongest good man in the race for President, being, as it were, under Communist control and direction."[15] The Chicago *Defender,* once having praised Wallace as an outstanding civil rights leader, now advised black Americans not to vote for him. It editorialized, "Negroes are being asked to get on the Wallace bandwagon on the grounds that Mr. Wallace can lead them out of the valley of tears and oppression. The more one studies the realities of the political picture today the more difficult it becomes to avoid the conclusion that Mr. Wallace can only lead Negroes up a blind alley."[16]

The man from Missouri made all the right moves in achieving his so-called miracle victory in 1948. Following advice given to him by presidential aide Clark Clifford in the fall of 1947,

Harry Truman handled Henry Wallace by continually seeking "to identify him and isolate him in the public mind with the Communists."[17] Furthermore Truman successfully negated G.O.P. nominee Thomas E. Dewey's attempt to capitalize on the Communist issue. Revelations about Alger Hiss and his alleged subversive activities were effectively dismissed by Truman with the comment, "They are simply a 'red herring' to keep from doing what they [the Eightieth Congress] ought to do."[18]

By taking credit for saving Greece and Turkey, initiating the Marshall Plan, and standing up to Joseph Stalin, the President refuted the criticism of Roosevelt's wartime diplomacy as being soft on Communism. At Boston the President emphasized not only his hatred for Communism but his determination to stop its advance, "There are some Republicans who have been trying to make you believe that your Government is endangered by Communist infiltration. That is a malicious falsehood. . . . I hate Communism . . . I have fought it at home. I have fought it abroad. . . . The Communist Party of the United States is today supporting a third party in an effort to defeat me."[19]

While Dewey, influenced by public opinion polls, began to play it safe with innocuous speeches and harmless generalities on the assumption victory was assured if he did not rock the political boat,Truman was conducting a whirlwind "give 'em hell" campaign. The President strove to reconstruct F.D.R.'s coalition. Winning back the allegiance of labor, liberals, minority groups, and farmers was vital, so Truman had to convince dissatisfied Democrats to rally and support their party at the polls. In Los Angeles Truman displayed how potent this "don't waste your vote" approach was. Although California was a potential Wallace stronghold, the President ultimately captured its electoral votes and with it another four-year stay in the White House. His convincing argument to doubtful Democrats was aimed at undercutting the appeal of the Progressive party. He insisted:

> The fact that the Communists are aiding and using the third party shows that this party does not represent American ideals. . . .
>
> The third party has no power in the Government and no chance of achieving power. The simple fact is that the third party cannot achieve peace, because it is powerless. . . .
>
> A vote for the third party plays into the hands of the Republican forces of reaction, whose aims are directly opposed to the aims of American liberalism. . . .

> I say to those disturbed liberals who have been sitting uncertainly on the outskirts of the third party: Think again. Don't waste your vote.[20]

An unexpected source of aid for the Democrats came from Norman Thomas. His chances of being elected President as the nominee of the Socialist Party of America were nil, but Thomas was deeply concerned lest the Progressive party draw off his supporters and ultimately supplant Socialists as the main third party. Traditionally the Socialist party drew left-wing–radical votes plus garnering additional strength from any measurable protest at the polls. Initial predictions, including one by the usually reliable James Farley, indicated the Progressive party would draw some 10 million votes. When a Wallace-endorsed American Labor Party candidate, Leo Isaacson, won a special election in New York's Twenty-fourth Congressional District, it did appear that the Progressives would inherit the radical vote.[21] Norman Thomas therefore aimed his sharpest campaign barbs at Henry Wallace in an effort to salvage his own ebbing party strength.

On September 11, 1948, Norman Thomas informed President Truman he was going to propose that the UN General Assembly take up the Berlin blockade issue. He suggested that all presidential aspirants be briefed by the State Department on this crucial issue, mainly so that it would "put Henry Wallace on the spot."[22] Eight days later in a speech at Buffalo, New York, Thomas unleashed an attack on Wallace. Speaking to the Mechanics Educational Society of America, he said in part, "I should be tempted to overlook Mr. Wallace's past, excuse the imperfections of his domestic platform, and join the good people who are backing his efforts to form a new party if the evidence did not clearly show that with his half unwilling compliance his party is dominated by the Communists who, as they have boasted, were its master builders, and has drawn up a foreign policy for America which might have been dictated by Stalin."[23]

Henry Wallace was not only a whipping-boy for Dixiecrats, Democrats, and Socialists but also the primary target of the Americans for Democratic Action. Since the membership of ADA read like a Who's Who of former New Dealers, its main appeal was to those desiring to identify themselves with traditional liberal policies. To carefully distinguish themselves from radicalism or subversion, their statement of basic principles contained the affirmation, "We reject any alliance with totalitarian forces,

Communist or Fascist."[24] ADA officials defended Wallace's right to disagree with them but criticized him severely for not repudiating Communist support. As Minneapolis Mayor Hubert Humphrey put it, "In my opinion, if you ask someone if he follows the Communist party line, that is not red-baiting. It is merely a matter of identification."[25]

In an effort to keep New Deal Democrats from supporting the Progressive party, the ADA issued a public statement. Titled "An Appeal to the Liberals of America," it claimed, "American liberalism is facing its most serious test in 1948. . . . The Wallace candidacy presents a fundamental challenge to the liberals of America—to their sense of political responsibility. We urge all followers of Franklin D. Roosevelt to oppose Henry Wallace and his Progressive party. We urge all followers of Franklin D. Roosevelt to vote on November 2 for Harry S. Truman and Alben W. Barkley."[26] This statement was signed by an impressive array of individuals who had served the late President: Dean Acheson, Will W. Alexander, Paul H. Appleby, Thurman W. Arnold, Francis Biddle, Adolf A. Berle, Jr., Thomas G. Corcoran, Elmer Davis, Abe Fortas, Paul Porter, Samuel I. Rosenman, and Grace Tully.

In order to defend itself from ADA attacks, the PCA took steps to counter the Communist issue. In a "not for publication" memorandum, Field Service Director Lillian H. Traugott prepared some answers for local officials. One suggested response to questions relating to Communists was, "PCA feels that hurling the word 'Communist' is a verbal device used by political propagandists of the Right to discredit the progressive movement in general and to divide progressives into rival camps. It succeeded in Germany. . . . To fall into their trap is merely to become dupes of their propaganda." Another recommended reply was, "Other groups crying 'Communism' with shrill voices are those who are committed to a soft peace for Germany." Yet another proposed answer went as follows: "If the ADA 'rejects any association with Communists or sympathizers with Communism' how will it determine who falls into these categories? Will it adopt a screening technique? Will it call in the FBI or the Un-American Activities Committee to serve as its private Gestapo?" On the one hand it was stated, "PCA's convention decisions . . . were not molded by any obsession with the Communist issue" and on the other it boasted, "Obviously liberals have found themselves in the past and find themselves today, in the same group with Communists. . . . As for the organization that does not exclude Communists, the only question that matters there, it seems to me, is do the members stand for and work for the organization's program."[27]

ADA's Arthur M. Schlesinger, Jr., wrote *The Vital Center* in 1949 to expose the Progressive party. The widely circulated polemic helped ruin whatever chances the Progressive party may have had to survive after its defeat in 1948. Conceding that "Wallace was plainly not a Communist," he went on to describe him as a "windfall for the Communists." Why? According to Schlesinger, "This well-intentioned, woolly-minded, increasingly embittered man was made to order for Communist exploitation; his own sense of martyrdom was swiftly generalized to embrace all friends of Soviet totalitarianism." Concerning the Progressive party he wrote, "From the start, the key jobs in the Wallace Progressive Party were filled by Communists or fellow travelers. Stalin himself, who never had lifted a finger to the CPUSA, sent a letter to Wallace, as if to a head of state, laying down a basis for international negotiations. By the time of the Philadelphia convention in July, 1948, Communist control was arrogant and shameless."[28]

Needless to say Henry Wallace also sought support from liberal intellectuals and members of the academic fraternity. Writing in *The Annals of the American Academy of Political and Social Science,* he endeavored to answer the question as to why a new party was needed. The "decisive mistake of the New Deal," he asserted, "was its failure to recognize that it had to break through the limitations of the old parties to forge a new party of the people if its program was to be developed and carried forward." Penning this statement prior to the advent of Truman's Fair Deal, Wallace promised to revive the reform impetus. The Progressive party was to be an instrument of progress; it would "fight for a broader democracy with the assurance that it will not be a transient party of protest but a major and lasting party." In conclusion he cataloged the failures of the two major parties: "The old parties seek to entrap us in a vicious circle in which freedom can be maintained only if we give them up, in which peace is to be had only by preparing for a greater war, in which depression is the only alternative to inflation. The New Party knows that the new era will and must be different. We are fighting and planning for the century of peace and the century of the common man."[29]

Having written many books during the Roosevelt years when he fulfilled the vital role of New Deal philosopher, Henry Wallace produced his last political work in 1948. Seeking to explain just what his views were and the philosophy behind them, he spent much time preparing *Toward World Peace.* It more than any other work clearly revealed his Christian idealism. With great sincerity he wrote, "We need to read the Sermon on the Mount and to reflect whether we are following a Christian doctrine when we throw our weight against the under-privileged." To Wallace such actions as rearmament, the Truman Doctrine, and cold-war militancy on the part of the United States were denials of those religious standards which had to be applied to international relations. How could the United States be a Good Samaritan when it held an atomic bomb in its hands instead of meat and drink for the world's poor? With a morally impassioned argument he contended, "If democracy does not stand for the Christian concept of the brotherhood of man, it will disappear because it will have lost its fundamental reason for being. The psychological dilemma of the West is that it does not act vigorously and enthusiastically in terms of its professed beliefs."[30]

Countering the Communist charge, Wallace wrote of his own dislike of Communism: "My first objection to Russian communism is the emphasis which it places on dialectical materialism as a complete explanation of the universe. I disagree. . . . I believe the final explanation of the universe lies in our faith in God who created it. And the tolerance I expect from the communists is a healthy respect for my right to believe this, without attempts on their part to prohibit or undermine my faith."[31]

Not only did Wallace reject Communism as a philosophy that contravened his religious principles he also believed reformed capitalism was a superior economic system. "Progressive capitalism believes that the wealth and resources of a country—including the channels of public information—must serve the whole people and not just a few." Elaborating on this, he explained, "The progressive capitalist believes in a mixed economy where, with co-operation and continuous planning, government, labor, industry, and agriculture operate through whatever mechanisms will produce most and distribute most widely and cheaply without 'boom and bust.' "[32]

The book's final judgment was that nothing "short of a change in the administration" could guarantee future peace and prosperity. Since the "Truman administration has disqualified itself," Wallace maintained, new leadership was needed to ensure new policies. "So today a New Party proclaims a crusade to rediscover the spirit of America." Would a change in presidents really help? "I am under no illusion that the misunderstandings of the past two years can be quickly eliminated," he conceded, "but for the sake of my grandchildren, I want to start the job before it is too late." In conclusion, Wallace implored, "Now is the time for believers in the general welfare to organize for action which, by bringing social justice and increased opportunity for service to the common man, will prevent internal discord and revolution in every country in the world."[33]

Toward World Peace made such an impression on the famed scientist Albert Einstein that he wrote the following words to Wallace's publisher: "Only men who are above the petty bickering of the day and without any selfish interest can save us from the threatening domestic and international situation. Such men were Roosevelt and Willkie, and such a man is Henry Wallace."[34] Not many voters, however, were persuaded by Wallace's passionate presentation.

In a dramatic attempt personally to bring an end to the cold war, just prior to the Progressive convention Henry Wallace had resorted to a type of open diplomacy. Bypassing the official channels, he sent an "open letter" directly to Joseph Stalin. In a New York City speech, sponsored by the National Wallace for President Committee, he reiterated the six proposals deemed a suitable basis for U.S.-Soviet reconciliation. They were armament reduction and outlawing weapons of mass destruction, stopping the export of weapons, resumption of trade between the United States and Russia, cultural exchange programs, free exchange of scientific information, and reestablishment of a United Nations Relief and Rehabilitation Administration.[35]

Joseph Stalin took immediate advantage of this opportunity to score a propaganda triumph. In a vaguely worded reply he made himself look like the bearer of an olive branch. The Kremlin leader replied, "I do not know whether the United States Government approves of Mr. Wallace's program as a basis for agreement between the U.S.S.R. and the United States. As far as the Government of the U.S.S.R. is concerned it considers that Mr. Wallace's program could serve as a good and fruitful basis for such an agreement and for the development of international cooperation, since the U.S.S.R. Government considers that, despite the differences in the economic systems and ideologies, the coexistence of these systems and a peaceful settlement of differences between the U.S.S.R. and the United States are not only possible but also doubtlessly necessary to the interests of general peace."[36]

While addressing a crowd at the Cow Palace near San Francisco on May 18, 1948, Wallace announced excitedly, "Yesterday I enjoyed the very satisfactory feeling that I had made a contribution to world peace. The reply of Premier Stalin to my open letter was an indication, I feel, that the Russians genuinely desire—just as most Americans desire—a peace to end the cold war."[37] Nothing ever came of this exchange except that Harry Truman in desperation sought to capture public attention himself with a peace gesture of his own. The President announced in a campaign speech that he was prepared to send Chief Justice Fred Vinson to Moscow on a special mission to iron out U.S.-Russian differences. Because all the normal diplomatic channels were readily available, Secretary of State George Marshall frowned upon this election gimmick and soon the ill-conceived stratagem was allowed to slip into oblivion.[38]

Almost all the vilification heaped upon Henry Wallace came in the form of calling him a Communist or one who sympathized with Russia. In a radio broadcast he rebuked newspapers for their scurrilous attacks: "Beware of men who cry 'Communism'; Karl Marx did not write the Sermon on the Mount."[39] His protestations went unheeded and his pleas unheard. Denials are themselves signs of political weakness, and the fact that Wallace had to issue disclaimers periodically only served to tarnish his public image further.

Despite persistent and stinging personal attacks upon him, Wallace never relented in his own denunciations of American foreign policy. A bipartisan approach, he claimed, simply condoned the "war-mad plans of Truman, Dewey, Vandenberg and Forrestal." Their course, "if permitted to come to full fruition, will destroy completely the civilization of the past 2,000 years and may destroy all human life on this planet."[40] His fears may have seemed exaggerated to his radio listeners, but to him humanity deserved a warning of impending doom if nuclear weapons were ever to be employed. Returning to Philadelphia once more at the close of the campaign, although exhausted from his crusade, Wallace made a final entreaty for public support. "A large Progressive vote will send a thrill of hope around the world," he predicted.[41]

Long before the ballots were counted, Henry Wallace knew he was not going to win. His only hope now was to pull a sufficiently large vote to insure the permanency of his party and thereby influence the future conduct of foreign affairs. He believed his campaign had forced Harry Truman to champion a liberal program far more progressive in nature than he would have otherwise. In the end Progressives placed their hopes for defeating Truman on two key states—New York and California. The President needed the electoral votes of at least one of them to win. Acknowledging defeat of the national ticket even before the ballots were counted, Hugh Bryson, chairman of the State Central Committee of California's Progressive party, sent out a statement "To Be Read At All Election Night Parties." It was both a concession and a call to make "every registered IPP [Independent Progressive Party] voter a club member." He outlined their future objective: "We can make our new party, first dubbed a 'third party' not only the second party but the first party of the land. That is our goal, that is the only way that the slogans of peace, freedom and abundance will cease to be slogans and become instead the rights of all our people."[42]

No political miracle saved Wallace's self-styled Gideon's army from a rout. Pulling a national total of only 1,157,140 votes was nowhere near the once predicted 10 percent of the total electorate. Only in New York, where the ALP was strong, did it anywhere near approach this percentage. Wallace's party drew 509,559 ballots there, which was 8.12 percent of the vote cast in that state. The tally in California was 190,381 or 4.73 percent of the number of total ballots.[43] The Progressive party drew its heaviest vote from minority, ethnic groups with three-fourths of its vote coming primarily from the Negro and Jewish communities.[44]

Harry Truman no doubt lost New York because of Wallace's campaign, and this was due to the strength of the ALP. Its astute state chairman, radical Vito Marcantonio of East Harlem, worked indefatigably for the presidential ticket of the Progressive party.[45] In other states, excepting California, the third-party effort fizzled miserably. Its base was too narrow and its voter appeal too limited. Tattered and torn, the battle-worn band who followed their leader to defeat now simply disbanded and went their separate ways.

What about Henry Wallace? The 1948 campaign was a transfiguring experience for him; he had sacrificed practically all for his convictions. Considering himself part of a grand historical drama, he gazed at the distant horizon but seldom looked down at the immediate political terrain. Starting out with a commitment to world peace and social justice, he moved further into the rigid confines of utopian dreams and unrealistic ideas. Once having moved further to the left without outright repudiation of the help of Communists and fellow travelers, it was all too easy for him to take the next step and defend their right to participate in the Progressive party, and then the next, until he was virtually in the position of continually apologizing for them. So it was also with his explanations of Soviet behavior. He was placed in the untenable predicament of justifying every Russian move no matter how outrageous it happened to be.

Bestowing a moral fervor upon each of his successive steps away from reality, Henry Wallace gradually alienated himself from the main body of liberal and progressive moderates. Emotionally fortified rationalizations made him suppose his extremist views were perfectly consistent with his personal philosophy. Friends thought differently but could no longer peruade him of the absurdity of his indefensible stand. Public hostility only served to reinforce his own determination not to yield to hysteria or falter because of the abuse that was heaped upon him.

As his involvement intensified, Wallace could no longer clearly discern between legitimate compromise and appeasement or national defense and preparations for aggression. By becoming too critical of American actions and totally uncritical of Soviet intentions, his very integrity was made suspect. Seeing himself as a prophet crying in the wilderness, he failed to subject his own beliefs to intense scrutiny. Frantically trying to launch the new era he believed Franklin D. Roosevelt had been bringing into existence, Wallace deluded himself into thinking the only changes that could take place were in terms of American policy. Trapped by circumstances and ringed by tormentors, Wallace's vertiginous behavior brought deep anguish to those who knew him well. His noble ideals soon became gigantic illusions; his lofty idiom degenerated into a campaign of strange-sounding cant. Lacking the vital ingredient of expertise in matters of international relations, the would-be prophet of peace allowed his idealism to run rampant. Once this happened, it was fatally easy to become a blind fanatic instead of a fearless preacher.

CHAPTER 13

THE KOREAN WAR AND THE RETREAT FROM POLITICS

"SOMETIMES people call me an idealist," Woodrow Wilson told an audience while campaigning for the League of Nations. "Well, that's the way I know I am an American. America, my fellow citizens . . . is the only idealistic nation in the world."[1]

Much like Wilson, Henry Wallace did not feel that his arduous efforts in the 1948 election campaign were in vain. For him the "idealism enshrined"[2] in the United Nations charter was not ephemeral but a lasting beacon to guide mankind to the harbors of perpetual peace. Since he envisaged a long voyage before the U.S. ship of state charted a correct course, Wallace had no immediate intention of ceasing his crusade. He did not consider defeat at the polls irrevocable; there was much work to be done to build a sound base for future campaigns. If he could prevent it, the Progressive party was not going to be disbanded or demobilized. Instead, it must resolutely undergo purification and revitalization for the tasks that lay ahead.

In keeping with this general plan and feeling that his personal discomfiture was unimportant in view of the critical prob-

A prophet is not without honour,
but in his own country. . . .
MARK 6:4

lems besetting the nation, Henry Wallace made one last appeal to Harry Truman. In a congratulatory message that contained neither concession of defeat nor praise for the victor, the vanquished Progressive party candidate informed the President, "You now have a unique opportunity to unite the world on the basis of putting millions to work producing peacetime goods who are now forging the implements of destruction. Peace with honor is possible. Peace with security and without appeasement is possible. Not a single American public interest need be sacrificed. But to attain this peace, you must stand up against the 'gluttons of special privilege' in the foreign field." Now was the time for Truman to "cut loose from the advice of the military and the reactionaries from the South and from Wall Street," he counseled, and to remember that "the Sermon on the Mount has become the only practical guide for the human race." If the President would but initiate steps for a reconciliation with the Soviet Union, Wallace promised the Progressive party would "support [you] in every move which can really contribute to the attainment of world peace and the advancement of a progressive America."[3]

Rexford G. Tugwell, who in the waning weeks of the campaign had all but withdrawn from the Progressive party, also sought to counsel Truman. Sending his suggestion to Press Secretary Charles Ross on November 15, 1948, he outlined his scheme. Why did not "Mr. Truman revive the idea of a mission to Moscow by Mr. Justice Vinson, but . . . enlarge it by adding Mr. Wallace?" This overture, Tugwell insisted, would "draw back to his support . . . the Progressives who voted the Wallace-Taylor ticket" while simultaneously assuring "all people everywhere of his determination to seek peace regardless of any opposing interest."[4] The proposal impressed President Truman so little he ordered his press secretary merely to acknowledge receipt of it and nothing more. This was done when Ross sent Tugwell the terse reply, "Thank you for your thoughtful letter of November fifteenth."[5]

Although Gideon's army, Wallace's own designation for his followers, was in complete disarray, party machinery was still very much intact. C. B. Baldwin lost no time in calling the national committee into session for a postelection look at future prospects. Seeking to revive party spirits at this November 13th meeting, Henry Wallace told the gathering "we come here not as a people who lost—but as people who won." While conceding that 2.5 percent of the popular vote and the election of one congressional candidate was not impressive in and of itself, he claimed many people "voted for the Democratic candidate for President only after we had forced him to compete with us on the peace program, on civil liberties, and on the revival of an expanded New Deal with an emphasis on lower prices and housing." He believed his own bold stand on civil rights and domestic issues had forced Truman to concern himself with minority rights and liberal legislation. Thus to some extent he was taking credit for the Fair Deal on the assumption the President would not ordinarily have moved to expand the New Deal. "These so-called liberals had better get right on foreign policy or we shall do our best to get a strong candidate out against them."[6] This constituted a warning that 1952 would bring another challenge from the Progressive party unless the direction of international relations altered drastically toward the position Wallace had advocated.

Voicing concern over the fact that the New Party was considered much too pro-Russian by many voters, he declared belatedly, "It is not the purpose of the Progressive party to apologize for Russia. We have fought—and shall continue to fight—for one world at peace," vowed Wallace. Reaffirming this basic contention, he concluded, "We believe we are being true to America, to humanity, and to all that is deepest and finest in the Judaic-Christian religion when we say this. As long as the Democratic Party is not prepared to act thusly we must continue to be militantly organized."[7]

Despite this well-intentioned appeal the Progressive party could not maintain itself. Gradually its supporters deserted, and only a few of the faithful remained in any way active in either state or local groups. The national organization soon became a skeleton of which C. B. Baldwin was the caretaker. As far as the public was concerned Henry Wallace was synonymous with the Progressive party, and his poor showing at the polls doomed it to an inevitable death. Wallace's faithful wife Ilo (who had never cared too much for the Progressive party and the people in it) pleaded with him to retire permanently from politics. Since he was still titular head of his party and as such felt a responsibility to keep it alive, he could not yet bring himself to remain silent on important issues.

When the Senate took up debate on the proposed North Atlantic Treaty Organization, Wallace could not refrain from voicing concern that such an alliance would be both unwise and unwarranted. "It violates the spirit and the letter of the United Nations Charter, . . . it irrevocably splits the world in two, . . . it imposes an impossible burden of arms both on Europe and America, . . . [and] it is leading to war not peace."[8] He still thought the West should take no overt step to bipolarize the world into two permanent warring camps. Little attention was paid to Wallace's protestations because of the threatening posture of the Soviet Union vis-à-vis the Atlantic Community.

By the time the Progressive party held its second national convention in Chicago on February 24, 1950, many significant events had taken place at home and abroad. NATO had come into existence as well as the rival Warsaw Pact; America started production on hydrogen weapons, while the Soviets were testing their thermonuclear device; and in general the cold war was at the peak of its intensity. Still worried that a frightful military confrontation might lead to total annihilation of the planet, Wallace told his small band of followers, "For the first time in history, civilization has reached a crisis brought about by the development of the means of its own self-destruction— the hydrogen bomb." Because a relaxation of tension between the Soviet Union and the United States was the only way he knew to prevent a miscalculation leading to a nuclear holocaust, Wallace called for "a public declaration by the North Atlantic Pact nations that they will not be the first to use atomic weapons . . . ," to be followed by "initiation of official public diplomatic negotiations between the United States and Russia to continue until an agreement has been reached providing for the renunciation of the use of atomic energy as a destructive weapon. This agreement will include a method of inspection through the U.N. to insure the carrying out of the agreement."[9]

Having had much time to reflect on the mistakes of the 1948 campaign, Wallace readily admitted that rejection of the Vermont Resolution had been a grievous error. Now, two years later, trying to make amends, he declared: "I know everybody in this hall really believes in this resolution and is willing to see the sense of it adopted in our statement on foreign policy. We must not allow anyone the slightest, legitimate reason for believing that any working member of the Progressive Party puts Rome, Moscow or London ahead of the United States."[10]

Going further, Wallace emphasized his own conviction that "our principles are vastly different from those of the Communist Party." In order to clear the air, he stressed the fact that "our philosophy is not based upon the principles of Marxism or Leninism." Instead, it rested squarely upon the concept of "reform by constitutional and democratic processes." Lecturing the assemblage on the importance of disassociating themselves from Communists, he insisted "we must make it clear that there are no concealed strings manipulating us." Leaving no doubt that the party should purge itself, Wallace concluded with finality, "The Communists have their party. . . . We have ours."[11]

Still hopeful that altruism would replace aggression and that service to humanity rather than self-interest would guide nations, Henry Wallace again reiterated his Christian idealism as a blueprint for united action on the part of all peoples and all countries. "We in the Progressive Party proclaim that the day of force is over," he maintained. "Jesus saw it in the year 30. Gandi saw it in 1920. The atomic scientists saw it in the fall of 1945." Reflecting his own intense feeling, he said, "True Christians cannot tolerate the thought of two nations stockpiling hydrogen bombs capable of destroying the planet." His eloquent peroration came from the heart: "Gideon fought for the Lord and for Israel. We must fight for the Lord and America, remembering always that the Lord is the Lord of all the world, and not of any one nation, race, class, or religion."[12]

There were more than a few at the Progressive party gathering who did not like their erstwhile leader's strong stand against accepting assistance from the American Communist Party. Since a good many of the left-wing ideologues remaining in its depleted ranks were by and large pro-Soviet in their sympathies, it was highly doubtful whether Henry Wallace would have been acceptable to them as a presidential candidate for 1952 (assuming he wanted to run again). The essential difference between Wallace and remaining diehards in the Progressive party was simply this: He wanted the United States to be a moral leader—an international Good Samaritan as it were—while the hard-line leftists wanted the United States to be made out a scapegoat for the world's ills, thus promoting Russia as the paladin of peace. This type of "peace movement" had become a major propaganda enterprise for European Communist parties culminating in the Stockholm Appeal of 1950. For most liberals any love affair that they may have had with the Soviet Union chilled when it became apparent that Kremlin leaders practiced *Realpolitik* with such cynical skill it would have surprised either Niccolo Machiavelli or Karl Marx. Whatever sentiment for trusting Russia that remained was killed by the Korean War. Only a coterie of naive pacifists or deluded Marxists could convince themselves that this overt aggression was not planned and precipitated by Communist leaders.

On June 25, 1950, when the so-called North Korean Peoples Army crossed the 38th parallel to invade the Republic of South Korea, Henry Wallace was deeply shocked. Heretofore he had held America chiefly responsible for the cold-war tension, but now he heard the stark news reports that related the flagrant aggression initiated by North Korea. He was frightened by the prospect of a nuclear confrontation between the United States and the Soviet Union. He had always assumed, perhaps erroneously, that war of any kind would automatically be an atomic holocaust of worldwide dimension. He did not anticipate the possibility of a limited war, nor did anyone else.

Although not enumerated specifically as a part of America's defense perimeter, President Truman responded to this overt act of aggression with direct orders for U.S. forces to defend the South Koreans. Because the Soviet representative was boycotting Security Council sessions, no Russian veto blocked attempts for a ceasefire resolution, nor were there any obstructionist tactics present to delay collective action. Subsequently the American forces became in large measure the United Nations' police force in Asia.

The Korean War constituted a moral crisis for Henry Wallace and precipitated a confrontation between himself and those remaining in positions of leadership within the Progressive party. A meeting of the executive committee was called for July 6, 1950. Gathered in New York City were the following people: Henry Wallace, C. B. Baldwin, John Camper, James Durkin, Lillian Hellman, James Imbrie, Leo Isaacson, Vito Marcantonio, Jack McManus, Paul Robeson, Arthur Schutzer, Alfred K. Stern, Katherine Van Orden, John Abt, Vaughn Albertson, and Louis Burnham. Negro physician Dr. John Camper presided over the all-important meeting to decide what stand the Progressive party would take relative to the fighting then taking place. Discussion began when copies of a speech by Representative Vito Marcantonio were passed out. The ALP-Progressive member of Congress was extremely critical of the UN police action. Almost immediately Henry Wallace found himself alone in defending the United Nations. From the news coming in from UN officials on the spot it seemed to him that North Korea was the obvious aggressor.

On July 8th Henry Wallace received a phone call from his wife Ilo, and he excused himself and promised to return the next day. Once back in South Salem, only a commuter's distance from Manhattan, he was given a message from UN Secretary-General Trygvie Lie. Therein was a memorandum entitled, "Legal Aspects of Security Council Action in Korea." It convinced Wallace that UN sanctions against North Korea were justified on both legal and moral grounds.

Returning to the meeting once more, Wallace argued for a statement which would condemn the action of Communist North Korea. Others contested this position vigorously. They continued spirited debate for several more days, and a compromise draft was finally hammered out. On the final day of the gathering, July 10th, Wallace offered amendments to make it a stronger indictment of Communist aggression, while Paul Robeson sought to weaken it. Again the final results did not please Wallace. He reserved final judgment, telling the assembled group he would call Baldwin the next day and inform him of his final decision.

On July 11 Henry Wallace telephoned "Beanie" Baldwin to notify him that he could not endorse the statement as it then stood. After he related the changes he deemed necessary to make it acceptable, Baldwin presented them to the executive committee. They in turn unanimously rejected all of them. When informed of this turn of events, Wallace let Baldwin know that under the circumstances he would be forced to issue his own public announcement. Out of deference to his former political cohorts, Wallace told them he would send them a copy of his statement before releasing it. This he did. Accompanying it was a suggestion that the executive committee send a wire to Premier Joseph Stalin in the name of the Progressive party, asking the Soviet leader to end the war. Wallace's proposed request would have read: "In the name of world peace and humanity we call upon you to stop the fighting in Korea, and to initiate action looking toward the Union of Soviet Socialist Republics' immediate participation in the United Nations Security Council as a preliminary to the seating of the New China as soon as peace and free elections are established in a unified, democratic Korea."[13]

John Abt moved that as a substitute for Wallace's recommendation the executive council merely send copies of their own resolution to the secretary general and to representatives of the UN's permanent membership. The "Statement of the National Committee of the Progressive Party on Korea and China," finally adopted on July 15, 1950, claimed the following to be true: "We are united in the conviction that the continuance of hostilities is not in the interest of the American people. It is not in the interest of world peace. . . . The universal demand of the whole Korean people is to exercise their inalienable right of self-determination by establishing a unified and independent government. . . . The Rhea regime does not meet that demand. . . . The United Nations cannot fulfill the high purpose of its charter and serve the people of the world so long as the 450 million people who compose the Chinese nation are excluded. . . ."[14]

Issuing his own statement on the same day, Henry Wallace laid the blame for hostilities squarely on the Kremlin. "Undoubtedly the Russians could have prevented the attack by the North Koreans and undoubtedly they could now stop the attack at any time they wish." He then asserted, "I was Vice-President of the United States during a great war and I can never forget that. As Secretary of Agriculture and as Vice-President I always advocated preparedness. In building the Ever-Normal Granary program . . . and serving as Chairman of the Supply Priorities and Allocations Board and the Board of Economic Warfare, I did much to prepare my country for victory in World War II. Just because I believe the present war in Korea could have been prevented is no reason why I should not support my country when it gets into serious trouble. . . ."[15]

The remnant remaining within the Progressive party did not agree with Henry Wallace on this issue. Their ideological rigidity, in fact, made them critical of U.S. intervention—not Soviet complicity in the breach of peace. Realizing how irreconcilable his position was with theirs, Wallace finally resigned from the party on August 4. Standing alone before a newsreel camera, he stated very simply his reason for quitting the organization he once led, "I resigned from the Progressive Party because I felt the party should support the United States and the United Nations in the Korean War."[16] No Orwellian "doublethink" or Communist doubletalk could camouflage the naked aggression of North Korea; hence the Korean War provided the *coup de grâce* for the Progressive party. What was left of its miniscule membership now eroded to a mere handful because of its subsequent line of action.

The only congratulatory message Wallace received from anyone in the Progressive movement came from Rexford G. Tugwell. The man who once served as Wallace's Assistant Secretary of Agriculture told his former chief, "I am very glad you decided as you did in the Korean matter. It was the only thing to do and not to have said so would greatly have weakened your moral position. This does not mean, as I understand it, that you retreat at all from criticism of the mistakes in the past. It merely means that you recognize reality. . . ."[17]

Hate mail from Communists and hard-core Progressives let Henry Wallace know he was no longer the great American they had once thought. One letter signed "Mrs. American Jewess" called him a "turncoat"; another included an article by Gil Green in the *Daily Worker,* which charged Wallace with being a jingoist and a betrayer of peace, with the notation: "How could you be so like a Judas?" Writing in the *Daily Worker* Joseph Starobin claimed Wallace was "obsessed with the theme that Russia is as much responsible for the war danger as the Truman administration. . . . Related to this obsession, there was a deep fear and hostility for American Communists, whom he could not understand except as 'Russian agents.' "[18] From then on Wallace was considered an enemy of the people and a lackey of the capitalists. The Communists no longer had any use for the man they once hailed as a man of peace and leader of the common man.

Not being bound by any crypto allegiance to the Soviet Union, Wallace spoke out against both Russian subversive activities and its warlike attitude on the international scene. Speaking at the Brooklyn Jewish Center in 1951, the former candidate of the Progressive party maintained, "Today I am convinced that Russia wants the Cold War, that she is willing to run the risk of a hot war, that she is out to dominate not merely the countries on her border but also countries with a Western culture through the medium of Moscow-trained Communists, and that she is trying to subject many governments through Moscow-trained native Communists or espionage agents." He predicted an ultimate break between Moscow and Peking, warning that "in the long run Chinese nationalism organized to utilize modern techniques in hatred of the United States can be even more dangerous to the United States than Hitler, Japan, or Stalin."[19]

Later from the pulpit of the Community Church in Boston, he confessed, "Up till recently I had not thought that Stalin might prove to be a devil in the same sense as Hitler and Mussolini." He warned, "Communism inevitably kills the spirit of individual initiative, the freedom on which science thrives, [and] spiritually because of the way in which it invades the sacredness of the human soul. . . ."[20]

In a most revealing sermon given at the Community Church of New York, slightly before his break with the Progressive party, Wallace stated clearly the basic religious thought underlying his political philosophy. Churches should cease condemning man as a "poor miserable sinner," he asserted, and instead should teach "that man has infinite possibilities when he is armed with the religion of potentialism instead of being depressed by the religion of guilt and fear." Enumerating some of the sources of his religious ideals, he said, "I have the profoundest respect for the great prophets and philosophers of the past from the time of Amos, Isaiah, Heraclitus, and Jesus on down to the days of Emerson, Whitman, Thoreau, William James, and Josiah Royce."[21]

"With religious rightists," Wallace's name for those adhering to traditional doctrines, he conceded, "we share a common belief in the Fatherhood of God and the Brotherhood of Man." As for any religion with supernatural aspects, Wallace exclaimed, "We are not ashamed of being idealists or even mystics. . . ." But the American religion whereof he preached was not one of ritual and ceremony only, rather it was "definitely leftist in character as was the religion of the Old and New Testament in the days when the prophets and Jesus spoke." It was radically reformist in nature seeking to change man and society. Without the influence of the past, orthodox religion could adjust to contemporary needs. In secular terms he thought the Communists had caught the revolutionary spirit of pristine Christianity. "Christianity and Communism have much in common if Communism would profess God and Christ and if Christianity would show some capacity to realize that the world is always changing and no prophet out of the past can ever give us a complete guide to the future."[22] As a secular religion some of the theoretical doctrines of Communism had a kinship with the Social Gospel, since both desired to make man happier on earth.

Universal harmony and abundance were possible, Wallace predicted, "only when capitalism in the United States is modified, Communism in Russia is modified and Christianity abandons its medievalism, abandons its link with nineteenth century capitalism and applies the spirit of Jesus against the background of twentieth century science." Man had the power to make the planet an earthly paradise or convert it into an inferno of death and destruction. In a final pastoral admonition he said, "As practical Americans we disagree sharply with those who would make the Kingdom of God of concern only to those who have passed on to life after death. The best way to praise God is right here on earth by helping Him unfold His joyous plan for all humanity."[23]

It saddened Wallace to see religion used negatively to reinforce prejudice and human selfishness or made to justify enmity against certain peoples. While delivering an Easter sermon over radio in upstate New York, he pondered aloud, "Sometimes I wonder what Jesus would say if he were to walk the earth again as a man and see the sins committed, the hatred poured out and the blood shed in his name." Expressing hope for the future, Wallace added the comment, "Roman force killed Jesus but his spirit lived and will continue to live until mankind ceases to rely on force as a test of righteousness."[24] Seeking constantly to inspire men to work for a better world, Wallace was aware, as he informed the authors in January, 1961, that "there is no magic way of fusing religion with democracy." He elaborated, "The prophets saw this when the situation was most desperate in the lands of both Judea and Israel. The new order can be preached but not imposed. It must come from the hearts of many millions when they understand in their very being what is coming to pass."[25]

As a political leader, Wallace often used religious imagery in his speeches; now when talking about religion, he relied on political phraseology. In this prophetic role as an elder statesman and speaking in a somewhat quasi-Orphic manner, Wallace tended to anticipate some of the tendencies that appeared in the decade of the sixties. He did not presume that man's moral imperfections or natural perversity prevented social reforms. His emphasis upon commitment, activism, and a dynamic faith were to appear in three distinct movements: namely, the civil rights crusade led by Dr. Martin Luther King, Jr.; the modern theology of "Christian Atheism" inspired by the writings of the Reverend Dietrich Bonhoeffer; and the New Left phenomenon based on the "politics of truth" of C. Wright Mills. One cannot say that Henry Wallace was either the founder or "father" of these, yet from his own experience and philosophy there were interesting parallels and points of similarity.

Whereas elements of the Progressive party crusade for peace resembled the stand taken by Vietnam "doves" and its objectives were radical considering the circumstances, the similarity was by no means identical. Wallace's ends-oriented philosophy did not ignore means as do the Students for a Democratic Society and other New Left groups. At all times he worked from within the established political system, and never did Wallace advocate the use of violence to thwart the will of the majority. He wanted to reform society through democratic means, not destroy democracy for the sake of ideological objectives. Henry Wallace was a reformer, not a revolutionary.

Following his break with the Progressive party and as the forties became the fifties, Wallace was to discover unpleasant truths about many of his former associates. It soon became evident to him that some whom he had trusted were all along dedicated to less than noble principles. To his horror Wallace found himself a target for anti-Communist hunters during an era of suspicion launched by Senator Joseph McCarthy of Wisconsin. Not only was his patriotism impugned but all he had done during many years of public service came under heavy attack. The 1950s were a painful period in which Henry Wallace strove to defend his achievements, his reputation, and a place of honor in history.

CHAPTER 14

ANTI-COMMUNIST HYSTERIA AND THE ORDEAL OF

THE Korean War gave impetus to a renewed emphasis upon antisubversion investigations by congressional committees.

Information uncovered by the House Un-American Activities Committee and based on testimony given by former Communists Whittaker Chambers and Elizabeth Bentley eventually led to the perjury conviction of both Alger Hiss and William R. Remington. These cases made sensational headlines because Hiss had been in the employ of both the Department of Agriculture and the State Department, while Remington had been in the Department of Commerce. Then came revelations about the existence of a secret Communist cell in the Agriculture Department, which was supposedly operated by Harold Ware during Henry Wallace's tenure as Secretary. Others with whom Wallace was closely associated also came under investigation, although there was no evidence of any wrongdoing. John Carter Vincent and Owen Lattimore were also charged at this time with conspiring to undermine the Chinese Nationalist government of Chiang Kai-shek. Self-confessed Communists such as Louis Budenz and Harvey Matusow added their testimony to those of other accusers, and soon Wallace

I will not fail thee, nor forsake thee.
JOSHUA 1:5

SLANDER

was caught in the web of doubt and suspicion along with other innocent people. No clear distinction was being made between intentional Communist subversion and those espousing liberal doctrines, some of which went awry during the postwar period.

Prolonged investigations by the House Un-American Activities Committee revealed that in the fall of 1943 a small amount of uranium materials (500 pounds of uranium oxide and 500 pounds of uranium nitrate) had been shipped to the Soviet Union. Immediately the allegation was made by some critics that Henry Wallace, as head of the Board of Economic Warfare, must have approved these shipments. Politically the implication was that this constituted a deliberate act on his part to help the Russians acquire material for an atomic bomb. Outraged by the implied charge of treason, Wallace asked to appear before the committee in person. Seeking assistance from Walter Freedman, former legal counsel for the export section of BEW, Wallace sought to clear his name simply by explaining the facts.

Voluntarily appearing before the committee on January 26, 1950, he told them, "Nothing having to do with uranium or the Manhattan Project ever came up before the Board of Economic

Warfare at any time . . . the relationship of the BEW to shipments to lend-lease areas, whether they were of a lend-lease nature or a cash nature, was purely pro forma and clerical, and there was no discretionary authority in the BEW whatever." As it turned out, the authorization for these uranium shipments, too small even for experimentation let alone production of nuclear weapons, had been cleared by the Lend-Lease Administration. Honoring Russian requests, they preferred not to arouse undue speculation about uranium rather than to prohibit its shipment.

Wallace claimed he never once advocated giving the Soviet Union technical details about the atomic bomb construction. He admitted backing Henry L. Stimson's proposal about sharing broad scientific theories and information about atomic energy with Russia and Britain. This he maintained did not involve mechanical details of technical knowhow. "The bulk of the people, and I think most Congressmen, don't understand the nature of science; that there isn't any secret and never was any secret." Referring to Secretary Stimson's plan made just before the aged statesman retired from the Truman administration, he said, "I told the Cabinet meeting that if they were placing their confidence in scientific secrecy, they were placing their confidence in a Maginot Line, and there was no security there."[1]

Privately Wallace tried to find out what lower echelon clerk actually signed the export order giving BEW approval for the exportation of the uranium. After many years of searching, he was unsuccessful. He also appealed to Albert Einstein, then at the Princeton Institute for Advanced Research, to organize a group of top-flight physicists to explain that the amount of uranium material gratuitously allowed to leave the country was woefully insufficient for the purpose of developing an atomic bomb.[2]

When Harvard historian William Henry Chamberlin quoted General Leslie R. Groves in the book *America's Second Crusade* to the effect that the Manhattan Project director deliberately withheld atomic information from the Vice-President, he inferred strongly that Henry Wallace had been considered a security risk. The next paragraph in Chamberlin's work dealt with the exposure of Dr. Klaus Fuchs, a scientist working for the British who did give atomic secrets to the Russians. Wallace was both angry and disheartened by the calumnious charge. He wrote General Groves on March 7, 1951, reminding him first, "I was not in your chain of command and it was not within your power to either submit or withhold reports from me." After relating to Groves his role with the Top Policy Committee, Wallace asserted, "You must realize, General Groves, that it is a very serious matter when you and Chamberlin put me in the same category with Fuchs." With considerable indignation, he defended his record:

> I am proud of having as Vice-President strengthened Roosevelt's convictions that the atomic bomb project was worth while and should be backed with adequate funds. . . . I am proud of the way in which as Secretary of Agriculture, I built up large stockpiles of wheat, corn, cotton, and rubber.
>
> I am proud of the way in which during the months immediately prior to Pearl Harbor I worked as Chairman of the Supply Priorities and Allocations Board with Donald Nelson to straighten out the mess in OPM which centered around the conflict between Knudsen and Hillman.
>
> I am proud of the way in which as Chairman of the Board of Economic Warfare, I backed Milo Perkins in getting adequate supplies of strategic materials from all over the world. . . . I cannot tolerate the way in which your interview has been used to place my war record in the same category as that of spies and traitors.[3]

Writing also to Henry Regnery, the publisher of *America's Second Crusade,* Wallace protested, "It is unfortunate that Chamberlin in fighting a real evil should find it necessary to pervert the truth. In process of time I know that history will take care of these distortions."[4] Waiting for historical vindication did not remove the immediate mental anguish to which Wallace was subjected. The years from 1950 to 1953 were filled with intense heartache and emotional torment. Repeatedly he would endeavor to correct perversions of the truth, only to have them reiterated. When the uranium controversy had no more political value, his trip to China became the target of abuse. Although Wallace had never refused to provide information to any investigating committee, Senator Pat McCarran (D-Nevada) took it upon himself to issue the former Vice-President a subpoena. Dated October 3, 1951, the first such calculated insult ever dealt him, Wallace was ordered to be present the next day at the federal building in New York City to appear before the Senate Subcommittee on Internal Security.[5]

What made this summons so ludicrous was its groundless nature. The self-admitted Communist Louis Budenz, now a star witness before various investigating committees, while no doubt providing some valuable information, made grossly exaggerated assertions about the role of John Carter Vincent and Owen Lattimore on the mission Wallace took to China. Upon learning of this testimony, Wallace immediately wrote a letter to Senator Homer Ferguson (R-Michigan) offering a rebuttal to what Budenz had said. He chose to contact Ferguson because this particular member of the Senate Subcommittee on Internal Security had voiced the opinion that much of Budenz's testimony was actually hearsay.[6] Later Wallace also wrote Senator McCarran, the Chairman, to inform him of the erroneous nature of what Louis Budenz had claimed.[7]

With the help of columnist Joseph Alsop, who knew the facts of Wallace's China mission because he was there in 1944, Wallace secured George Ball as his attorney. This was done to make sure Senator McCarran did not turn the hearing into a morass of political prosecution. It never occurred to Wallace to use either the first or fifth amendment to keep from incriminating himself; he merely wanted a fair hearing to make his position clear. Whereas he had already given Senator Ferguson all the facts and the committee knew the contents of his actual report to President Roosevelt, Wallace now made it available for publication, hoping it would put an end to misrepresentations and fabrications. With the cold war at fever pitch, the former Vice-President was ensnared in a net of innuendo and guilt by association that defied reason and justice. Anti-Communist crusaders were looking for scapegoats, not explanations, and this made rational exposition well-nigh impossible.

The demise of Chiang Kai-shek and his eventual expulsion from the mainland by the Red Chinese was caused by many factors, not the least of which was the ineptitude of the Nationalist leader himself. Mistakes in judgment did play their part, but these decisions were made in good faith and under difficult circumstances. Every American official sent to China during World War II or shortly thereafter seems to have become enmeshed in the controversy. No less a personage than General George C. Marshall became a suspect in this alleged plot, as Senator Joseph McCarthy and his Red-hunting colleagues, with the help of the so-called China Lobby, endeavored to explain away Chiang's failures and the Communists' success by placing the total blame on supposed traitorous actions of certain Americans.

Whatever counsel Henry Wallace received from those who accompanied him to China, he advised President Truman on September 19, 1951, "As both Mr. [John Carter] Vincent and Secretary of State Dean Acheson have stated, Mr. Vincent took no part in the preparation of my formal report to President Roosevelt on July 10, [1944] and to the best of my knowledge was not aware of its contents." He made it clear, "I wrote the July 10 report myself and went to the White House to present it to the President." This was already known by the McCarran committee, as well as his claim that he "did not recommend any political coalition between the government of Chiang Kai-shek and the Chinese Communists."[8] All this was again repeated and rehashed, but the conservative chairman from Nevada turned a deaf ear to Wallace. Nothing Wallace said found its way into the committee's ultimate report to the Senate.

The tempest did not subside nor did the ordeal end. Two years after his first letter to Senator Homer Ferguson, Wallace sent another missive to this Michigan Republican pleading with him to help bring an end to this nightmare. "How would you feel," he posed the question, "if you had been sent by the President of the United States in time of war to attain a specific military objective against the enemy and then that mission was completely misinterpreted and falsely so by a government agency eight years later?" Poignantly Wallace pleaded with one whom he considered to be decent and honorable that his service to America not be relegated to the ash can of scorn and ridicule. He confessed, "It is a humiliating experience when a man who has served his country to the best of his ability in high public office for 12 years, is dragged before a Senate Committee (the first subpoena served was designed to give me less than a day's notice) and then to have no attention paid to his sworn, public testimony in the final report. May God grant that you may never have to undergo such an experience. If you do have to I am sure you would want to set the record straight for the sake of your children and grandchildren. . . . My daughter Jean is delivering this to your residence by hand because Mrs. Wallace and myself believe that this will make more likely the giving of your personal attention."[9]

Lest there be any misunderstanding about it, Henry Wallace at no time denied that some Communist infiltration into the councils of government had existed during the war; in fact he was convinced, much to his dismay, that espionage did take place. What he objected to so vehemently was the deliberate falsification and unfair smears connected with the investigations. Rather than these inquiries being kept judicious and relevant and thus exposing the real culprits, they were allowed to become hysterical inquisitions. With sorrow he came to realize that some Progressive party officials whom he had trusted were men with divided loyalties. After having initially cooperated with Professor Curtis MacDougall of Northwestern University (who was once a member of the Progressive party) in a history of the movement, Wallace lost interest in the project and refused to render any more assistance. It never occurred to him to challenge men's motives; and when it became evident that certain individuals had used his peace crusade for their own ends, this was but another cross for Wallace to bear. Too many people now viewed Wallace's entire career through the Red-hued lenses of the Progressive party.

The enigma of Whittaker Chambers remains as one of the unsolved riddles of the McCarthy era. In sworn testimony before government investigating committees and in his book *Witness,* Chambers pointed the accusing finger at Alger Hiss. This confrontation was dramatic and tragic in its consequences for both men. Hiss, though convicted of perjury, still maintained his innocence long after Chambers was dead. Tangentially Wallace became involved in this affair when Chambers claimed a secret Communist enclave, the Ware cell, existed in the Agriculture Department during the 1930s. Becoming aware of this charge only after reading what Chambers wrote in the *Saturday Evening Post* in an article titled, "I Was the Witness: The Tragedy of Alger Hiss," Wallace was intrigued by this strange man; and in a letter to Chambers he told him the second installment of his memoirs was "one of the most gripping human documents I have ever read."[10] Since it contained errors, he politely let both Chambers and Ben Hibbs, editor of the *Post,* know about it.

The truth about Harold Ware, Wallace explained, was that "Ware began as a dollar-a-year man under President Coolidge in 1925. At the time when, according to Chambers, Ware was setting up a Collective Farm in Russia he was serving as a collaborator with the U.S. Department of Agriculture while Herbert Hoover was President. Ware was not in the USDA or the AAA when Roosevelt was President and I was Secretary."[11] If the guilt by association formula was authentic, then presumably both the Coolidge and Hoover administrations were strongholds of subversion.

In his letter to Hibbs, which he also sent to Presidential Secretary Joseph Short so that President Truman would be aware of his rebuttal, Wallace took Chambers to task not only for obvious errors of fact but for overstating his case. Those in the Ware group were, according to Chambers, engaged in activities "much more dangerous . . . than espionage." Why? Because they allegedly influenced policy. Wallace reminded Chambers, who apparently was not aware of it and whose great memory seemed to falter when it came to facts regarding the Agriculture Department, that those named by the various ex-Communists as being coconspirators had in fact been purged from the AAA by him in 1935. This so-called "purge" was well known. Again stating the simple facts, Wallace explained: "Granting the Communist infiltration for policy-making purposes is a serious matter, I must emphatically state that most if not all of the men named by Chambers as in the AAA, left the AAA prior to July 1, 1935, and most of them as a result of my much publicized 'purge' of February, 1935. I did not know these men were Communists, I purged them because I disagreed with the suggestions they put forward to influence policy. For years I have been bitterly criticized by the liberals for what I did then."[12] Wallace was unaware that Alger Hiss was not even in the service of the AAA during this time, but Chester C. Davis did know this and helped implement the purge as chief administrator of the Triple-A program. Hiss, although technically a part of the Triple-A, had been loaned to the Nye committee previously and never returned after other young liberals were dispersed because of their objections to certain AAA policies.[13]

Ben Hibbs acknowledged Wallace's complaint by admitting, "You are quite right about Harold Ware, and I am sorry that Whittaker Chambers made this error in his book."[14] Whereas Wallace's correction was placed in the letters to the editor column, it hardly compensated for the wide distribution of the initial error. This episode tends to make one suspect of Chambers's credibility, since he built up Harold Ware to be a big-time spy and then did not know he left the Agriculture Department in 1932.

The self-revelations and compulsion to tell all made ex-Communists national figures. Too often everything they said was taken at face value even when their veracity was subject to question. One such informer, Harvey Matusow, wrote a candid confession in 1955, *False Witness,* in which he admitted adjusting his testimony to fit the needs of Senator Joseph McCarthy or any other investigating committee. A simple technique of smear, he found, was merely to claim that books written by Henry Wallace, Owen Lattimore, or whomever he desired to indict were being sold in Communist bookstores. Matusow, for instance, while before the Senate Internal Security Subcommittee on March 13, 1952, "deliberately dropped big names." Later acknowledging his wrongdoing he wrote, "I implicated Henry Wallace by saying I had seen and sold a pamphlet of his that was printed by the Institute of Pacific Relations." Likewise, he divulged the fact that his testimony was climaxed "with the dramatic assertion that Owen

Lattimore's books were used as the official Communist Party guide on Asia." Commenting on the accuracy of these insinuations, he said, "Once again, I told a complete falsehood." According to Matusow the blacklist publication *Counterattack* singled out many individuals just because they "had identified" themselves with Henry Wallace's Progressive Party."[15]

The agony of having to defend his honest intentions and to disentangle fact from fiction did not cause Wallace to lose faith in the ultimate public acquittal that would come when the American people understood all facets of the story. Unlike contemporary radicals of the New Left or Communists of the Old Left, he never advocated subversion or storm-trooper confrontation tactics. Speaking before the Harvard Law School Forum in 1953, Henry Wallace vowed, "To me a liberal is one who believes in using a nonviolent, tolerant, and democratic way the forces of education, publicity, politics, economics, business, law and religion to direct the ever-changing and increasing power of science into channels which will bring peace and the maximum of well-being both spiritual and economic to the greatest number of human beings." He warned that the "great peril of liberalism is its tendency to become materialistic." Most liberals raised in the John Dewey tradition of democracy and science believe neither in God nor in a future life," he elaborated. "It is because of this fundamental attitude that so many liberals are looked on with suspicion by so many small town and farm people." From his agrarian years to old age his concept of progressive capitalism envisioned a practical fusion of growing democracy, scientific advancement, and religious enlightenment to provide the basis for an abundant and peaceful life for all. "The methods of Progressive Capitalism are empirical and not doctrinaire."[16] Liberals, he said, must never become rigid, materialistic, or irreligious.

After the demise of Senator Joseph McCarthy of Wisconsin (he was censured by his peers for his behavior), the fanaticism and hysteria of the anti-Communist movement began to subside. At long last the scurrilous character assassinations ceased. The damage to Wallace's reputation could not be undone merely because the tormentors were at last silenced. When New Deal cohorts or those who had served with him in the Truman administration began to write their memoirs, he found himself either ignored or his position grossly distorted. The same phenomenon occurred when historians began to write about the thirties and forties. His contributions were either ignored or interpreted in terms of post-1948 events. As if to protect Franklin D. Roosevelt and themselves from guilt by association and to disassociate themselves from him, those who had once been his most active political allies minimized Wallace's important role and perverted his career.

When, for example, Alben W. Barkley wrote his memoirs (*That Reminds Me*) in 1954, he revived the myth about Wallace's alleged mysticism as the reason for his political behavior in 1948. Such rumors, given impetus originally by George Peek and to some extent by Rexford G. Tugwell, reoccurred continually during Wallace's career. Without malice no doubt, former Vice-President Alben Barkley maintained that as early as 1940 Wallace was "beginning to be troubled by some of the symptoms . . . of the increasing mysticism which later made it possible for the left-wing groups to exploit him." This remark made Wallace sigh in disbelief, since the Kentuckian was one political figure he had always held in high esteem. Dejectedly he sat down at his typewriter and wrote his former friend a lengthy letter. "It was not mysticism," he declared, "which made me want to see a settlement with Russia before she was strong economically and before she had the atom bomb. It was not mysticism which made me want to see the firm foundation for an abiding peace laid as soon as possible. It was not mysticism which made me want a really strong United Nations. The extreme left wingers never did like me personally but they did think they could twist my doctrine of peace for their own purposes. Mysticism did not enter into the picture in the slightest degree unless you wish to call the Doctrine of Christ mysticism."[17]

Publication of *The Forrestal Diaries,* edited by Walter Millis, was another source of grief. Wallace protested to the publisher that Forrestal's reference to him as being "completely, everlastingly and wholeheartedly in favor of giving it [the atomic bomb] to the Russians" was "a lie."[18] Viking Press officials promised to add a footnote to subsequent editions so that his denial would be made known. Although James Forrestal, Truman's Secretary of Navy, saw fit to condemn Wallace, he made no derogatory comment about Henry L. Stimson, the one who initially proposed the idea of sharing atomic scientific information with the Soviet Union. Whenever criticism of Stimson's plan was made, it was consistently Henry Wallace who was the target of abuse, not the Secretary of War.

Another painful episode arose when William Hillman compiled a book of documents called *Mr. President, Personal diaries, private letters, papers, and revealing interviews of Harry S. Truman Thirty-Second President of the United States of America.*

This 1952 publication contained some unflattering, diarylike quotations about a person designated merely as "Mr. X." Truman was cited as labeling this individual as follows: "X is a pacifist 100 per cent. He wanted us to disband our armed forces, give Russia our atomic secrets and trust a bunch of adventurers in the Kremlin Politburo." This and other references prompted Henry Wallace to wire President Truman while the latter was vacationing at Key West, Florida. Getting right to the point, the telegram read: "The press has been after me to comment on your diary reference to Mr. X . . . of the Hillman book. They believe that by Mr. X you meant me. . . . After reading this incredible diary entry made in your own handwriting I could not believe my eyes. Therefore I ask you to confirm or deny that Mr. X is I. If I receive no answer by noon on Monday or if the answer is no comment I shall take it that you meant me by Mr. X."[19]

Predictably an answer came back from Press Secretary Joseph Short indicating that the President "does not wish to comment or elaborate on the Hillman book."[20] Learning to live with frustration at this stage in his life, Wallace wired back, "Deeply appreciate the courtesy of your reply but am very sorry the President refused to comment."[21] Such protests offered little consolation; yet Wallace felt obliged to contest what he believed were twisted interpretations of his past actions.

After the first volume of Harry Truman's *Memoirs* was issued in 1955, Wallace again felt the former President had not presented an accurate description of him or his actions. "First, there was never at any time a single bitter word between President Truman and myself," attested Wallace. "Second, in the light of events today, I rejoice in what I stood for in 1946." He was referring to his anticipation of Truman's own Point Four Program and President Eisenhower's attempt to make coexistence a workable means of U.S.–Russian understanding. "Third, . . . I can enumerate only a few of the essential facts which Mr. Truman has evidently forgotten. I quote verbatim from my notes made at the time: 'September 10, 1946. At the meeting with the President, I went over page by page, with him, my Madison Square Garden Speech, to be given on September 12. Again and again, he said, "That's right; yes, that is what I believe." He did not have a single change to suggest. He twice said how deeply he appreciated my courtesy in showing him my speech before I gave it.' "[22]

Henry Wallace perhaps suffered the greatest blow to his pride and personal feelings when Arthur M. Schlesinger, Jr., completed the early volumes of *The Age of Roosevelt*. Attempting to evaluate Wallace's behavior, Schlesinger interpreted his political philosophy in psychological terms. Among other things, he stated: "Wallace was, in Westbrook Pegler's phrase, a 'spiritual window-shopper,' moved by both the experimental curiosity which interested William James in psychical research and by the prairie mysticism which led so many of his fellow Iowans into weird sects when they retired to California. Without fully believing it all, he probably found release (or refuge) in Roerich's theosophical potpourri as other men might in sex or liquor."[23]

Frances Perkins informed Wallace she was reviewing the second volume for the *Atlantic Monthly* and that she was "really very annoyed at the way in which he invaded your private life." The former Labor Secretary, then teaching at the New York State School of Industrial and Labor Relations at Cornell University, also thought Schlesinger had relied too heavily on materials supplied by Rexford G. Tugwell (i.e., writings, interviews, and his unpublished New Deal Diary at the Franklin D. Roosevelt Library). She conceded that "a stupendous bit of work has been done" by Schlesinger, but confided, "I don't trust Rex Tugwell's private diary to be anything more than exoneration."[24]

Frances Perkins took a rather strong exception to Schlesinger's statement about Wallace's supposed mystic personality, but did not explicitly mention this in her public review. In a letter to the authors, however, she volunteered her own opinion of Henry Wallace: "Mr. Wallace was a sincere and deeply religious man with a definite religious orientation. I knew Mr. Wallace well and under circumstances where it was natural that I should understand this aspect of his nature [she attended the same Episcopal church that he did]. He was firmly grounded in the Old Testament as well as in the great revelation of the New Testament and his basic philosophy certainly was based on sincere religious convictions. I dare say that historians, including Mr. Schlesinger, are oblivious to these signs and I have never agreed with Mr. Schlesinger's attitude on Mr. Wallace as shown in his second volume [*The Coming of the New Deal*]."[25]

Columnist Drew Pearson once told Henry Wallace very candidly that his public relations instincts were not sound. "It was my thought," he wrote as an old friend, that you were "misunderstood by a lot of people back in 1948."[26] He suggested that Wallace listen more to his wife, who did not hide her ill-will for many of his close associates in the Progressive party. She counseled against the idea of writing memoirs, although her husband had voluminous private papers. Wallace ultimately decided against it. To prepare his own version of what had transpired during his many years in public service would have consumed much valuable time. His own inclination was to spend the remaining years of his life in scientific work and humanitarian endeavors. Wallace once wrote Donald Murphy, his colleague when he edited the family's farm journal in the 1930s, that he was "more interested in the truth of the future than . . . in the half-truths of the past."[27] The result was that Henry Wallace, ordinarily a prolific writer, never published his own account of the many controversies in which he was involved.

CHAPTER 15

PROFILE OF A SCIENTIST: THE FINAL CONTRIBUTION

CLOSE FRIEND Boris Pregel, chairman of the board of the New York Academy of Sciences and president of Canadian Radium and Uranium Company, wrote Henry Wallace in 1960 to tell him, "Glancing back fifteen years, people, if they would have memory, would have seen how exact were your predictions about the economy, scientific developments, the labor situation, and the necessity for coexistence."

Viewing Wallace as a man before his time, he noted with a tinge of irony, "the most conservative Republicans are advancing such ideas about cooperation with U.S.S.R., which certainly would have led a few years ago to the most thorough investigation by the Committee on Un-American Activities." Times had changed, it was true. To console Wallace, Pregel added the comment, "All this proves only one thing–it is difficult and painful to be a pioneer in any field and especially in state affairs." He concluded, "It takes a great man like yourself to look around without bitterness, and feel satisfied to see the righteousness of your thinking."[1]

Professor Marcus Bach, director of the Foundation for Spiritual Understanding and formerly of the University of Iowa's

But love ye your enemies, and do good, . . . hoping for nothing again; and your reward shall be great. . . .
LUKE 6:35

School of Religion, received much intellectual stimulation from corresponding with Wallace and also saw him as one far ahead of his times. So much so, he wrote, "The inspiration of your ideas and the creativity that sparks them, together with your *Weltanschauung,* are qualities all too rare and all too needed."[2] Those who carelessly or in some cases callously denigrated Wallace often did not truly comprehend the religioscientific nature of his philosophy. With historical perspective it becomes clear that throughout Wallace's entire life he strove to discover both the forces that controlled nature's evolution and the moving element in human progress, so that he might use that knowledge to make life more bountiful for all people. Unlike most public figures who dealt only with short-range objectives but in accordance with the prophetic calling he felt, Wallace sacrificed peace of mind and public adulation to project goals and ideals for the long-range future. There is a tendency to tire of reformers who challenge convention and run too far ahead of the prevailing mood. Wallace knowingly often courted disfavor and rejection in his self-styled crusades to make the world safe for humanity.

If this made him appear erratic, one must attribute this to

the duality of his nature; that is to say, he was a philosopher and prophet as well as statesman and scientist.

Whether it was Oswald Spengler, Henry Adams, Brooks Adams, or Flinders Petrie the Egyptologist, Henry Wallace was intrigued by thinkers who sought to explain the underlying reasons for the rise and fall of different civilizations. In a public talk given in 1959, Wallace elaborated on the implications of these cyclical explanations of history, "Under these doctrines of civilization, a new race is formed by both genetic and ideological crossbreeding and after awhile there is evolved a somewhat new attitude toward the universe, what might be called a new religion. This new feeling for both God and Nature manifests itself first in a succession of art forms, cathedrals, sculpture, literature, music, softness, and decay. The whole process presumably takes a thousand and or fifteen hundred years to complete itself. . . ."[3]

During his New Deal days Wallace had assigned to himself the herculean task of altering attitudes (i.e., preaching the religion of reform in practical terms) to prevent both American society and Western civilization from sinking into a state of deterioration. From the advent of the atomic age his concern heightened lest mankind either destroy the planet outright or pollute the atmosphere with radiation so as to alter adversely man's genetic heredity code. Before a Memorial Day audience Wallace again reminded those who would listen that the "atmosphere-polluting hydrogen bomb [must] . . . make the people of all the world comprehend that the abolition of war is the only practical way of insuring the safety of our nation, of all nations, of humanity itself." Because atomic war would instigate one final downward cycle for all mankind, the ethics of men must change with the precepts of the Sermon on the Mount becoming the commonly accepted norm of behavior. "Always heretofore these ideas of Jesus and the prophets even in Christian lands have been discarded as wild and fantastic," he admonished.[4]

Writing down some of his thoughts, possibly for a talk that was never delivered, Henry Wallace expressed his innermost feelings about the Progressive party crusade of 1948. He confessed, "Undoubtedly I made many mistakes in what I said during the 1948 campaign, but I do not think it was a mistake to write what I did in 1948 in my book *Toward World Peace*: 'My fundamental faith is that when the bulk of mankind looks over the atomic abyss and confronts suicide face to face, we shall finally pull back and reach for the firm ground of international righteousness. There is nothing that will save us but belief in the unity of all mankind.' "[5]

Despite this premonition Wallace did not despair. He saw a final ray of hope that the tremendous existential confrontation facing mankind would force humans to take a "leap of faith." For this reason he very strongly believed that, as he told a college audience in 1955, "mass destruction makes mandatory the introduction of moral principles into a system of world order."[6] In truth, as he conceived it, science had made it absolutely necessary for all men to practice the morality inherent in Christianity. This was necessary if *Homo sapiens* were to survive on the planet, and this specter drove him to preach unceasingly his message of making religious principles work on the international scene.

The possibility of making atomic energy serve mankind excited Henry Wallace. After receiving some of a mildly radioactive compound from Boris Pregel (who was an expert in radiation), the then Vice-President began his first experiments with the effects of alpha rays on plant growth. This testing was expanded later at Farvue Farm by using gravel-filled tanks (30′ x 2′) in which to raise tomatoes. A liquid radioactive nutrient containing 10 parts of radium to 10 trillion parts of water and other substances was pumped into the tanks. To his surprise Wallace found tomatoes grown in radioactive fertilizer were superior to those raised with normal methods, and the new technique increased output some 30 percent.[7] This initial success prompted him to encourage his son to try similar experiments with chickens.

Always hopeful that science might find ways and means of making new knowledge of benefit to the human race, Wallace used the royalties from his last book ($4,458) to set up a financial grant for furthering basic research in neurophysiology. According to the terms of the trust fund, "Infra-red detectors will be procured and/or developed for the detection of long-wave infra-red radiation from nerves and nervous systems."[8] Supervision of grants was bestowed upon the Round Table Foundation with Paul de Kruif, Milo Perkins, and publisher Eugene Reynal as trustees.

Once in retirement Wallace expanded all his research activities. He renewed his genetic experiments with corn and sought to develop new varieties of strawberries and gladioli. It was truly a labor of love for him to rise early in the morning to tend his plants. His reaction to living things was not that of mere manipulator or statistician, although he kept meticulous records, but of one who appreciated the beauties and mysteries of nature. Thrilled anew each day, he looked forward to his work in guiding the evolutionary process for the betterment of certain species. It was a basic conviction with him that a scientist must possess, using

Albert Schweitzer's phrase, "a sense of reverence for life itself." Explaining his philosophy to the students of George Washington University in St. Louis, Wallace attested, "In genetics it is a rare privilege to watch life change generation after generation in response to different environments and different types of selection pressures. . . . More and more it seems to me that the future belongs to the artists, the bio-chemists, the geneticists, the psychologists and those ministers of the gospel who really believe that the spirit of God came to earth that we might live and have it more abundantly in ever changing and more joyous forms."[9]

Having absorbed this religioscientific outlook from George Washington Carver when the "Wizard of Tuskegee" was a student at Iowa State College (now Iowa State University), Wallace too felt that the manifestation of divine power was God's imminent presence in living things. Deeply admiring the black genius who taught him when he was a child, he maintained a lifelong friendship with Carver. Out of kindness to Wallace's father, who was then a professor at the Ames, Iowa, campus, the former slave-turned-scientist introduced the young boy to the study of botany. Speaking at the dedicatory ceremonies for Carver Hall at Simpson College (where Carver had attended as an undergraduate), Henry Wallace spoke about the famed scientist, "Carver, himself, always believed his most important inspirations came directly from God. But his relationship with God was not something vague and mystical, an ecstatic experience which would evaporate with the rising of the sun. The school of hard knocks and the training he had received at Ames made him try to attain his ideals in a very practical way. He believed God was using him as an instrument to help his neighbors live better, both white and colored."[10]

Most scientists deliberately inculcated in themselves a spirit of detached aloofness and cold objectivity toward the subject of their observation. Wallace, to the contrary, was convinced an observer would overlook important aspects of his experiment unless he developed a personal relationship with the plant or animal being studied. Today this practice of displaying "tender loving care" toward experimental plants and animals is not dismissed as readily as it was when Wallace and Carver were its lone exponents. The subsequent blending of this scientific pantheism with Wallace's Social Gospel Christianity gave a unique cast to his religiousness and became an essential key to understanding his overall philosophy.

Henry Wallace not only excelled in the field of applied genetics but capitalized upon his research through the channels of the

Pioneer Hi-Bred Corn Company. Its success made it one of the largest commercial producers of hybrid seed corn in the world. Wanting to keep Pioneer in the forefront, he alerted its staff to the possibilities of conducting pure research. He wrote Fred Lehmann, Jr., his old friend and then president of the company, "We are more definitely pioneers in the chicken game than we were in the corn game. . . . In a sense what we have done is not research but rather empirical testing. . . . Some people are very good at weeding out the ideas which other people discover. Both types are essential in an organization. The time has certainly come to re-assess our poultry research (and our corn too for that matter)."[11]

Since genetic theories applicable to plants or animals had relevance to humans, Wallace often thought about their implications pertaining to the betterment of the human race. He confided to fellow scientist Boris Pregel, "The effect of any type of atomic rays existing to some extent in nature, on evolution, fascinates me greatly." His goal, he added, was to "improve the quality of life, not for one generation only but for succeeding generations."[12] How could this be done? One way was to alter the fundamental hereditary pattern in living things via radiation, thus changing the reproductive code itself. The other approach was the development of hybrids by inbreeding to obtain dominant and recessive traits and then crossbreeding these to bring together complementary and desirable genetic characteristics.

In this process of breeding for hybrid vigor the Wallace technique differed from that of other geneticists. He liked to inbreed up to seven or eight times before employing the crossing procedure. This was almost double the number used by others. Also in contrast to the usual practice he thought it inadvisable to disregard recessive traits. Wallace speculated "that on the average many semideleterious characters of a complex nature may be helpful and not merely to be tolerated when properly covered up by a 'good dominant.' " What concerned him was the question, "Who knows which of these so-called inferior sorts may have had just one block of superior genes to contribute at some critical future juncture when the environment may have changed?"[13] For instance, he pointed out in one of his lectures the value of a "recent transfer of a whole block of genes from a wild grass called Aegilops Umbellata into wheat to give greater leaf rust resistance."[14] If all the so-called wild varieties of plants disappeared, no more raw material would exist for hybrid breeding. To prevent the disappearance of open-pollinated corn, another such source, Wallace was instrumental in acquiring primitive strains from Latin America so they could be preserved in a germ plasm bank. When he went to China in 1944, one of the items Wallace brought back was a sample of early maize that had existed in an unchanged state for centuries. Only by preserving breeding stock in its natural state could care be taken that new hybrid plants might be developed if strange diseases or different environmental conditions arose due to alteration of radiation levels in the atmosphere.

Among geneticists there existed a running debate over the relative importance of inherited traits versus environmental factors. This is often referred to as the nature or nurture controversy. In his experiments with chickens, where he produced a strain of Leghorn that had less body weight but yielded more in egg production, Wallace came to the conclusion: "I am convinced that care and feeding, especially feeding, of the inbreds . . . has a great deal to do with the outcome. . . . My belief is that we have been inclined a little too much to slide along in the belief that the various inbreds are fixed entities. To a degree they are, but I am also convinced that food is tremendously important."[15] Thus when the Lysenko controversy raged in Russian scientific circles over this same issue, Wallace believed "Lysenko, or rather Michurin, has something to contribute." He held this opinion while conceding, "I have no doubt, however, that the geneticists in America would not agree with me on this particular point."[16]

From his own deductions gained from empirical testing, Wallace definitely felt that in humans the nutritional, educational, and cultural factors were as important as the hereditary ones. This explained his great interest, while in politics, in raising the living standards of minority groups. Much of their alleged inferiority, he claimed, existed only because of social and educational deprivation as well as poor food during the early developmental years. His concept of "genetic democracy" meant that with proper nurture, despite so-called inequalities of intelligence or physical features, all men of all races were basically equal. Inequalities developed because of poverty, lack of education, and paucity of opportunity, not deficient heredity. Some psychologists have been coming to the conclusion that I.Q.'s are not fixed at birth but can be raised substantially with excellence in education. Statistics from Japan, a nation which learned to drink milk because of U.S. aid in the postwar era, indicate a dramatic increase in the size and weight of the contemporary generation of children. When Wallace was lampooned for "advocating a quart of milk for every Hottentot," this type of practical improvement of the human race was the objective he had in mind.

With the discovery of the existence of deoxyribonucleic and the ribonucleic acids (DNA and RNA), it seemed possible to control heredity in human beings. Nobel prize winner George W. Beadle of the California Institute of Technology, speaking at the 1959 Resources for the Future forum in Washington, D.C., posed the query, "Can we go on indefinitely defending as a fundamental freedom the right of individuals to determine how many children they will bear, without regard to the biological or cultural consequences?" With reservations he intimated, "We could in fact apply the knowledge we have attained in directing our own evolutionary futures. . . ."[17]

Answering Professor Beadle in a paper titled "Genetic Differentials and Man's Future," Henry Wallace acknowledged existing problems stemming from birth defects and overpopulation. The former, he thought, could be prevented by keeping genetic (or genealogical) records to prevent transmission of certain traits; the latter he had always thought could be dealt with by raising the level of food production in underdeveloped countries, while educational and technological standards were being raised through aid from advanced nations. However, he opposed any tampering with genetic diversity which resulted from random mating. Wallace was filled with apprehension that such interference might be used for the detriment of mankind rather than its betterment. "Man is on the threshold of controlling everything but himself," he warned, and thereby came once again to his most cherished principle: "Science has unwittingly made the Sermon on the Mount mandatory as an ultimate guide to international relations." "No genetic bomb has yet been dropped," stated Wallace—contemplating the implications of controlling the code of heredity as physicists manipulated the power of the atom —"I hope it may never be." He believed science must never become a party to the dehumanization of men. "Pure materialism working through atomic energy and biochemistry will destroy that spirit which I believe to be at the heart of all creative work." He realized and had preached for many years that "religion as well as sociology and politics . . . adapts itself to the new knowledge." Yet he feared the divine spark in man might well be extinguished if science engaged in "planned genetics." The "mystery of life will grow greater, not less, as our knowledge expands," argued Wallace, imploring that men might "find the wisdom and knowledge to reconcile our past with an ever more rapidly changing future."[18]

Addressing the Pioneer Club of Des Moines in the year 1962, Wallace enjoyed reminiscing about his Iowa background. He did not talk much about his political career, but again speculated on the future effects of science. "The spirit of man," he reminded his listeners, "increasingly immerses itself in sub-atomic particles, electricity, DNA, messenger RNA, enzymes, amino acids, computing machines, TV in the heavens to make possible one world, and subtleties without number, none of which bothered our pioneer ancestors." Accelerated technology, he vowed, should be used first to eliminate poverty and hunger rather than giving such a high priority to such spectaculars as flights to the moon. Universal social justice achieved by application of science would prevent starving people from harboring "hatred, violence, and envy in their hearts."[19]

Condemning the Soviet Union for deliberately inciting revolution and wars of liberation for its own selfish purposes, Wallace predicted, "Sooner or later Russia will understand that long-time self-interest demands that she stop her destructive leadership of the Common Man. No nation can get long-time security by promoting hatred and violence. This is especially true today when science and technology are galloping so fast. Those who fan misery into violence will reap the whirlwind."

Noteworthy on this occasion was the veteran reformer's unequivocal rejection of revolutionary tactics being promulgated by a younger generation. Defending the democratic process, he vowed, "The genius of the U.S. is reform—not revolution." Contrary to the affirmations of the New Left, he claimed, "We proved Jefferson wrong when he said we needed a revolution every 20 years." His reminder to fellow Hawkeyes pointed out, "If reform comes fast enough and wisely enough, there never need be a revolution."[20]

To the youthful "Now" generation surrounded with affluence yet suffering from alienation or lack of purpose in life, he proffered some sage advice. Recalling the wisdom of his beloved grandfather, Wallace offered the gentle admonition, "Neither education nor wealth nor improvements nor comforts nor conveniences can change to any great extent the fundamental problems of existence, . . . nothing blesses except right living—'Thou shalt love the Lord thy God with all thy soul and with all thy mind. Thou shalt love thy neighbor as thyself.' " To this counsel he attested, "So spoke Moses, so spoke Jesus, and so wrote my Grandfather as he looked three generations ahead."[21]

The last few years of Wallace's life spent laboring amid his many experiments at Farvue Farm were filled with joy and contentment. Bitter memories receded as he immersed himself in work with flowers and strawberries. Using seeds bombarded with radioactive material, he developed a beautiful variety of gladiolus. His final efforts were devoted to perfecting a stunning shade of blue.[22] The strawberry had long interested him. Even as a teenager in Iowa he kept test plots of this plant. By cross-pollinating various types, he strove to produce a virus-resistant strain. He hoped to develop a commercial variety which combined the tangy taste of wild strawberries with the desirable characteristics of size and marketability. This led him to cross the *fraise des bois* (or *vesca*), a wild strawberry from Europe, with domestic types from America. He also worked with the *moschata,* or musky strawberry, which Franklin D. Roosevelt had called to his attention and which had an unusually fine flavor. In the definitive study on the subject of breeding and cultivating this plant, *The Strawberry: History, Breeding and Physiology,* George M. Darrow described the technical aspects of Wallace's experimentation as follows: "To Wallace, his most intriguing project in recent years has been his efforts to introduce *vesca* and *moschata* flavors into the domestic strawberry. Based on the work of Haig Dermen's application of colchicine to produce polyploids, that of Darrow in crossing tetraploid *vesca* with the domestic berry, and that of D. H. Scott in making a 10-ploid form which was 3/4 American and 1/4 wild European, Mr. Wallace converted the 10-ploid plants into 8-ploids in order to cross with other octoploids which he hoped could furnish size, firmness and color while retaining the taste of the wild European berry."[23]

On his 115-acre estate Wallace raised many such exotic plants as Yugoslav lettuce—a Chinese herb with a high vitamin C content—wild plums, assorted types of grapes, and an odd assortment of flora from all over the world. But by all odds the plant that captivated him most was corn. He not only experimented with it for many years but studied its origins and background. With Dr. William Brown (Pioneer's chief geneticist) in 1956, Wallace wrote an authoritative history, *Corn and Its Early Fathers.* In an address given to the American Philosophical Society that same year, Wallace propounded an imaginative set of deductions based on his exhaustive examination of how corn was developed. This led to a historical interpretation of American development which might well be labeled an "agricultural thesis" or more accurately the "corn thesis." Sketching the past in broad strokes, he outlined the following schematic projection of history: "The genius of Western Civilization has been to set up . . . great systems of mutual interdependence which involved endless divisions of labor, tireless scientific research, huge transportation systems, and ever enlarging markets. Corn as it has expanded in the Midwest since 1783 has played a substantial part in this modern phenomenon which looks eventually to a vast world market." Corn had provided the American Indian with sustenance, and it was also the grain that allowed the pioneers to move from the coastal regions to the heartland of the United States. "Midwestern corn and the livestock produced from corn had the most profound effects on Eastern United States and Western Europe. No rapidly growing hinterland has ever made its economic power so widely and so beneficially felt."[24]

Furthermore he claimed the midwestern Corn Belt developed the "most productive agricultural civilization the world has ever seen." Cities grew and industrialization took place only because ample food supplies were always present. Not only were foodstuffs provided in large amounts but they had great nutritional value. From this fact he contended, "Abundant, high quality animal protein is the basis of the energetic, vital living which is the outstanding characteristic of the people of the United States." Whereas the virgin land of the old frontier was gone forever, the "new frontier" still beckoned. New approaches and novel solutions to food problems "will come out of the laboratories of scientific research provided we maintain our social structure by using our present superabundance constructively."[25] This also inferred, of course, continual advances in social and economic mechanisms to insure equitable distribution of scientifically induced affluence. To Wallace science, economics, politics, and foreign policy were inextricably linked together. Undergirding all, of course, was religion.

Critics had constantly called Henry Wallace's concern for underdeveloped countries a manifestation of his give-away mentality, but they overlooked the implicit practicality of such foreign aid programs. Chances for world stability, higher living standards, and international peace would be greatly enhanced if less-endowed nations prospered beyond the point of mere economic survival. Everybody gained when abundance was widespread. Often lost amid the altruistic rhetoric uttered by Wallace was wise counsel, given purely on its merits as sound economic policy.

During his later years Henry Wallace continued to make frequent trips to Mexico and Central America. His abiding interest in the welfare of Latin America prompted him to do what he could as a private citizen toward rendering assistance to the people of that region. Inducing American foundations to continue their aid and contributing his personal service in the nature of a science adviser, he used his expertise in genetics to increase food production and to improve its quality. Particularly in Mexico his efforts were duly appreciated. Hybrid corn was unknown in a land that had grown this grain for centuries. For thirty years prior to 1960 Mexico's corn yield seldom exceeded ten bushels per acre; with hybrids it was slowly being pushed upward. Since hybrids have to be developed especially for each region, Wallace worked to produce corn adapted to growing conditions in Mexico and Central America. He spent much time trying to breed a corn plant for use in Guatemala that would both produce in high altitudes and resist *achaparramiento* (a stunting disease).

In 1964 after his last visit to Central America, he addressed the Production Credit Association of Harlan, Iowa. With Latin America in ferment at the time, Henry Wallace made a point of explaining how revolutionary agitation could be stopped if Latins had higher living standards. One prime requisite was a more productive agriculture. Whereas he had supported the Alliance for Progress, he believed many additional practical devices could be used to bring lasting reforms to the Western Hemisphere. He contributed both his services and financial assistance to the Escuela Agricola Panamericana in Honduras (an agricultural school) and arranged for graduates of Iowa State University to serve as agronomy advisers elsewhere in Central America. Indians of Guatemala, for instance, did not know how to use hybrid seed, fertilizers, insecticides, or the latest farming techniques. Without such concrete aid, he warned there would be more Castrolike takeovers and more evidence of Red Chinese infiltration. "Demagogues and hot-headed students will preach revolution, while generals and large landowners will use repression." This dismal pattern in Latin America was unfortunate, and it would remain so unless the United States displayed leadership, Wallace argued. The American government must induce legitimate changes before it was too late. His final words were a prayer that young Latin Americans would not become Communists. Again showing his disdain for revolutionaries, he implored, "May God in his knowing wisdom grant that they take on the idealism of Christian democracy instead of the atheism of one of the Marxist parties."[26]

Each day of these last years was filled with work. Interspersed with trips to Mexico or Central America were talks to small groups or guest appearances as a lay preacher in various churches. He was invited to participate in a World Food Forum by Agriculture Secretary Orville L. Freeman, who later wrote Wallace, "You may be sure that your advice and counsel is more than welcome here in the Department where you are held in both affection and respect."[27] John F. Kennedy saw to it that the aging man was sent an inauguration invitation; this courtesy had never been extended to him since 1944.

An unusual experience occurred in 1963 when television station WNDT (New York City's educational channel) invited Wallace to participate in a special program. Among the guests besides himself were James Farley, Thomas G. Corcoran, Ernest Lindley, and James Roosevelt. The highlight of this 90-minute feature came when moderator Richard D. Heffner played a recorded film version of Franklin D. Roosevelt delivering his 1933 inaugural address. One TV critic described the effect as "stunning." In a review of this specific show he described what happened after the former friends of F.D.R. heard that golden voice and once again felt his peculiar charisma. "As it ended, the studio cameras quickly switched to closeups of the old New Dealers, catching such expressions of poignancy and yearning remembrances as one seldom sees on faces trained to hide inner feelings from the public gaze."[28]

As the decades slipped past, Henry Wallace drifted into oblivion as far as the American public was concerned. He was busy and content; in fact with the exception of visits from intimate friends he enjoyed the solitude so dear to a scientist. On occasion school children asked and were permitted to see and hear about his various experiments. His library holdings reflected a wide literary taste and a desire to keep up on world affairs. Sitting before his white fireplace with book in hand during the winter season provided him ample time to keep abreast of contemporary events. Writing an occasional article or keeping up with his correspondence, which he often typed himself, constituted his only outside activity. He refused to engage in politics of any kind. Although Wallace let it be known he supported Dwight D. Eisenhower for the presidency, he never involved himself in any political campaign. When he was approached to comment on Ezra Taft Benson's agricultural policies during the Eisenhower years, he generally spoke well of Ike's Agriculture Secretary. He agreed with Benson that commodity surpluses had to be reduced and, with some disagreement on methods, Wallace never uttered any substantial criticism of the man who held the same position he once devoted so much time to filling.[29] After being the recipient of so many political attacks, he felt much disposed to remain silent rather than add to the burdens of a conscientious public official trying to do his job.

Old memories were revived for Henry Wallace when he received a letter from his Uncle Dan of Walker, Minnesota. Included in this communication was a note of condolence from Bernard Baruch—a message of consolation sent to Dan when his brother Henry C. Wallace died in 1924. Henry A. was so moved by Baruch's comforting words, which he had never before seen, that he wrote him to say: "It was such a lovely letter and showed such an understanding of my father as he really was, that I could not forbear writing you my warm appreciation. . . . The other day I spent some time reading the book you gave me many years ago on Popular Delusions and Crowd Madness [the exact title was *Extraordinary Popular Delusions and the Madness of Crowds* by Charles Mackay]. The more I looked into this book the more I realize that it is a great compendium of wisdom. We have agreed and disagreed on many things. But that is no reason why I should not express my appreciation."[30]

Wallace remained mentally alert and physically strong to an amazing degree into his seventies. He could still play tennis and boasted of his ability to do twenty push-ups in rapid succession. While on a trip to Central America in 1964, he wanted to examine one of the pyramids of Guatemala; despite his advanced age of seventy-six, he thought nothing of climbing to the top. After descending, he noticed a peculiar numbness in one of his legs. A limp developed after he returned home, and finally the discomfiture forced him to see a doctor. Medical experts at the Mayo Clinic noted a deterioration in the muscle but initially could not diagnose its cause. He subsequently went to Germany for special treatment. There his tonsils were removed and he was treated for a sinus condition on the assumption this would relieve the increasing paralysis. Tests finally confirmed the worst. He had become afflicted with the rare disease called "amyotrophic lateral sclerosis," an incurable illness resulting in slow atrophy of the muscles. This was the same malady that had struck down the iron man, baseball player Lou Gehrig of the New York Yankees.

Because of his strong Christian faith and inner will, Henry Wallace endured great suffering with stoic bravery. Eventually he was forced to rely on crutches, and only near the end would he use a wheelchair. His speech was affected, and immense effort was needed to communicate with others. Knowing his case was terminal, he wasted no time in self-pity; instead, he wanted to make one last contribution to humanity. So that medical scientists might gain more knowledge of this unusual disease, he invited doctors at the National Institute of Health at Bethesda, Maryland, to conduct tests on him. Serving as a human guinea pig Wallace allowed them to remove sections of muscle tissue for microscopic examination. His hope was that intensive tests and other experiments conducted on him might lead to the extinction of this dreadful disease. Respite from his suffering came on Thursday, November 18, 1965. With his beloved wife Ilo at his bedside in the hospital at Danbury, Connecticut, the end came quietly for Henry Wallace. His body had finally succumbed to the ravages of a spreading paralysis, but his gallant spirit triumphed even in death. The official autopsy report stated coldly in clinical terms that death resulted from "a respiratory arrest due to a chronic neuromuscular ailment and lateral sclerosis"; but that description failed to record the undaunted courage of a man waiting patiently until released from life by his Maker.[31]

Henry Wallace was many things: scientist, economist, philosopher, politician, journalist, preacher, and humanitarian. He wanted to be known most of all as a prophet of peace and plenty. Vice-President Hubert Humphrey eulogized him best when he said "but above all he was a good man."[32] Everything Wallace did as a public servant was meant to help mankind. No doubt he made mistakes, and for this he paid the most extreme penalty exacted in politics—journalistic pillorying and ultimate exile from public esteem. Yet he did not become a bitter or cynical man. For all his efforts to reconcile Soviet aims to American objectives in foreign policy, the Kremlin thanklessly labeled him an "enemy of mankind." He tried to make amends for wrongs done to others and sought reconciliation with past political foes. His old adversary Harry Truman paid him final tribute by saying: "I am sorry as I can be. Henry Wallace was an asset to this country."[33]

Once when asked what he would have done if he had succeeded Franklin D. Roosevelt as President, Henry Wallace answered honestly, "I . . . don't know whether I would have been able to handle it. The responsibility is tremendous."[34] He served America best by being the conscience of a nation and its constant protagonist for peace. If he saw visions visible to no other man, it was because his gaze extended far beyond that of others. If controversy was his constant companion, it was because he fought relentlessly for what seemed right to him. If he failed at times, it was because his efforts were dedicated to the attainment of enormously difficult objectives. Never did this man waver when the call of duty beckoned. Service to God and man was to him the very meaning of life itself. Confidant and friend Henry C. Taylor once assured his agrarian colleague "the Wallace family is an institution."[35]

If good deeds are remembered after men die, then former Secretary of Agriculture Orville L. Freeman uttered a most appropriate memorial when he said, "History cannot ignore him, and we shall not forget him. No single individual has contributed more to the abundance we all enjoy today than Henry Wallace."[36]

SELECT BIBLIOGRAPHY

MANUSCRIPT COLLECTIONS

Bancroft Library. Papers of Robert W. Kenny.
Catholic University of America. Papers of Philip Murray.
Clemson University. Papers of James F. Byrnes.
Columbia University. Oral History Collection: Will W. Alexander, Louis H. Bean, Samuel B. Bledsoe, Harvey Bundy, Rudolph M. Evans, Mordecai Ezekiel, Edward J. Flynn, Bernard L. Gladieux, Gove Hambidge, Fred Henshaw, John B. Hutson, James LeCron, Arthur Krock, Henry L. Stimson, Oscar C. Stine, Norman Thomas, and Rexford G. Tugwell.
Cornell University. Collection of Regional History. Papers of Augustus L. Richards.
Duke University. Papers of Harry Slattery, Josiah Bailey, William Watts Bell, and thc Socialist Party of America.
Franklin D. Roosevelt Library. Papers of Franklin D. Roosevelt and Henry Agard Wallace.
Harry S. Truman Library. Papers of Harry S. Truman, Alfred Schindler, Charles S. Murphy, John Redding, and J. Howard McGrath. Oral History Collection: William L. Batt, Jr., John Franklin Carter, Kenneth M. Birkhead, Jonathan Daniels, Harry B. Vaughan, William J. Bray, and Samuel C. Brightman.
Harvard University. Papers of Joseph C. Grew.
Iowa State University. Iowa State Historical Collection: Henry Agard Wallace.
Library of Congress. Papers of Henry Agard Wallace, Cordell Hull, Jesse Holman Jones, and Thomas Connally.
Michigan Historical Society. Papers of Frank Murphy.
National Archives. Files of the Supply Priorities and Allocations Board.
Princeton University. Papers of Bernard M. Baruch.
State Historical Society of Wisconsin. Papers of Henry C. Taylor, Harry W. Bolens, and the Americans for Democratic Action.
Syracuse University. Papers of Dorothy Thompson.
University of Iowa. Papers of Henry Agard Wallace, the Progressive Party, and the Iowa Authors' Collection.
University of Kentucky. Papers of Alben W. Barkley.
University of Oklahoma. Papers of Robert S. Kerr and Helen Gahagan Douglas.
University of Oregon. Papers of the Progressive Party.
University of Washington. Papers of Ethan Allen Peyser.
Washington, D.C., State Department Building. Papers of Mordecai Ezekiel.
Washington National Records Center. Files of the Board of Economic Warfare.
Yale University. Papers of Irving Fisher and the Walter Lippmann Collection.

PERSONAL INTERVIEWS AND CORRESPONDENCE

Clinton P. Anderson, George Beadle, Joseph F. Bickman, McGeorge Bundy, Vannevar Bush, James F. Byrnes, Bruce Catton, Clark M. Clifford, Benjamin V. Cohen, E. U. Condon, Leo T. Crowley, Chester C. Davis, Goldwaithe H. Dorr, Mordecai Ezekiel, Abe Fortas, Phyllis Gelbman, Bernard L. Gladieux, Leslie R. Groves, Alvin H. Hansen, Philip H. Hauser, John H. Hazard, George F. Kennan, Robert W. Kenny, Leon H. Keyserling, Frank Kingdon, Max Lerner, James L. McCamy, Helen Hill Miller, Walter Millis, Raymond

Moley, Robert Nathan, Robert Oppenheimer, Edwin W. Pauley, Claude Pepper, Frances Perkins, Milo Perkins, Boris Pregel, James Roosevelt, Alfred Schindler, Michael Straight, Strom Thurmond, Glen H. Taylor, Jerry Voorhis, Henry A. Wallace, James W. Wallace, James Wechsler, John F. Wharton, and M. L. Wilson.

PUBLIC PAPERS

Lord, Russell, ed. *The Century of the Common Man, Selected from Recent Public Papers.* New York: Reynal and Hitchcock, 1943.

———, ed. *Democracy Reborn, Selected from Public Papers and Edited with an Introduction and Notes.* New York: Reynal and Hitchcock, 1944.

Rosenman, Samuel I., collator. *The Public Papers and Addresses of Franklin D. Roosevelt, with a Special Introduction and Notes by President Roosevelt.* Vols. 1–4, New York: Random House, 1938; vols. 5–9, New York: Macmillan, 1941; vols. 10–13, New York: Harper, 1950.

COLLECTED DOCUMENTS

Bernstein, Barton J., and Matusow, Allen J., eds. *The Truman Administration: A Documentary History.* New York and London: Harper and Row, 1966.

The China White Paper August 1949. Stanford Univ. Press, 1967.

GOVERNMENT DOCUMENTS AND PUBLICATIONS

Baruch, Bernard M., Conant, James B., and Compton, Karl T. *Report of the Rubber Survey Committee September 10, 1942.* Washington, D.C.: GPO, 1942.

Foreign Relations of the United States Diplomatic Papers 1943 Volume V The American Republics. Washington, D.C.: GPO, 1965.

Foreign Relations of the United States Diplomatic Papers 1944 Volume IV Europe. Washington, D.C.: GPO, 1966.

Foreign Relations of the United States Diplomatic Papers 1944 Volume VI China. Washington, D.C.: GPO, 1967.

Public Papers of the Presidents of the United States Harry S. Truman, 8 vols. Washington, D.C.: GPO, 1966.

BOOKS AND ARTICLES BY HENRY A. WALLACE

BOOKS

Wallace, Henry A. *Christian Bases of World Order.* New York and Nashville: Abingdon-Cokesbury, 1943.

———. *Our Job in the Pacific.* New York and San Francisco: American Institute of Pacific Relations, 1944.

———. *Price of Free World Victory, The.* New York: L. B. Fischer, 1942.

———. *Sixty Million Jobs.* New York: Reynal and Hitchcock, 1945.

———. *Soviet Asia Mission.* New York: Reynal and Hitchcock, 1946.

——— and Brown, William L. *Corn and Its Early Fathers.* East Lansing: Michigan State Univ. Press, 1956.

Toward World Peace. New York: Reynal and Hitchcock, 1948.

ARTICLES

"A New Dealer Looks at the New Frontier," *Journal of Farm Economics,* vol. 44 (May 1962).
"Foundations of Peace," *Atlantic,* vol. 169 (Jan. 1942).
"How I'd Stop the March of Stalin," *Coronet,* vol. 29 (Nov. 1951).
"Reconversion Days" *Vital Speeches,* vol. 10 (Feb. 1, 1944).
Review of *Imperial Germany and the Industrial Revolution,* by Thorstein Veblen, *Political Science Quarterly,* vol. 55 (Sept. 1940).
"Students of Today—The Leaders and Builders of Tomorrow," *Vital Speeches,* vol. 9 (Feb. 15, 1943).
"Wallace Report on China," *Current History,* vol. 18 (Jan. 1950).
"Wallace Tells His Story," *U.S. News and World Report,* vol. 34 (Jan. 1953).
"Where I Went Wrong," *This Week,* vol. 29 (Nov. 1951).
"Why a Third Party in 1948?" *Annals of the American Academy of Political and Social Science,* vol. 259 (Sept. 1948).

NEWSPAPERS AND MAGAZINES

Baltimore *Sun,* Chicago *Defender,* Chicago *Sun-Times, Christian Science Monitor, Current History,* Detroit *News, Foreign Affairs, Foreign Commerce Weekly,* Milwaukee *Sentinel, Newsweek,* New York *Herald Tribune,* New York *Post,* New York *Times,* St. Louis *Post-Dispatch, The Nation, The New Republic, Time, U.S. News and World Report, Vital Speeches, Wall Street Journal,* Washington *Post,* Washington *Star,* Washington *Times-Herald.*

BOOKS

Acheson, Dean. *Present at the Creation, My Years in the State Department.* New York: W. W. Norton, 1969.
Byrnes, James F. *Speaking Frankly.* New York and London: Harper, 1947.
Compton, Arthur Holly. *Atomic Quest, a Personal Narrative.* New York: Oxford Univ. Press, 1956.
Davis, Kenneth S. *Experience of War: The United States in World War II.* Garden City: Doubleday, 1965.
Divine, Robert A. *Second Chance, the Triumph of Internationalism in America during World War II.* New York: Atheneum, 1967.
Fehrenbach, T. R. *F.D.R.'s Undeclared War 1939 to 1941.* New York: David McKay, 1967.
Feis, Herbert. *The China Tangle, the American Effort in China from Pearl Harbor to the Marshall Mission.* New York: Atheneum, 1965.
Filene, Peter G., ed. *American Views of Soviet Russia 1917–1965.* Homewood, Ill.: Dorsey, 1968.
Frye, Alton. *Nazi Germany and the American Hemisphere, 1933–41.* New Haven and London: Yale Univ. Press, 1967.
Halle, Louis J. *The Cold War as History.* New York and Evanston: Harper and Row, 1967.
Janeway, Eliot. *The Struggle for Survival, a Chronicle of Economic Mobilization in World War II,* vol. 53 of *The Chronicles of America Series,* Allan Nevins, ed. New Haven: Yale Univ. Press, 1951.
Kingdon, Frank. *An Uncommon Man, Henry Wallace and 60 Million Jobs.* New York: Reader, 1945.
Lord, Russell. *The Wallaces of Iowa.* Boston: Houghton Mifflin, 1947.

Macdonald, Dwight. *Henry Wallace, the Man and the Myth.* New York: Vanguard, 1947.

MacDougall, Curtis D. *Gideon's army.* New York: Marzani & Munsell, 1965. 3 vols.

Nogee, Joseph L. *Soviet Policy towards International Control of Atomic Energy.* Notre Dame: Univ. Notre Dame Press, 1961.

Phillips, Cabell. *The Truman Presidency, the History of a Triumphant Succession.* New York: Macmillan, 1966.

Rogow, Arnold A. *James Forrestal, a Study of Personality, Politics, and Policy.* New York: Macmillan, 1963.

Rosenman, Samuel I. *Working with Roosevelt.* New York: Harper and Brothers, 1952.

Schapsmeier, Edward L. and Frederick H. *Henry A. Wallace of Iowa: The Agrarian Years, 1910–1940.* Ames: Iowa State Univ. Press, 1968.

Schmidt, Karl M. *Henry A. Wallace: Quixotic Crusade 1948.* Syracuse: Syracuse Univ. Press, 1960.

Shannon, David A. *The Decline of American Communism, a History of the Communist Party of the United States since 1945.* New York: Harcourt, Brace, 1959.

Smith, Alice Kimball. *A Peril and a Hope, the Scientists' Movement in America: 1945–47.* Chicago and London: Univ. Chicago Press, 1965.

Steinberg, Alfred. *The Man from Missouri, the Life and Times of Harry S. Truman.* New York: Putnam, 1962.

Ulam, Adam B. *Expansion and Coexistence: The History of Soviet Foreign Policy, 1917–67.* New York: Praeger, 1968.

Wright, Gordon. *The Ordeal of Total War 1939–1945.* New York, Evanston, and London: Harper and Row, 1968.

ARTICLES

Adams, Mildred. "Wallace: Liberal or Star-Gazer," *New York Times Magazine,* Sept. 15, 1946.

Childs, Marquis W. Review of *Democracy Reborn,* edited by Russell Lord, *The Saturday Review of Literature,* vol. 28 (Sept. 9, 1944).

Hale, William Harlan. "What Makes Wallace Run?" *Harper's,* vol. 196 (Mar. 1948).

Herring, Hubert. "Henry III of Iowa," *Harper's,* vol. 186 (Feb. 1943).

Jackson, Gardner. "Henry Wallace: A Divided Mind," *Atlantic,* vol. 182 (Aug. 1948).

Kempton, Murry. "The Progressives' Long Winter," *The Nation,* vol. 170 (Mar. 11, 1950).

Lindley, Ernest K. "Observations on the Wallace-Jones Feud," *Newsweek,* vol. 22 (July 26, 1943).

Phillips, Cabell. "That Baffling Personality, Mr. Wallace," *New York Times Magazine,* Feb. 8, 1944.

Stone, I. F. "The Anti-Wallace Plot," *The Nation,* vol. 157 (Dec. 19, 1942).

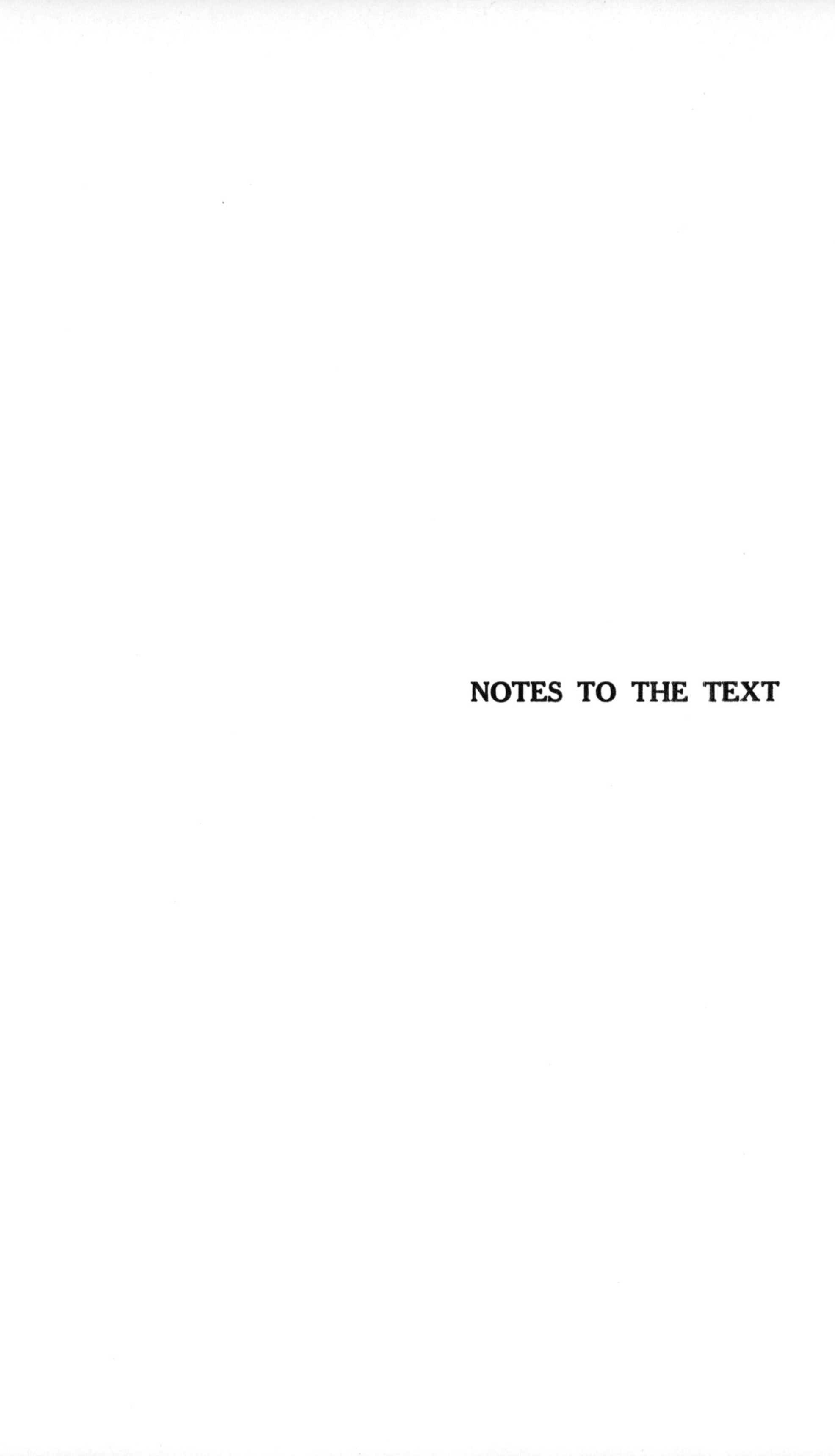

NOTES TO THE TEXT

SOME paperback editions have been cited. For the convenience of the reader commonly used abbreviations are listed in the preliminary pages after the Introduction.

CHAPTER 1

1. F.D.R. may also have been influenced by Woodrow Wilson's method of mobilization. See Frederic L. Parson, "The American War Government," *American Historical Review*, 26 (Oct. 1920): 54–76.

2. This portion of his career is covered by E. L. and F. H. Schapsmeier, *Henry A. Wallace of Iowa: The Agrarian Years*, 1910–1940 (Ames, 1968).

3. During the 1940 presidential campaign Westbrook Pegler sought to malign Wallace by publishing letters supposedly written to Nicholas Roerich (described by the press as a White Russian mystic). In a diary-type statement in his papers Wallace explained that most of these were forgeries and the rest "were written in rather high flown language." They were peddled to the highest bidder evidently to get even for recalling the Roerich Expedition. This expedition to China in 1936 was originally F.D.R.'s idea and not Wallace's. Statement on Nicholas Roerich, n.d., HAW-UI.

4. David Lynch to HAW, Jan. 9, 1941, and HAW to Michael Francis Doyle (chairman, electoral college of the United States), Feb. 11, 1941, HAW-UI.

5. Washington *Times-Herald*, Mar. 25, 1941.

6. FDR to HAW, July 9, 1941, HAW-FDRL.

7. Samuel I. Rosenman, collator, *The Public Papers and Addresses of Franklin D. Roosevelt, with a Special Introduction and Explanatory Notes by President Roosevelt*, 13 vols. (New York, 1950), 1941 vol., pp. 290-91, 350-51. Hereinafter cited as *FDR-Public Papers*.

8. FDR to HAW, Sept. 16 and Dec. 31, 1941, HAW-FDRL. The best accounts of preparedness steps taken at this time are in Eliot Janeway, *The Struggle for Survival, a Chronicle of Economic Mobilization in World War II* (New Haven, 1951) and Donald M. Nelson, *Arsenal of Democracy* (New York, 1946).

9. *Wall Street Journal*, Oct. 16, 1941.

10. As quoted in Springfield (Mass.) *Republican*, Oct. 20, 1941.

11. HAW to W. W. Waymack, Apr. 11, 1941, HAW-FDRL.

12. HAW to FDR, Aug. 29, 1941, HAW-FDRL.

13. HAW to FDR, Nov. 8, 1941, HAW-FDRL.

14. Text of speech in New York *Times*, Nov. 13, 1941.

CHAPTER 2

1. HAW, "Farmers and the War," address over NBC radio, Mar. 14, 1942, Omaha, Nebr., HAW-UI.

2. Arthur Holly Compton, *Atomic Quest, a Personal Narrative* (New York, 1956), p. 62.

3. Wallace's role in the Top Policy Committee is best described in "Testimony of HAW before House Committee on Un-American Activities Committee," Jan. 25, 1950, and HAW to Leslie R. Groves, Mar. 7, 1951, HAW-UI. Other accounts may be found in H. D. Smyth, *A General Account*

of the Development of Methods Using Atomic Energy for Military Purposes under the Auspices of the United States Government, 1940–1945 (Washington, D.C., 1945), pp. 32–150; Richard G. Hewlett and Oscar E. Anderson, Jr., *The New World, 1939–1946* (University Park, Pa., 1962), pp. 18–19, 44-52; and the Oral History Memoir of Henry L. Stimson, COHP.

4. HAW to FDR, Dec. 18, 1941, HAW-FDRL.
5. HAW to FDR, Aug. 7, 1942, HAW-FDRL.
6. HAW to FDR, July 11, 1942, HAW-FDRL.
7. HAW to FDR, Dec. 9, 1942, HAW-FDRL.
8. FDR to HAW, Dec. 10, 1942, HAW-FDRL.
9. HAW, Memorandum for the President—subject: Necessity for prompt action to adopt the sugar program to defense needs, Apr. 8, 1941, HAW-LC.
10. HAW to FDR, Apr. 13, 1942, and Memorandum for the President urging an anti-inflation program, Apr. 1942 (signed by HAW, Claude Wickard, Leon Henderson, Marriner S. Eccles, and Harold Smith), HAW-LC.
11. Supply Priorities and Allocations Board Minutes, Meeting 15, Dec. 8, 1941, WPB file, RG 179 (National Archives, Washington, D.C.). Hereinafter referred to as NA.
12. *FDR-Public Papers,* 1941 vol., pp. 294-95 and 1942 vol., pp. 242-43.
13. HAW to Addison M. Parker, Jan. 16, 1942, HAW-LC.
14. Cordell Hull, *The Memoirs of Cordell Hull,* 2 vols. (New York, 1949), II, p. 1154.
15. FDR to HAW, Apr. 23, 1942, HAW-FDRL. Dean Acheson discusses this administrative conflict in *Present at the Creation, My Years in the State Department* (New York, 1969), pp. 39–42.
16. HAW to FDR, Apr. 16, 1942, HAW-FDRL.
17. HAW to Sumner Welles, Apr. 20, 1942, HAW-FDRL.
18. Kenneth Davis, *Experience of War, the United States in World War II* (Garden City, 1965), pp. 165–69.
19. James Reston, "The Assistant President," New York *Times,* Oct. 12, 1941.
20. FDR to HAW, Dec. 23, 1941; HAW to Harold Ickes, Nov. 19, 1941; Harold Ickes to HAW, Jan. 14, 1942; Harold Ickes to FDR, Apr. 14, 1942; memorandum of agreement marked "Accepted in principle," Jan. 20, 1942—all in HAW-LC.
21. Donald M. Nelson, *Arsenal of Democracy: The Story of American War Production* (New York, 1946), p. 7 ff.

CHAPTER 3

1. HAW to FDR, Feb. 24, 1942, HAW-FDRL.
2. HAW to FDR, Jan. 31, 1942, HAW-FDRL.
3. HAW to FDR, Feb. 4, 1943, HAW-FDRL.
4. HAW to FDR, May 22, 1943, HAW-FDRL.
5. Sondra R. Herman, *Eleven against War, Studies in American Internationalist Thought, 1898–1921* (Stanford, 1969), pp. 150–78.
6. HAW, review of *Imperial Germany and the Industrial Revolution,* by Thorstein Veblen, *Political Science Quarterly,* 55 (Sept. 1940): 435-45.
7. HAW, "America's Part in World Reconstruction," Dec. 28, 1942, copy of text in Papers of Mordecai Ezekiel (State Department, Washington, D.C.).
8. Ibid.

9. Ibid.
10. H. S. Latham to HAW, June 12, 1942, HAW-LC.
11. Donald M. Stuart to HAW, June 1, 1942, HAW-LC.
12. FDR to HAW, May 4, 1942, HAW-FDRL.
13. HAW, "The Price of Free World Victory," May 8, 1942, copy of text in Ezekiel Papers.
14. Ibid.
15. Ibid.
16. Ibid.
17. Eleanor Roosevelt to HAW, July 31, 1942, HAW-FDRL.
18. Louis Lochner, ed. and trans., *The Goebbels Diaries* (Garden City, 1948), p. 306.
19. HAW, *Christian Bases of World Order* (New York and Nashville, 1943), pp. 9–10, *passim.*
20. Ibid.
21. Ibid.
22. Ibid.
23. HAW to FDR, June 5, 1942, and Feb. 5, 1943, HAW-FDRL.
24. Russell Lord, ed., *Henry A. Wallace, the Century of the Common Man, Selected from Recent Public Papers* (New York, 1943), pp. 58.
25. FDR to HAW, Aug. 30, 1943, HAW-FDRL.
26. Memorandum from HAW to General Watson (for the President), Feb. 13, 1943, HAW-LC.

CHAPTER 4

1. Alton Frye, *Nazi Germany and the American Hemisphere, 1933–1941* (New Haven and London, 1967), p. 120 ff.
2. HAW to FDR, June 5, 1936, HAW-FDRL.
3. HAW to FDR, Dec. 23, 1936, HAW-FDRL.
4. HAW, "Pan America," *New York Times Magazine,* July 9, 1938, as quoted in Russell Lord, ed., *Henry A. Wallace, Democracy Reborn, Selected from Public Papers and Edited with an Introduction and Notes* (New York, 1944), p. 160. Hereinafter cited as *HAW-Public Papers.*
5. Ibid., p. 161.
6. David Cronon, *Josephus Daniels in Mexico* (Madison, 1960), pp. 255–71; Joseph L. Morrison, *Josephus Daniels, the Small-d Democrat* (Chapel Hill, 1966), pp. 213–14.
7. Oral History Memoir of James LeCron, COHP.
8. Josephus Daniels, *Shirt-Sleeve Diplomat* (Chapel Hill, 1947), pp. 347-49.
9. HAW to FDR, Dec. 26, 1940, HAW-UI.
10. HAW to Sumner Welles, Dec. 24 and 26, 1940, HAW-UI.
11. FDR to HAW, Jan. 10, 1941, and Cordell Hull to HAW, Jan. 6, 1941, HAW-UI.
12. Nelson A. Rockefeller to HAW, Jan. 31, 1941, and Feb. 26, 1942, HAW-UI.
13. HAW to Jean Wallace, Nov. 16, 1942, HAW-UI.
14. Dr. E. N. Bressman (director, Agricultural Division, Office of Inter-American Affairs) to HAW, Nov. 29, 1941, HAW-LC.
15. HAW to Nelson A. Rockefeller, Nov. 3, 1941, HAW-LC. Rockefeller's exemplary work with Latin America is discussed in Alex Morris, *Nelson Rockefeller, a Biography* (New York, 1960).

16. Armando Medina to HAW, Mar. 22, 1942, HAW-LC.
17. As quoted in New York *Times,* Sept. 17, 1942.
18. Ibid.
19. "Use of Labor Clause in U.S. Contracts for Procurement of Strategic Materials," n.d., BEW–General Committee Minutes, Records Analysis Division-Foreign Economic Administration, RG 169 (Federal Records Center, Suitland, Maryland). Hereinafter cited as FRC.
20. "The Policy of the Department of State with Reference to the Inclusion of Labor Clauses in Purchase Contracts," n.d., RG 169, FRC.
21. Carlton Savage to Cordell Hull, May 28, 1943, with enclosure: "Address of Senator Robert A. Taft at the Grove City College Commencement," May 22, 1943, Papers of Cordell Hull (Library of Congress).
22. Press release from the office of the Vice-President, Feb. 23, 1943, HAW-LC.
23. Baltimore *Sun,* Apr. 26, 1943.
24. Claude G. Bowers to Cordell Hull, Mar. 29, 1943, copy in HAW-LC.
25. Edwin C. Wilson to Cordell Hull, Mar. 26, 1943, copy in HAW-LC. See other flattering reports from American ambassadors and embassy officials in *Foreign Relations of the United States Diplomatic Papers 1943, Volume Five, the American Republics* (Washington, D.C., 1965), pp. 55-75.
26. *El Panama America,* Mar. 24, 1943.
27. *HAW-Public Papers,* pp. 227–28.
28. HAW to FDR, Mar. 23, 1943, and FDR to HAW, Apr. 6, 1943, HAW-LC.
29. Charles A. Thompson and Walter H. C. Laves, *Cultural Relations and U.S. Foreign Policy* (Bloomington, Ind., 1963), pp. 36–39.
30. Mordecai Ezekiel, "Henry A. Wallace, Agricultural Economist," *Journal of Farm Economics,* 48 (Nov. 1966): 789.

CHAPTER 5

1. Martin Dies to HAW, Mar. 28, 1942, HAW-LC.
2. "Statement of the Vice-President," Mar. 29, 1942, HAW-LC.
3. Ibid.
4. Further accounts of the techniques employed by the committee relative to this episode are found in August Raymond Ogden, *The Dies Committee, a Study of the Special House Committee for the Investigation of Un-American Activities 1938–1944* (Washington, D.C., 1945), pp. 260–67, and Walter Goodman, *The Committee, the Extraordinary Career of the House Committee on Un-American Activities* (New York, 1964), pp. 132–40, 162–66.
5. Elaborate discussions of the entire Communist issue are found in Earl Latham, *The Communist Controversy in Washington from the New Deal to McCarthy* (Cambridge, Mass., 1966), and Frank Warren III, *Liberals and Communism, the "Red Decade" Revisited* (Bloomington, Ind., and London, 1966).
6. *Daily Worker* (New York), Sept. 20, 1942.
7. New York *Times,* Aug. 1, 1942.
8. Richard L. Strout, "Three Views on Postwar Problems," *Christian Science Monitor,* Aug. 1, 1942.
9. Walter Lippmann, *U.S. Foreign Policy, Shield of the Republic* (Boston, 1943), p. 37.
10. Ibid., pp. 50–51. For an expanded discussion on his criticism of Roosevelt administration foreign policy see E. L. and F. H. Schapsmeier,

Walter Lippmann: Philosopher-Journalist (Washington, D.C., 1969), pp. 82–104.

11. Bascom N. Timmons, *Jesse H. Jones, the Man and the Statesman* (New York, 1956), pp. 50–167.

12. Arthur M. Schlesinger, Jr., *The Age of Roosevelt,* 3 vols. (Boston, 1960), II, pp. 430–33.

13. Jesse H. Jones with Edward Angly, *Fifty Billion Dollars, My Thirteen Years with the RFC (1932–1945)* (New York, 1951), p. 427.

14. "Statement by Dr. Earl M. Bressman before the Senate agricultural subcommittee investigating industrial alcohol and synthetic rubber," June 5, 1942, copy in HAW-UI.

15. Joseph Borkin (Department of Justice), "Confidential Memorandum for Harold Young" (special assistant to the Vice-President), July 14, 1942, HAW-LC.

16. "Report of the Rubber Survey Committee," Sept. 10, 1942, copy in HAW-LC. See also Bernard M. Baruch, *The Public Years, My Own Story* (New York, 1960), pp. 301–7, and Margaret Coit, *Mr. Baruch* (Boston, 1957), pp. 516–17.

17. U.S. Senate, 77th Cong., 2d sess., Special Committee Investigating the National Defense Program, *Investigation of National Defense,* Senate Rept. 480, pt. 5 (Washington, D.C., 1942), p. 71 (See also Repts. 10, 110, and 440). The excellent work of this committee is documented in Donald H. Riddle, *The Truman Committee: A Study in Congressional Responsibility* (New Brunswick, 1964).

18. Milo Perkins to William R. Jeffers, Jan. 2, 1943, copy in Papers of James F. Byrnes (Clemson University).

19. William R. Jeffers to Milo Perkins, Jan. 9, 1943, copy in Byrnes Papers.

20. HAW to William R. Jeffers, Jan. 12, 1943, copy in Byrnes Papers.

21. HAW to James F. Byrnes, Jan. 12, 1943, Byrnes Papers.

22. HAW to FDR, Jan. 25, 1943, HAW-FDRL.

23. HAW to Jesse Jones, Jan. 19, 1943, Jones Papers.

24. Jesse Jones to HAW, June 2, 1943, Jones Papers. A "Memorandum of agreement between the Secretary of Commerce and the chairman of the Board of Economic Warfare," dated Apr. 3, 1943 had seemingly set the stage for solution of the RFC-BEW administrative conflict.

25. HAW to Jesse Jones, June 3, 1943, Jones Papers.

26. HAW to FDR, June 1, 1943, copy in Jones Papers.

27. HAW to FDR, June 10, 1943, HAW-UI.

28. U.S. Congress, Joint Committe on Reduction of Nonessential Expenditures, *Hearings on Reduction of Nonessential Federal Expenditures,* 78th Cong., 1st sess., 1943, pp. 2371–73; Senator Kenneth McKellar to HAW, June 29, 1943, HAW-UI. He corrected his error relative to congressional appropriations but still remained antagonistic to the BEW's existence.

29. Joint Committee on Reduction of Nonessential Expenditures, *Hearings,* pt. 7, Apr. 5, June 1 and 22, 1943, pp. 2298–2388.

30. Ibid.

31. Senate Subcommittee on Appropriations, *Hearings on H.R. 2828,* 1943, pp. 3–12, 38–41.

32. Transcript of telephone conversation dated June 25, 1943, HAW-UI.

33. Memorandum to the Vice-President from Milo Perkins, June 30, 1943, HAW-UI.

34. Senate Subcommittee on Appropriations, *Statement by Vice-President Wallace, Chairman, Board of Economic Warfare, June 29, 1943,* pp. 359–71.

35. Statement of Vice-President as quoted in New York *Times,* July 1, 1943.
36. Jones, *My Thirteen Years with the RFC,* p. 498.
37. "Reply of Jesse H. Jones, Secretary of Commerce, to Vice-President Wallace, July 5, 1943," press release, Jones Papers.
38. HAW to James F. Byrnes, July 1, 1943, HAW-UI.
39. As quoted in New York *Times,* July 1, 1943.
40. Ibid.
41. Ibid.
42. James F. Byrnes to HAW, July 6, 1943, HAW-FDRL and Byrnes to Jesse Jones, July 6, 1943, Jones Papers.
43. Jesse Jones to James F. Byrnes, n.d. [ca. July 7, 1943], Jones Papers.
44. HAW to FDR, July 12, 1943, as quoted in Russell Lord, *The Wallaces of Iowa* (Boston, 1947), pp. 510–11.
45. Ibid.
46. Milo Perkins to Senator Carter Glass, July 5, 1943, HAW-FDRL.
47. FDR to HAW and Jesse Jones, July 15, 1943, HAW-FDRL.
48. White House press release, July 15, 1943, and FDR to Leo T. Crowley, July 15, 1943, HAW-FDRL.
49. Jones, *My Thirteen Years with the RFC,* p. 328.
50. Leo T. Crowley to Jesse Jones, July 28, 1943, Jones Papers.
51. *FDR-Public Papers,* 1943 vol., p. 298 ff.
52. Quintin M. Sanger, "BEW-OEW-FEA Foreign Procurement and Development Responsibilities," RG 169, FRC.
53. Leo T. Crowley to authors, Mar. 3, 1964.
54. Milo Perkins to HAW, July 29, 1943, HAW-UI.

CHAPTER 6

1. I. F. Stone, "Why Wallace Spoke Out," *The Nation,* 167 (July 10, 1943): 36; "Mr. Wallace Walks the Plank," *The New Republic,* 109 (July 20, 1943): 93–95; *PM,* (New York), July 25, 1943.
2. Addison M. Parker to HAW, Mar. 16, 1944, HAW-UI.
3. Dan Wallace to HAW, Mar. 28, 1944, HAW-UI.
4. *HAW-Public Papers,* p. 233.
5. *PM* (New York), July 25, 1943.
6. *HAW-Public Papers,* pp. 239–40.
7. Ibid., p. 240.
8. Ibid.
9. As quoted in Washington *Post,* July 27, 1943.
10. As quoted in Baltimore *Sun,* July 28, 1943.
11. *HAW-Public Papers,* p. 193.
12. As quoted in Washington *Times-Herald,* July 25, 1943.
13. Guy Irving Burch to HAW with enclosure, "A Blind Spot in World Politics," July 11, 1943, HAW-FDRL.
14. HAW to Guy Irving Burch, July 13, 1943, HAW-FDRL.
15. Ibid.
16. HAW to FDR, Sept. 8, 1943, HAW-LC.
17. Address by the Vice-President to the Chicago United Nations Committee to Win the Peace, Sept. 11, 1943, as quoted in Washington *Star,* Sept. 12, 1943.
18. Ibid.
19. As quoted in New York *Herald Tribune,* Sept. 11, 1943.
20. Published as "Sustained Yield," *The Land,* 2 (Spring 1943): 273 ff.

21. HAW, "Soil Defense," *The Land,* 1 (Winter 1941): 49–50.

22. HAW, "A Billion People," *The Land,* 2 (Fall and Winter 1942–43): 242.

23. John Carter Vincent to HAW with letter from Dr. Tseng Yang-fu, June 14, 1943, HAW-FDRL.

24. HAW to Major General Philip B. Fleming, June 17, 1943, and Fleming to Dr. Tseng Yang-fu, June 23, 1943, HAW-FDRL.

25. HAW, *Our Job in the Pacific* (New York and San Francisco, 1944), p. 5.

26. Ibid., pp. 23, 45.

27. Gunnar Myrdal, *Asian Drama, an Inquiry into the Poverty of Nations,* 3 vols. (New York, 1968), II, pp. 1241–1384. Other works paralleling ideas of Wallace are Michel Cépède, et al., *Population and Food* (New York, 1968), pp. 5–35, and Lester R. Brown, "The Agricultural Revolution in Asia," *Foreign Affairs,* 46 (July 1968): 688–98.

28. HAW, *Our Job in the Pacific,* p. 40.

29. Ibid., pp. 30–39.

30. As quoted in Washington *Times-Herald,* June 29, 1944.

31. As quoted in *Christian Science Monitor,* June 29, 1944.

32. Report of Senator Hugh Butler, Dec. 20, 1943, copy in HAW-UI.

CHAPTER 7

1. HAW to Cordell Hull, Mar. 25 and Apr. 25, 1944, HAW-UI.

2. Memorandum, John Carter Vincent to Lauchlin Currie (marked "strictly confidential"), dated Jan. 23, 1944, copy in HAW-UI.

3. Ibid. This memorandum was forwarded to him by Lauchlin Currie. See HAW to John Carter Vincent, May 6, 1944, HAW-UI.

4. Frances Perkins to HAW, July 25, 1944 (written after Wallace returned; she refers to her warning), HAW-LC.

5. Harold Young to Robert Kenny, Jan. 10, 1944, HAW-UI; Jake More (Democratic state chairman of Iowa) to HAW, Feb. 10 and Apr. 18, 1944; HAW to Jake More, Apr. 25, 1944, HAW-UI.

6. HAW to Stephen Early with enclosure, "Press and radio release," May 19, 1944, HAW-FDRL.

7. HAW, *Soviet Asia Mission* (New York, 1946), p. 130.

8. Ibid., pp. 136–37.

9. Ibid., pp. 137–38.

10. Ibid., p. 141.

11. HAW to Marshal Joseph Stalin, June 17, 1944, in *Foreign Relations of the United States Diplomatic Papers 1944, Volume IV Europe* (Washington, D.C., 1966), pp. 972–73.

12. HAW, *Soviet Asia Mission,* pp. 147–49.

13. *Foreign Relations of the U.S., Volume IV Europe,* pp. 968–71.

14. HAW, "Where I Went Wrong," *This Week,* Sept. 7, 1952, pp. 7, 29–30.

15. HAW, *Soviet Asia Mission,* pp. 154–55.

16. John Carter Vincent, "Summary Notes of Conversations between Vice-President Henry A. Wallace and President Chiang Kai-shek, June 21–24, 1944" *The China White Paper, August, 1944* (Stanford, 1967), pp. 549–60.

17. HAW to FDR, June 28, 1944, *Foreign Relations of the United States Diplomatic Papers 1944, Volume VI China* (Washington, D.C., 1967), pp. 234–35.

18. "Summary Report of Vice-President Wallace's Visit in China," July 10, 1944, *Foreign Relations of the U.S., Volume VI China,* pp. 240–44.

19. FDR to Chiang Kai-shek, July 14, 1944, *China White Paper,* p. 560.

20. In defense of his position see: "Wallace Tells His Story," *U.S. News and World Report,* 34 (Jan., 1953), p. 22 ff.; "Wallace Reports on China," *Current History,* 18 (Jan., 1950), pp. 104–7; HAW, "My 1944 Trip to China," ms. (intended for *The New Leader*), Oct. 22, 1951, HAW-UI. An overall historical account is contained in Herbert Feis, *The China Tangle, the American Effort in China from Pearl Harbor to the Marshall Mission* (New York, 1965).

21. HAW, *Soviet Asia Mission,* pp. 187–94.

22. Samuel I. Rosenman, *Working with Roosevelt* (New York, 1952), pp. 442–43.

CHAPTER 8

1. As published in Washington *Post,* July 15, 1944.

2. Harold Young to Marshall Field (Chicago *Sun),* May 27, 1944, and to George Creel *(Colliers),* June 13, 1944, HAW-LC.

3. Edwin W. Pauley to authors, Sept. 3, 1963 with enclosure, "Why Truman Is President," by Edwin W. Pauley as told to Richard English. Other accounts appear in Edward J. Flynn, *You're the Boss* (New York, 1947) and George E. Allen, *Presidents Who Have Known Me* (New York, 1950).

4. Lord, *Wallaces of Iowa,* p. 529.

5. HAW, "The Role of the Vice-President," address to Harvard Law School Forum, Mar. 30, 1956, HAW-UI.

6. *FDR-Public Papers,* 1944 vol., p. 199.

7. Pauley to authors, Sept. 3, 1963.

8. As quoted in Cleveland *Plain Dealer,* July 20, 1944.

9. Pauley to authors, Sept. 3, 1963.

10. Address of the Honorable Henry A. Wallace, as chairman of the Iowa delegation, seconding the nomination of President Roosevelt—Democratic National Convention, Chicago, Illinois, July 20, 1944, text in HAW-UI.

11. Ibid.

12. Alfred Steinberg, *The Man from Missouri, the Life and Times of Harry S. Truman* (New York, 1962), p. 207. Truman speaks of yet another note reading, "Bob, it's Truman. F.D.R.," *Memoirs,* 2 vols. (Garden City, 1956), I, p. 191.

13. Authors' notes on convention proceedings.

14. Flynn, *You're the Boss,* p. 198; Richard C. Bain, *Convention Decisions and Voting Records* (New York, 1960), 263–67.

15. James C. Hagerty, "Big City Bosses Win Over Hillman," New York *Times,* July 22, 1944.

16. HAW, "How a Vice-President Is Picked—Inside Look at U.S. Politics," *U.S. News and World Report,* 90 (Apr. 16, 1956): 86–89.

17. Telegram, FDR to HAW, July 21, 1944, as quoted in Lord, *Wallaces of Iowa,* p. 537.

18. Mark Sullivan, "Wallace's Chances," Washington *Post,* July 7, 1944.

19. As quoted in Pueblo (Colorado) *Chieftan,* July 11, 1944.

20. Copy of campaign speech in Papers of Harry A. Slattery (Duke Univ.).

21. As quoted in Providence *Journal,* July 23, 1944.

22. As quoted in Ottumwa (Iowa) *Courier,* July 22, 1944.
23. As quoted in Washington *Star,* Dec. 5, 1944.
24. *HAW-Public Papers,* pp. 225–26.
25. Rosenman, *Working with Roosevelt,* pp. 438–39.
26. Harold Young to Lynn Landrum, Apr. 24, 1942, HAW-LC.
27. Eleanor Roosevelt, *This I Remember* (New York, 1949), p. 220.
28. Walter Reuther to HAW, Aug. 17, 1944, HAW-LC.
29. William Shirer to HAW, Aug. 16, 1944, HAW-LC.
30. Sumner Welles to HAW, July 22, 1944, HAW-LC.
31. James W. Lucas to HAW, July 20, 1944, HAW-LC.
32. Upton Sinclair to HAW, July 22, 1944, HAW-LC.
33. Paul de Kruif to HAW, Aug. 2, 1941, HAW-LC.
34. Rudolph M. Evans to HAW, n.d. [ca. July or Aug. 1944], HAW-LC.
35. James D. LeCron to HAW, Aug. 2, 1944, HAW-LC.
36. Abe Fortas to HAW, July 25, 1944, HAW-LC.
37. Senator Carl Hatch to HAW, Aug. 8, 1944, HAW-LC.
38. Max Lerner to HAW, July 25, 1944, HAW-LC.
39. Robert Nathan to HAW, July 26, 1944, HAW-LC.
40. Felix Frankfurter to HAW, July 23, 1944, HAW-LC.
41. Nelson A. Rockefeller to HAW, n.d. [ca. July or Aug. 1944], HAW-LC.
42. Milo Perkins to HAW, July 23, 1944, HAW-LC.
43. Archibald MacLeish to HAW, July 21, 1944, HAW-LC.
44. Elmo Roper to HAW, July 27, 1944, HAW-LC.
45. Telegram, Frank P. Graham to HAW, July 21, 1944, HAW-LC.
46. David E. Lilienthal to HAW, July 28, 1944, HAW-LC.
47. Nancy McInery to HAW, Aug. 2, 1944, HAW-LC.
48. Senator James Mead to HAW, Aug. 4, 1944, HAW-LC.
49. William L. Batt to HAW, n.d. [ca. July or Aug. 1944], HAW-LC.
50. HAW to William Agar, Aug. 12, 1944, HAW-LC.
51. HAW to George S. Counts, Aug. 10, 1944, HAW-LC.
52. HAW to Franklin P. Adams, Aug. 7, 1944, HAW-LC.
53. HAW to Josephus Daniels, Aug. 7, 1944, HAW-LC.
54. As quoted in Chicago *Defender,* Sept. 2, 1944.
55. HAW, "The New Liberalism," address to Independent Voter's Committee of the Arts and Sciences for Roosevelt, Sept. 21, 1944, copy in Ezekiel Papers.
56. Telegram, FDR to HAW, quoted in Augusta (Georgia) *Chronicle,* Nov. 14, 1944.
57. Addison M. Parker to HAW, Nov. 9, 1944, HAW-UI.
58. Jay G. Hayden, "What to Do with Wallace," Detroit *News,* Nov. 27, 1944.
59. *Wall Street Journal,* Nov. 28, 1944.
60. Redford E. Mobley, "'Hank' May Lick Jesse Jones Yet," Akron *Beacon Journal,* Nov. 19, 1944.
61. Grace Tully, *F.D.R. My Boss* (New York, 1949), p. 190.
62. Jones, *My Thirteen Years with the RFC,* pp. 278–79.
63. Ibid., pp. 282–83.

CHAPTER 9

1. U.S. Senate, 79th Cong., 1st sess., Committee on Commerce, *Hearings on S. 375* (Washington, D.C., 1945), pp. 24–25.

2. Ibid., pp. 54–56.
3. *U.S. Congressional Record,* 79th Cong., 1st sess., 1945, vol. 91, pt. I, p. 1167.
4. Ibid, p. 1180.
5. William D. Leahy, *I Was There* (New York, London, and Toronto, 1950), pp. 293–94.
6. FDR to HAW, Nov. 27, 1944, HAW-FDRL.
7. *FDR-Public Papers,* 1944–45, vol., p. 41.
8. As quoted in J. T. Salter, ed., *Public Men in and out of Office* (Chapel Hill, 1956), p 98.
9. HAW to FDR, Feb. 28, 1945, HAW-FDRL.
10. Winston S. Churchill, *The Second World War,* 4 vols. (New York, 1962), IV, p. 407.
11. HAW, *Sixty Million Jobs* (New York, 1945), p. 91.
12. Ibid., p. 93.
13. Ibid., pp. 52–53.
14. Ibid., p. 125.
15. HST to HAW, Sept. 10, 1945, HSTL.
16. Alvin H. Hansen, *Economic Policy and Full Employment* (New York and London, 1947), p. 307.
17. HAW, *Sixty Million Jobs,* p. 208.
18. HAW, "In Memorial of Franklin D. Roosevelt," Churchman award dinner, New York City, June 4, 1945, copy in Papers of Alfred Schindler, HSTL.
19. Memorandum by George Kennan titled, "Russia's International Position at the Close of the War with Germany," n.d. [ca. 1945], *Foreign Relations of the United States Diplomatic Papers 1945, Volume V Europe* (Washington, D.C., 1967), p.858.
20. Leon H. Keyserling to authors, Feb. 18, 1964; Robert Nathan to authors, Feb. 26, 1964; and interview with Mordecai Ezekiel, Dec. 19, 1963.
21. For a complete story of the political fight involved in its passage see Stephan Kemp Bailey, *Congress Makes a Law, the Story behind the Employment Act of 1946* (New York, 1964).
22. Two works helpful in understanding the details and mechanics of the proposed legislation are Karl Schriftgiesser, *Business and Public Policy, the Role of the Committee for Economic Development: 1942–1967* (Englewood Cliffs, 1967), and Edward S. Flash, Jr., *Economic Advice and Presidential Leadership, the Council of Economic Advisers* (New York and London, 1965).
23. Statement by Secretary of Commerce before Senate Committee on Banking and Currency, Aug. 28, 1945, in Schindler Papers.
24. Edwin G. Nourse, *The 1950's Come First* (New York 1951), p. 8.
25. Memorandum, HAW to HST, Dec. 4, 1945, HSTL.
26. HAW to HST, Feb. 6, 1946, HSTL.
27. HAW to HST, Jan. 22, 1946, HSTL.
28. HST to HAW, Jan. 24, 1946, HSTL.
29. Statement by Secretary of Commerce, Oct. 11, 1945, Schindler Papers.
30. HAW, "The Significance of the Atomic Age," unpubl. ms., Oct. 11, 1945, HAW-UI.
31. Address by Secretary of Commerce, Jan. 10, 1946, Schindler Papers.
32. Statement by Secretary of Commerce, Jan. 22, 1946, Schindler Papers.
33. Statement by Secretary of Commerce, Jan. 25, 1946, Schindler Papers.
34. Address by Secretary of Commerce, Feb. 16, 1946, Schindler Papers.
35. Statement by Secretary of Commerce, Feb. 21, 1946, Schindler Papers.
36. Address by Secretary of Commerce, Apr. 7, 1946, Schindler Papers.
37. Statement by Secretary of Commerce before Special Committee on Atomic Energy, Jan. 31, 1946, Schindler Papers.

38. HAW, "Why Is the Control and Development of Atomic Energy a World Problem?" CBS, July 31, 1946, Schindler Papers.
39. Elting E. Morison, *Turmoil and Tradition, a Study of the Life and Times of Henry L. Stimson* (New York, 1964), pp. 532–34.
40. Henry L. Stimson to HST with enclosure, "Memorandum for the President, subject: Proposed action for control of atomic bomb," Sept. 11, 1945, and diary entry for Sept. 25, 1945, Henry L. Stimson Diary (Sterling Memorial Library, Yale Univ.).
41. Senator Clinton P. Anderson to authors, Aug. 9, 1963.
42. Walter Millis, ed., *The Forrestal Diaries* (New York, 1951), p. 95.
43. HAW to Leo Crowley, Oct. 18, 1951, HAW-UI.

CHAPTER 10

1. As quoted in Alexander Werth, *Russia at War, 1941–1945* (New York, 1964), p. 944.
2. Hopkins-Stalin conference record, Moscow, May, 1945, copy in Byrnes papers.
3. HAW to HST, June 5, 1945 with enclosure, letter of Sumner Welles to HAW dated June 1, 1945, HSTL.
4. As quoted in Truman, *Memoirs,* I, pp. 555–56.
5. Address by General Walter Bedell Smith to the National Council of American-Soviet Friendship, n.d., ms. in Papers of Walter Bedell Smith (Dwight D. Eisenhower Library).
6. Memorandum from Richard H. Hippelheuser to Philip M. Hauser, July 17, 1946, HAW-UI.
7. HAW to HST, July 23, 1946, Schindler Papers.
8. Otto Nathan and Heinz Norden, eds., *Einstein on Peace* (New York, 1960), p. 375 ff.
9. Baruch, *The Public Years,* p. 369.
10. HST to Bernard M. Baruch, July 10, 1946, Papers of Bernard M. Baruch (Princeton Univ.).
11. Joseph L. Nogee, *Soviet Policy towards International Control of Atomic Energy* (Notre Dame, 1961), pp. 22–32.
12. Statement by Senator Tom Connally regarding Council of Foreign Ministers meeting, Paris, May 18, 1946, Papers of Thomas Terry Connally (Library of Congress).
13. Winston Churchill, Address at Westminster College, Fulton, Missouri, Mar. 5, 1946, in Barton J. Bernstein and Allen J. Matusow, eds., *The Truman Administration: A Documentary History* (New York and London, 1966), p. 217.
14. Statement respecting the issues before the Peace Conference at Paris, Connally Papers.
15. Remarks by Secretary of Commerce at a dinner given in honor of Mrs. Eleanor Roosevelt by the Woman's Joint Congressional Committee of Washington, Mar. 14, 1946, Schindler Papers.
16. "Headline Edition," ABC broadcast from Washington, D.C., Mar. 15, 1946, Schindler Papers.
17. Address by Secretary of Commerce in honor of W. Averell Harriman given by the American Society for Russian Relief, New York City, Mar. 19, 1946, Schindler Papers.
18. Address by Secretary of Commerce before the Mexican Labor Organization, Mexico City, Sept. 5, 1946, Schindler Papers.

19. Address by Secretary of Commerce at Jackson Day meeting under the auspices of Democratic National Committee, Los Angeles, Apr. 18, 1946, Schindler Papers.

20. Address by Secretary of Commerce to Michigan Citizen's Committee, Detroit, May 7, 1946, Schindler Papers.

21. Address by Secretary of Commerce at tenth anniversary dinner of American Labor Party, New York City, May 24, 1946, Schindler Papers.

22. Address by Secretary of Commerce to joint meeting of Liberal Voters League and National Citizens Political Action Committee, St. Louis, June 14, 1946, Schindler Papers.

23. Allan Nevins, *Herbert H. Lehman and His Era* (New York, 1963), pp. 304–7.

24. The one person to whom almost all Henry Wallace's agrarian colleagues point when discussing the Commerce Secretary's involvement in his peace crusade is Calvin B. Baldwin. They invariably held that "Beanie" Baldwin unduly influenced Wallace, hence leading him into the third-party venture against the better judgment of others. For a discussion of Baldwin's background see: Sidney Baldwin, *Poverty and Politics, the Rise and Decline of the Farm Security Administration* (Chapel Hill, 1968).

25. Truman, *Memoirs,* I, pp. 557–61; Oral History Memoirs of Samuel Bledsoe and Bernard Gladieux, COHP.

26. Stuttgart address by Secretary Byrnes, Department of State *Bulletin,* 15 (Sept. 15, 1946): 496 ff.

27. Press conference of Sept. 12, 1946, *Public Papers of the Presidents of the United States, Harry S. Truman, Containing the Public Messages, Speeches and Statements of the President January 1 to December 31, 1946* (Washington, D.C., 1962), pp. 426–28.

28. George Curry, *James F. Byrnes,* in *The American Secretaries of State and Their Diplomacy,* Robert H. Ferrell and Samuel Flagg Bemis, eds., (New York, 1965), pp. 255–57.

29. Cited in Curtis D. MacDougall, *Gideon's army,* 3 vols. (New York, 1965), I, p. 67.

30. Herbert E. French to HAW, Oct. 29, 1955, HAW-UI.

31. Many versions of this speech exist. The authentic text (sans omissions at the podium) is contained in Memorandum from Vi Lonski to Mildred Eaton (HAW's personal secretary), Sept. 20, 1946, with enclosure marked, "Copy of Mr. Wallace's September 12 speech as it was delivered at the Garden," HAW-UI.

32. Ibid.

33. Ibid.

34. *Public Papers of the Presidents, Harry S. Truman, 1946,* p. 427.

35. Press release, Department of Commerce, Sept. 16, 1946, Schindler Papers.

36. Thomas Connally with Alfred Steinberg, *My Name Is Tom Connally* (New York, 1954), p. 302.

37. Arthur K. Vandenberg, ed., *The Private Papers of Senator Vandenberg* (Boston, 1952), p. 301.

38. Press release, Department of Commerce, Sept. 18, 1946, Schindler Papers.

39. James F. Byrnes, *Speaking Frankly* (New York, 1947), p. 240.

40. Cabell Phillips, *The Truman Presidency, the History of a Triumphant Succession* (New York and London, 1966), p. 153.

41. Curry, *James F. Byrnes,* p. 270.

42. Ibid.

43. William Hillman, *Mr. President, Personal diaries, private letters,*

papers, and revealing interviews of Harry S. Truman (London, 1952), pp. 109–11.

44. Truman, *Memoirs,* I, p. 560.

45. Lord, *Wallaces of Iowa,* p. 582. Truman records Wallace as answering, "If that is the way you want it, Mr. President, I will be happy to comply."

46. HAW to HST, Sept. 20, 1946, Schindler Papers.

47. Presidential press and radio conference no. 83, Sept. 20, 1946, HSTL.

48. Truman, *Memoirs,* p. 560.

49. Speech by Henry A. Wallace on the night of his resignation from the cabinet, Sept. 20, 1946, HAW-UI.

CHAPTER 11

1. HAW to Henry C. Taylor, Dec. 28, 1946, Papers of Henry C. Taylor (State Hist. Soc. Wisc., Madison).

2. Frank Murphy to HAW, Oct. 16, 1946, Papers of Frank Murphy (Mich. Hist. Coll., Ann Arbor).

3. HAW to Frank Murphy, Oct. 22, 1946, Murphy Papers.

4. HAW, *The Fight for Peace* (New York, 1946), Introduction.

5. Notes of meeting with Mr. Wallace and his aide Mr. Hauser, 10 A.M., Friday, Sept. 27, 1946; statement prepared by Mr. Wallace's representative, Mr. Hauser, after Baruch-Wallace conference on September 27 and accepted by Mr. Baruch (in which errors of fact are admitted); alternate statement proposed by Mr. Wallace over telephone to Mr. Baruch on Sept. 30th (in which no errors are admitted), Papers of Bernard M. Baruch (Princeton Univ. Library).

6. Telegram, Baruch to HAW, Oct. 2, 1946, Baruch Papers.

7. *The New Republic,* 115 (Dec. 23, 1946): 862–63. Hereinafter cited as *NR.*

8. Michael Straight to authors, Sept. 27, 1963.

9. Anita McCormick Blaine to HAW, Sept. 24, 1946, and HAW to Anita McCormick Blaine, Nov. 19, 1946, HAW–UI.

10. HAW to Jake More, Jan. 8, 1947, HAW-UI.

11. Donald Bruce to HAW, Sept. 24, 1946, and Kingsley Martin to HAW, Nov. 28, 1946, HAW-UI.

12. Interview with Robert Kenny, Aug. 13, 1963.

13. MacDougall, *Gideon's army,* I, p. 116.

14. Interview with Robert Kenny, Aug. 13, 1963.

15. James Roosevelt to authors, June 14 and Aug. 21, 1963.

16. Paul de Kruif to Harold Young, Jan. 27, 1947, HAW-UI.

17. Aubrey Williams to HAW, Apr. 30, 1959, HAW-UI.

18. HAW, "The Truman Doctrine—or a Strong UN," *NR,* 116 (Mar. 31, 1946): 11–21.

19. Memorandum from Jennie Lee to executive director of ADA, Apr. 29, 1947, Papers of the Americans for Democratic Action (State Hist. Soc. Wisc.).

20. "The President's News Conference of April 10, 1947," in *Public Papers of the Presidents, Harry S. Truman 1947,* p. 203.

21. MacDougall, *Gideon's army,* I, p. 134.

22. Ibid., p. 135.

23. Copy of resolution in Truman Papers, HSTL.

24. Arthur Vandenberg as quoted in David E. Lilienthal, *The Journals of David E. Lilienthal,* 3 vols. (1964), II, pp. 169–70.

25. HST to Louis E. Starr, Apr. 16, 1947, HSTL.

26. Copy of article by Robert S. Allen, "President Denounces Wallace in Letter to VFW Commander," HSTL.

27. Henry L. Stimson, "The Challenge to Americans," *Foreign Affairs,* Vol. 26 (Oct. 1947), as quoted in J. Joseph Huthmacher, ed., *Twentieth-Century America, an Interpretation with Readings* (Boston, 1966), pp. 373–74.

28. Senate speech by W. Lee O'Daniel, Apr. 23, 1947, *Congressional Record,* 80th Cong., 1st sess., as quoted in Huthmacher, ed., *Twentieth-Century America,* p. 381.

29. Address by Walter Lippmann to Phi Beta Kappa of William and Mary College (1948) as quoted in E. L. and F. H. Schapsmeier, *Walter Lippmann: Philosopher-Journalist,* p. 115.

30. George C. Marshall's speech at Harvard University, June 5, 1947, in Norman A. Graebner, ed., *Ideas and Diplomacy, Readings in the Intellectual Tradition of American Foreign Policy* (New York, 1964), pp. 732–33.

31. HAW, "My Alternative for the Marshall Plan," *NR,* 118 (Jan. 12, 1948): 13–14.

32. Irving Fisher to HAW, Sept. 30, 1946, Papers of Irving Fisher (Yale Univ. Library).

33. Edmund Stillman and William Pfaff, *Power and Impotence: The Failure of America's Foreign Policy* (New York, 1967), p. 21.

34. HAW, "Thoughts at Christmas," *NR,* 117 (Dec. 22, 1947): 12–13.

35. HAW, "Stand Up and Be Counted," *NR,* 118 (Jan. 5, 1948): 4.

36. Ibid.

CHAPTER 12

1. Communist party platform—1948, as quoted in Kirk H. Porter and Donald Bruce Johnson, *National Party Platforms, 1840–1960* (Urbana, 1961), p. 429.

2. As quoted in MacDougall, *Gideon's army,* II, p. 571.

3. Address by Henry A. Wallace at Second National Convention of the Progressive Party, Chicago, Feb. 24, 1950, in Papers of Progressive Party (Univ. Iowa). Hereinafter cited as Progressive Party Papers-UI.

4. Notes on Progressive Party Convention by Norman Thomas, in Papers of Socialist Party of America (Duke Univ.).

5. A short but excellent account of the Progressive Party Convention is found in David A. Shannon, *The Decline of American Communism, a History of the Communist Party of the United States Since 1945* (New York, 1959), pp. 164–175.

6. Glen H. Taylor to authors, Sept. 20, 1963.

7. Glen H. Taylor, "I Take My Stand with Henry Wallace," Distributed by the National Wallace for President Committee, copy in Papers of Oregon Progressive Party (Univ. Oreg.).

8. As quoted in Shannon, *The Decline of American Communism,* p. 160.

9. James A. Wechsler, *The Age of Suspicion* (New York, 1953), p. 227.

10. James Loeb, Jr., to Harry Girvitz, Jan. 27, 1948, with enclosure, "To Be Frank," by Dr. Frank Kingdon, in Papers of Americans for Democratic Action (State Hist. Soc. Wis.). Hereinafter cited as ADA Papers.

11. As quoted by Shannon, *The Decline of American Communism,* p. 161.

12. S. C. Brightman (assistant director of publicity, Democratic National Committee) to Senator Robert S. Kerr, Jan. 19, 1948 with enclosure: "Statement of Senator J. Howard McGrath for *Capital Comment*," in Papers of Robert S. Kerr (Univ. Okla.).

13. As quoted in Los Angeles *Daily News*, Oct. 2, 1948.

14. Statement of Robert F. Wagner on Henry Wallace's announcement of his decision to run for President on an Independent party ticket, Dec. 29, 1947, HSTL.

15. Statement by A. Philip Randolph, Oct. 25, 1948, in Socialist Party Papers.

16. Chicago *Defender*, Mar. 27, 1948.

17. Phillips, *The Truman Presidency*, p. 198.

18. President's press conference of August 5, 1948, in *Public Papers of the Presidents, Harry S. Truman 1948*, p. 433.

19. Address by the President at Boston, Mass., Oct. 27, 1948, HSTL.

20. Address by the President at Los Angeles, Calif., Sept. 23, 1948, HSTL.

21. Memorandum from Marjorie Hill to Bert Witt (PCA executive director—Southern California chapter) titled, "Major Points of Concentration, Comments on Victory of Leo Isaacson in New York," Progressive Party Papers-UI.

22. Norman Thomas to HST, Sept. 11, 1948, HSTL.

23. Address by Norman Thomas to Mechanics Educational Society of America, Buffalo, N.Y., Sept. 19, 1948, Socialist Party Papers.

24. "Brief Statement of ADA Principles," Feb. 8, 1947, ADA Papers.

25. Address by Mayor Hubert Humphrey to ADA Convention, Washington, D.C., Mar. 29, 1947, ADA Papers.

26. "An Appeal to the Liberals of America," n.d., ADA Papers.

27. Memorandum from Lillian H. Traugott (PCA—field service director) to state directors, n.d., copy in ADA Papers.

28. Arthur M. Schlesinger, Jr., *The Vital Center, the Politics of Freedom* (Boston, 1949), pp. 115–18.

29. HAW, "Why a Third Party in 1948?" *The Annals of the American Academy of Political and Social Science*, 259 (Sept., 1948): 10–16.

30. HAW, *Toward World Peace* (New York, 1948).

31. Ibid.

32. Ibid.

33. Ibid.

34. Albert Einstein to Eugene Reynal [1948], copy in HAW-UI.

35. New York *Times*, May 12, 1948.

36. Ibid., May 18, 1948.

37. Address at Cow Palace, San Mateo County, May 18, 1948, Progressive Party Papers-UI.

38. Truman, *Memoirs*, II, pp. 213–17; Robert H. Ferrell and George C. Marshall, in *The American Secretaries of State and Their Diplomacy*, Robert H. Ferrell and Samuel Flagg Bemis, eds. (New York, 1966), pp. 250–58.

39. Radio broadcast, NBC, Sept. 13, 1948, Progressive Party Papers-UI.

40. Radio broadcast, NBC, Sept. 20, 1948, Progressive Party Papers-UI.

41. Address at Philadelphia, Oct. 30, 1948, Progressive Party Papers-UI.

42. Memorandum from Hugh Bryson, "To Be Read at All Election Night Parties," Oct. 29, 1948, Progressive Party Papers-UI.

43. Cited from election statistics in Karl M. Schmidt, *Henry A. Wallace: Quixotic Crusade 1948* (Syracuse, 1960), pp. 331–35.

44. For a complete analysis of voting patterns see Samuel Lubell, *The Future of American Politics* (New York, 1956), p. 220 ff.

45. Alan Schaffer, *Vito Marcantonio, Radical in Congress* (Syracuse, 1966), pp. 182–86. See also Milton C. Cummings, Jr., *Congressmen and the Electorate, Elections for the U.S. House and the President, 1920–1964* (New York and London, 1966), pp. 149–50.

CHAPTER 13

1. As quoted in Ronald Steel, *Pax Americana* (New York, 1967), p. 3.
2. Ibid., p. 16.
3. HAW to HST, Nov. 5, 1948, HSTL.
4. Rexford G. Tugwell to Charles G. Ross, Nov. 15, 1948, HSTL.
5. Charles G. Ross to Rexford G. Tugwell, Nov. 26, 1948, HSTL.
6. Address to the National Committee of the Progressive Party, Chicago, Nov. 13, 1948, Progressive Party Papers-UI.
7. Ibid.
8. Letters from HAW to members of the U.S. Senate, July 5, 1949, HAW-UI.
9. Address to Second National Convention of the Progressive Party, Chicago, Feb. 24, 1950, Progressive Party Papers-UI.
10. Ibid.
11. Ibid.
12. Ibid.
13. Minutes of the meeting of the Executive Committee, Progressive Party, on the situation in Korea and China, July 6–15, 1950, and HAW to C. B. Baldwin, July 13, 1950, HAW-UI.
14. Statement of the National Committee of the Progressive Party on Korea and China, adopted at a meeting in New York City, July 15, 1950, HAW–UI.
15. Personal statement by Henry A. Wallace on the Korean situation, July 15, 1950, HAW-UI.
16. As quoted in Schmidt, *Quixotic Crusade*, p. 307.
17. Rexford G. Tugwell to HAW, July 17, 1950, HAW-UI.
18. Found in box containing hate mail (1950), HAW-UI.
19. HAW, "Where I Stand," Brooklyn Jewish Center, Jan. 2, 1951, HAW-UI.
20. HAW, "March of the Common Man: Constructive or Destructive," Community Church, Boston, Jan. 21, 1951, HAW-UI.
21. Address at the Community Church of New York, Dec. 4, 1949, Progressive Party Papers-UI.
22. Ibid.
23. Ibid.
24. Easter sermon delivered by Henry A. Wallace over radio at Peekskill, New York, n.d., Progressive Party Papers-UI.
25. HAW to authors, Jan. 12, 1961.

CHAPTER 14

1. Testimony by Henry A. Wallace before the Committee on Un-American Activities, House of Representatives, 81st Cong., 2d sess., Jan. 26, 1950, copy in HAW-UI.
2. HAW to Albert Einstein, Jan. 30, 1959, HAW-UI.

3. HAW to General Leslie R. Groves, Mar. 7, 1951, HAW-UI.
4. HAW to Henry Regnery, Sept. 13, 1951, HAW-UI.
5. Subpoena to HAW, signed by Senator Patrick McCarran, Oct. 3, 1951, HAW-UI.
6. HAW to Senator Homer Ferguson, Aug. 25, 1951, HAW-UI.
7. HAW to Senator Pat McCarran, Sept. 13, 1951, HAW-UI.
8. HAW to HST, with enclosure, Sept. 19, 1951, HSTL.
9. HAW to Senator Homer Ferguson, Mar. 12, 1953, HAW-UI.
10. HAW to Whittaker Chambers, Feb. 19, 1952, HAW-UI.
11. HAW to Ben Hibbs, Mar. 3, 1952, copy in HSTL.
12. HAW to HST, Mar. 4, 1952, HSTL.
13. Interview with Chester C. Davis, Aug. 9, 1963.
14. Ben Hibbs to HAW, Feb. 22, 1952, HAW-UI.
15. Harvey Matusow, *False Witness* (New York, 1955), pp. 104, 110, *passim.*
16. HAW, "Liberalism Re-Appraised," address to Harvard Law School Forum, May 1, 1953, HAW-UI.
17. HAW to Alben W. Barkley, May 21, 1954, Papers of Alben W. Barkley (Univ. Ky.).
18. Phyllis Gelbman (Viking Press) to authors, Dec. 11, 1963; Walter Millis to authors, Aug. 23, 1963.
19. Telegram, HAW to HST, Mar. 12, 1952, HSTL.
20. Telegram, Joseph Short to HAW, Mar. 16, 1952, HSTL.
21. HAW to Joseph Short, Mar. 16, 1952, HSTL.
22. Statement with regard to Harry S. Truman's memoirs, concerning the period Sept. 10 to Sept. 18, 1946, HAW-UI.
23. Arthur M. Schlesinger, Jr., *The Age of Roosevelt,* 3 vols. (Boston, 1960), II, p. 33.
24. Frances Perkins to HAW, Mar. 20, 1959, HAW-UI.
25. Frances Perkins to authors, June 19, 1963.
26. Drew Pearson to HAW, Dec. 30, 1960, HAW-UI.
27. HAW to Donald R. Murphy, Aug. 15, 1949, HAW-UI.

CHAPTER 15

1. Boris Pregel to HAW, Jan. 18, 1960, HAW-UI.
2. Marcus Bach to HAW, Mar. 29, 1960, HAW-UI.
3. HAW, "The Ten Year Look Ahead," GE Crotonville Conference, Mar. 17, 1959, HAW-UI.
4. Memorial Day address, Bedford Village, N.Y., May 30, 1955, HAW-UI.
5. Notes with no title or date, ca. 1956, HAW-UI.
6. HAW, "Making Explosives Constructive," Keuka College, Keuka, N.Y., Apr. 25, 1955, HAW-UI.
7. HAW, "Radioactivity and Plant Growth," *NR,* 117 (Oct. 13, 1947): 11; *The Produce News,* Oct. 18, 1947; and interview with Boris Pregel, Jan. 17, 1970.
8. Terms of grant for Round Table Foundation, Apr. 1, 1949, HAW-UI.
9. HAW, "Science and Economic Problems," address at George Washington Univ., St. Louis, Mo., Sept. 25, 1956, HAW-UI.
10. HAW, "The Uniqueness of George Carver," dedication of Carver Hall, Simpson College, Oct. 5, 1956, HAW-UI.

11. HAW to Fred Lehmann, Jr., Mar. 21, 1953, HAW-UI.
12. HAW to Boris Pregel, Nov. 11, 1953, HAW-UI.
13. HAW, "Small Plots and Big Men," address at Mt. Carmel, Conn., Aug. 16, 1955, HAW-UI.
14. HAW, "Comments on Origin and Utilization of Germ Plasm in the U.S.A., meeting of Section O, AAAS, Chicago, Ill., Dec. 28, 1959, HAW-UI.
15. HAW to Fred Lehmann, Jr., Aug. 15, 1949, HAW-UI.
16. HAW to Professor Schmidt, Jan. 4, 1949. For an explanation of Lysenko's views see Zhores A. Medvedev (trans. by I. Michael Lerner), *The Rise and Fall of T. D. Lysenko* (New York, 1969).
17. George W. Beadle, "Molecules, Viruses, and Heredity," in Henry Jarret, ed., *Science and Resources, Prospects and Implications of Technological Advance* (Baltimore, 1959), pp. 20–21.
18. Ibid., pp. 26–28.
19. HAW, "Reminiscing—and a Look into the Future," address to Pioneer Club, Des Moines, Iowa, Sept. 8, 1962, Iowa Authors' Collection (Univ. Iowa).
20. Ibid.
21. Ibid.
22. HAW, "Hybridizing for Health and Vigor in Glads," unpubl. ms., [ca. 1965], HAW-UI.
23. George M. Darrow, *The Strawberry: History, Breeding and Physiology* (New York, Chicago, and San Francisco, 1966), pp. 209–10.
24. HAW, "Corn and the Midwestern Farmer," reprinted from *Proceedings of the American Philosophical Society,* 100 (Oct., 1956): 455, *passim.*
25. Ibid.
26. HAW, "Corn and People," address to Harlan [Iowa] Production Credit Association, Oct. 14, 1964, Iowa Authors' Collection.
27. Orville L. Freeman to HAW, May 25, 1963, as quoted in memorandum from Dorothy F. Stackpole to Mrs. Henry A. Wallace, Dec. 11, 1969.
28. Hallowell Bowser, "Reunion on Channel 13," *Saturday Review,* 46 (Apr. 6, 1963): 18–19.
29. HAW to James A. Farley, Jan. 29, 1954, and HAW, "Background of the Farm Program," NBC, Apr. 1, 1954, HAW-UI.
30. HAW to Bernard M. Baruch, Jan. 13, 1952, Baruch Papers.
31. John Wheeler, "How Henry Wallace Offered Self for Tests to Aid Others," Chicago *Sun-Times,* Dec. 12, 1965.
32. As quoted in Milwaukee *Sentinel,* Nov. 19, 1965.
33. Ibid.
34. As quoted in Chicago *Sun-Times,* Nov. 20, 1965.
35. Henry C. Taylor to HAW, Aug. 25, 1958, HAW-UI.
36. As quoted in "Henry A. Wallace," memorial brochure published by the Pioneer Hi-Bred Corn Company (1965).

INDEX